LIBRARY OF NEW TESTAMENT STUDIES

683

formerly the Journal for the Study of the New Testament Supplement series

Editor
Chris Keith

Editorial Board
Dale C. Allison, Lynn H. Cohick, R. Alan Culpepper, Craig A. Evans,
Jennifer Eyl, Robert Fowler, Simon J. Gathercole, Juan Hernández Jr.,
John S. Kloppenborg, Michael Labahn, Matthew V. Novenson,
Love L. Sechrest, Robert Wall, Catrin H. Williams, Brittany E. Wilson

The Cosmic Journey in the Book of Revelation

Apocalyptic Cosmology and the Experience of Story-Space

Joel M. Rothman

LONDON • NEW YORK • OXFORD • NEW DELHI • SYDNEY

T&T CLARK
Bloomsbury Publishing Plc
50 Bedford Square, London, WC1B 3DP, UK
1385 Broadway, New York, NY 10018, USA
29 Earlsfort Terrace, Dublin 2, Ireland

BLOOMSBURY, T&T CLARK and the T&T Clark logo are trademarks of
Bloomsbury Publishing Plc

First published in Great Britain 2023
Paperback edition published in 2025

Copyright © Joel M. Rothman, 2023

Joel M. Rothman has asserted his right under the Copyright,
Designs and Patents Act, 1988, to be identified as Author of this work.

For legal purposes the Acknowledgements on p. xi constitute an extension
of this copyright page.

All rights reserved. No part of this publication may be reproduced or
transmitted in any form or by any means, electronic or mechanical,
including photocopying, recording, or any information storage or retrieval
system, without prior permission in writing from the publishers.

Bloomsbury Publishing Plc does not have any control over, or responsibility for,
any third-party websites referred to or in this book. All internet addresses given
in this book were correct at the time of going to press. The author and publisher
regret any inconvenience caused if addresses have changed or sites have
ceased to exist, but can accept no responsibility for any such changes.

Library of Congress Cataloging-in-Publication Data

Names: Rothman, Joel M., author.
Title: The cosmic journey in the book of Revelation : apocalyptic cosmology
and the experience of story-space / by Joel M. Rothman.
Description: London ; New York : T&T Clark, 2023. |
Series: The library of the New Testament, 2513-8790 ; 683 |
Includes bibliographical references and index. |
Summary: "This volume uses narrative theory to provide a new interpretation
of the relationship of cosmic spaces in the Book of Revelation"– Provided by publisher.
Identifiers: LCCN 2022050790 (print) | LCCN 2022050791 (ebook) |
ISBN 9780567710321 (hb) | ISBN 9780567710369 (pb) |
ISBN 9780567710338 (epdf) | ISBN 9780567710352 (epub)
Subjects: LCSH: Biblical cosmology. | Bible. Revelation–Criticism, interpretation, etc.
Classification: LCC BS2825.6.C6 R68 2023 (print) | LCC BS2825.6.C6 (ebook) |
DDC 228/.06–dc23/eng/20230516
LC record available at https://lccn.loc.gov/2022050790
LC ebook record available at https://lccn.loc.gov/2022050791

ISBN: HB: 978-0-5677-1032-1
PB: 978-0-5677-1036-9
ePDF: 978-0-5677-1033-8
ePUB: 978-0-5677-1035-2

Series: Library of New Testament Studies, volume 683
ISSN 2513-8790

Typeset by Newgen KnowledgeWorks Pvt. Ltd., Chennai, India

To find out more about our authors and books visit www.bloomsbury.com
and sign up for our newsletters.

For those who opened the scriptures to me
For those who showed me the sky-emu

Contents

Acknowledgements			xi
1	Introduction		1
	1.1	Cosmic journeys	1
	1.2	Scholarship on cosmology in Revelation	6
		1.2.1 Structural cosmology	6
		Heaven or sky or firmament	7
		Earth	9
		Below earth	11
		Spherical cosmos	12
		1.2.2 Dynamic cosmology	13
		1.2.3 Rhetorical cosmology	16
	1.3	Conclusion: Apocalypse and cosmos	19
2	Methodology		21
	2.1	Hearer assumptions	22
	2.2	Visionary narrative	24
	2.3	Time	27
	2.4	Space	28
	2.5	Movement, events and narrative inferences	29
	2.6	Ideological comparison	30
	2.7	Conclusion: A visual-narrative reading	31
3	Assumptions and existing conceptions		33
	3.1	The sources	33
	3.2	Earth	35
	3.3	Below the earth	38
		3.3.1 The two regions	38
		3.3.2 Relocation	43
	3.4	Skies	44

		3.4.1	The sky-structure	44
		3.4.2	Spaces above and below the sky-structure	51
		3.4.3	Conflicted spaces, human spaces and the God-space	53
	3.5	Cosmic disorder and existing means of repair		56
	3.6	Conclusion: Existing assumptions		57
4	The sky-journey, the sky-structure and the God-space			59
	4.1	The earth-space		59
	4.2	The journey through the sky-structure		61
	4.3	The nature of the sky-structure		62
		4.3.1	Material composition	62
		4.3.2	Opacity	64
		4.3.3	Single layer	66
	4.4	The God-space		67
		4.4.1	Seeing the layout	67
		4.4.2	Nature of the space	72
			Defined by the Throne	72
			Limited accessibility to humans	75
	4.5	Conclusion: Structures and spaces		77
5	Four cosmic layers in operation			79
	5.1	The position of stars		79
		5.1.1	Position of stars in ancient sources	80
		5.1.2	Stars in Revelation 1–3	81
		5.1.3	No stars above the sky-structure	81
		5.1.4	Assumed position of sun, moon and stars in Rev. 6.12-14	82
	5.2	Four cosmic layers in the narrative (Rev. 9.1-11)		83
		5.2.1	Narrator, focalizer, character	83
		5.2.2	What is the star, and where has it come from?	83
			Excursus: What purpose the angel interpretation?	88
		5.2.3	Locating the abyss through narrative and visual perspective	89
		5.2.4	Nature of the abyss	91
		5.2.5	The abyss and Hades	94
	5.3	The Throne and the sub-Throne cosmos (Rev. 5.6-14)		96

	5.4	Mid-heaven	97
	5.5	Conclusion: The fourfold cosmos	98
6	The distinct natures of the two sky-spaces (Rev. 12)	101
	6.1	Narrator, focalizer, character	102
		6.1.1	There and back again	102
		6.1.2	Earthly position in Revelation 10	103
		6.1.3	Earthly position continues	105
	6.2	Narrative structure and narrative resonances	106
	6.3	The embedded narratives in the cosmic structure	107
		6.3.1	Star wars in the sky-heaven	107
		6.3.2	Battle angels in the sky-heaven	111
		6.3.3	Legal battles in the hyper-heaven	112
	6.4	Conclusion: A consistent hyper-heaven	113
7	Cosmic change (Rev. 20–22)	117
	7.1	No cosmos but the Throne (Rev. 20.11-15)	118
		7.1.1	Narrator, focalizer, character	118
		7.1.2	Deletions in story-space	119
	7.2	Cosmos restructured	121
		7.2.1	Story-space again	121
		7.2.2	God-space merges with earth-space	122
	7.3	Outside the cosmos: The lake of fire	125
		7.3.1	Locating the non-location	125
		7.3.2	Experiencing the lake of fire	133
	7.4	Real cosmos replaced?	136
		7.4.1	Existing scholarship	137
		7.4.2	A narratological contribution	138
		7.4.3	This earth and this moment	140
	7.5	Conclusion: Cosmos anew	141
8	The ideological import of the cosmic structure	143
	8.1	Imperial space: Architecture, ritual, myth	143
	8.2	Alternative spatial construction	147
	8.3	Complementary sky-spaces	150

	8.4 Appropriate action in cosmic context	152
	8.5 Conclusion: Living in the cosmos	156
9	Conclusion	157

Bibliography 161
Index of Ancient Literature 171
Index of Modern Authors 185

Acknowledgements

This book is a modest revision of a thesis submitted to the University of Divinity, Australia, for the degree of Doctor of Philosophy. I am grateful to the university for supporting this research. I am especially grateful to my supervisors, Keith Dyer and Robyn Whitaker, who encouraged me to keep going and pushed me to refine my thinking. Ian Paul and Sean M. McDonough also provided helpful feedback prior to publication.

My family, friends and communities were part of the journey, including Whitley College, Westgate Baptist Community and Sanctuary Baptist Church. Thankyou.

I live on the land of the Djargurd Wurrung people. Empire intruded into this place. As it wounded the people, so it scarred the mountain. Yet this land and sky have sustained me and helped inspire this book. For Wombeetch Puyuun and his people, to whom much rent is owed, I offer this book as my promissory note.

1

Introduction

1.1 Cosmic journeys

Cosmology is a central concern in much of the apocalyptic literature. There are extended descriptions of the number of heavens, the distances between each heaven, the 'geography' within each heaven, the storehouses of rain and snow, the cosmic means of future punishment, the abodes and prisons of powerful beings, and the path of the sun and moon as they traverse the heavens. Descriptions of cosmic geography include the ends of the earth and the significant beings and cosmic geographic features found there, as well as the regions beneath the earth. This cosmological concern is particularly strong in those apocalypses in which the seer is taken on a journey into the sky.[1] By comparison with these apocalypses the cosmological dimension of Revelation is less explicit; Revelation does not describe the gates of the sun, the place where clouds go to collect rainwater or the cosmological basis for a national calendar. Yet Revelation's narrative operates in a 'relatively coherent imagined geography',[2] a story-space co-extensive with the cosmos on the horizontal and vertical axes. This cosmic story-space carries just as much theological significance as the more complex cosmological assertions of the other apocalypses.

In describing the assumptions and ideas in ancient writings, I use the term 'cosmology' for conceptual frameworks that explain the nature of the universe and its parts. Cosmological conceptions can relate to size, shape, structure and material composition; to stability and longevity; to the movements of parts within the whole; and to status as animate or inanimate, ordered or disordered. Cosmological conceptions describe and explain observed phenomena in the sky and on the earth, and also spaces and phenomena that were beyond observation in ordinary human experience. In ancient cosmologies the earth is a highly significant part of the cosmos, so in this context cosmology rightly includes areas of interest that modern people would classify as geology or meteorology; mountains and rivers can be significant cosmological features, and rainfall can be a significant part of the workings of the

---

[1] This is especially noteworthy in *1 Enoch*, *2 Enoch* and *3 Baruch*, but is commonly present in apocalypses that feature cosmic journeys.
[2] Steven J. Friesen, *Imperial Cults and the Apocalypse of John: Reading Revelation in the Ruins* (Oxford: Oxford University Press, 2001), 152.

cosmos. Even a human city can function as the centre of reality within a conceptual framework explaining the nature of the universe and its parts.³

In 2008 Sean M. McDonough commented that within the New Testament, Revelation is the 'climax of cosmology', and lamented the lack of a book-length treatise on the question.⁴ Since then a few studies have examined some aspects of Revelation's cosmology from particular perspectives. This study makes a further contribution, examining the operation of Revelation's narrative in cosmic story-space and the way in which that narrative defines the spaces and situates the hearers. While scholarship commonly assumes a three-tiered cosmos in Revelation, I argue that Revelation's narrative operates in a four-tiered cosmos, with the hyper-heaven sitting above the sky-heaven, earth and abyssal depths – a cosmic story-space that is recreated in the imagination of the hearers.⁵ I aim to show that this specifically four-tiered cosmos has significance not only for recognizing the narrative moves within the text but also for understanding the impact of the text on its hearers.

This study is inspired, in part, by *Social Science Commentary on the Book of Revelation* by Bruce J. Malina and John J. Pilch, a challenging, sometimes insightful, and deeply flawed work.⁶ Since publication in 2000, this book has remained at the fringes of critical scholarship, partly because of its own failure to converse with wider Revelation scholarship. I am not persuaded by its premise that John's intended audience is a learned prophetic circle, educated in the most sophisticated astrology/astronomy of their time, and the most up-to-date cosmological models of Greek theoreticians, and trained to interpret astral prophecy through this lens.⁷ I find the cosmological conclusions based around a spherical earth tenuous and at odds with what is actually happening in the narrative. And yet their insistence on understanding Revelation's cosmos and its inhabitants in ancient terms is an important corrective to the natural tendencies of all modern readers. The direction of my own work has been greatly influenced by their challenge to take seriously John's experience of a journey into the sky and consider what he actually saw and where he saw it. I have, however, found it fruitful to consider not the real experience of John the real author but the experience described for the character John in the present form of the text – and this in conversation with the experience of the implied hearer, which is very similar to, but not identical with, the experience of the character John.

Like John, the hearers are taken on a journey through the cosmos. Drawing from narrative theory, I argue that in this experience Revelation's cosmic story-space is

---

³ Friesen, *Imperial Cults*, 4.
⁴ Sean M. McDonough, 'Revelation: The Climax of Cosmology', in *Cosmology and New Testament Theology*, ed. Jonathan T. Pennington and Sean M. McDonough (London: T&T Clark, 2008), 178.
⁵ The term 'hyper-heaven' is suggested by the Greek term ὑπερουράνιος. Plato speaks of gods going up through the vault of heaven and standing on its outer surface, the ὑπερουράνιος. Plato, *Phaedrus* 247b-c. Eusebius of Caesarea wrote of 'those things which lie above the vault of heaven ... the region above the heavens [ὑπερουράνιος]'. Eusebius, *Historia Ecclesiastica* 10.4.70. Translation Arthur Cushman McGiffert, *The History of the Church, By Eusebius* (Overland Park: Digireads, 2018). See also Aelius Aristides, *Orationes* 49.398; Clement, *Protrepticus* 4.
⁶ Bruce J. Malina and John J. Pilch, *Social-Science Commentary on the Book of Revelation* (Minneapolis: Fortress Press, 2000).
⁷ Malina and Pilch, *Social-Science*, 12–13, 19, 77.

Introduction

recreated in the imagination of the hearers; spaces are mapped in relation to each other, and the nature of the spaces is developed by the narrative.[8] Of particular note is the space that I have come to call sky-heaven and the space that I have come to call hyper-heaven.

I argue that in Revelation, sky-heaven and hyper-heaven each has its own significance. Contrary to the predominant scholarly view, Revelation does not exhibit tension in its portrayal of heaven, between heaven as a site of conflict and heaven as the realm in which God truly reigns. Rather, the hearers are shown a sky-heaven characterized by archetypal conflict between powerful sky-beings and a hyper-heaven defined by full recognition of the Throne. I will show that this characterization is consistent throughout Revelation, with sky-heaven and hyper-heaven each playing a distinct role in the narrative.

Such cosmological considerations are more than just esoteric speculation in ancient texts such as Revelation and the other apocalypses; rather, they promote particular ways of understanding the world and living in it. For example, if we consider the composite work known as *1 Enoch* we see that its cosmological descriptions serve a number of ethical and rhetorical functions. The Book of Watchers (*1 En.* 1–36) initially portrays a cosmos in which 'the consistent operation of nature is a paradigm for human obedience to God's commandments'.[9] Enoch directs the reader to consider what happens in the sky, how the luminaries do not deviate from their path (οὐ παραβαίνουσιν τὴν ἰδίαν τάξιν) but rise and set according to their role in the cosmic order (*1 En.* 2.1). Likewise, the reader is to live a moral, ordered life. There is a hint that this includes participation in the seasonal festivals (τοὺς φωστῆρας ... ἐν ... ταῖς ἑορταῖς αὐτῶν φαίνονται. *1 En.* 2.1). In a later section of the Book of Watchers (*1 En.* 17–36) the picture is modified, and a small number of sky-beings (stars) are portrayed as having deviated from their correct path; their captivity and impending punishment serve as a negative example to the readers.[10]

These themes recur in subsequent parts of *1 Enoch*. The Astronomical Book (*1 En.* 72–82) is devoted to the orderly cosmic movements in line with days, months, seasons and years and yet warns that 'in those days ... many of the chiefs of the stars shall make errors in respect to the orders given to them; they shall change their courses and functions and not appear during the seasons which have been prescribed for them' (*1 En.* 80.5-6).[11] The reader is further warned not to be 'like the sinners in the computation of the days' (*1 En.* 82.4). By following a simple calendar consisting of twelve months times thirty days, and failing to add the four additional days that bring the year to 364 days, sinners fail to live in accord with the true cycle of the cosmos and

---

[8] 'Verbal story-space ... is what the reader is prompted to create in imagination.' Seymour Benjamin Chatman, *Story and Discourse: Narrative Structure in Fiction and Film* (Ithaca: Cornell University Press, 1978), 104.
[9] Harry Alan Hahne, *The Corruption and Redemption of Creation: Nature in Romans 8.19-22 and Jewish Apocalyptic Literature*, Library of New Testament Studies, vol. 336 (London: T&T Clark, 2006), 38.
[10] Hahne, *Corruption*, 166.
[11] Translation E. Isaac, '1 (Ethiopic Apocalypse of) Enoch', in *The Old Testament Pseudepigrapha*, ed. James H. Charlesworth, vol. 1 (Garden City: Doubleday, 1983), 5–90.

the God who so orders the cosmos.¹² This concern is developed further in *Jubilees*, with its insistence that the orderly movements of the cosmos determine the one correct national calendar by which community life is ordered (*Jub.* 4.17-18; 6.32-38).

In many apocalypses humans are linked with the cosmos, particularly the earth and lower skies as the 'human part' of the cosmos. In *3 Baruch* the human cosmos extends into the four lower skies, where the human seer is taken and shown the course of the sun and moon (*3 Bar.* 6.1–9.7), the place where clouds collect the rainwater that enables the growth of human crops (*3 Bar.* 10.6-9) and the places in the skies where deceased humans dwell (*3 Bar.* 2.2-7; 3.1-8; 4.1-5; 10.1-5).¹³ This shares some similarities with the *Ascension of Isaiah*, in which the cosmos of living human beings includes the earth and (the underside of) the firmament, these two spaces being a mirror image of each other (*Asc. Isa.* 7.10). The connection between humans and 'the mountains, and the hills … and the desert, and the trees, and the angel of the sun, and that of the moon' is such that the voice of judgement can address all these together as 'this heaven and this earth' (*Asc. Isa.* 4.18). The connection between humans and their cosmos can mean that sinful or disordered living by human beings results in damage to the earth and seasonal harvests (*Jub.* 23.17-18) while ordered/righteous living is connected with the cleansing of the land and productivity of crops (*Jub.* 7.34-37; 50.1-5). Alternatively, the distinction between the human-proximate cosmos and the higher cosmos can be used in service of a more sectarian ideology; the *Ascension of Isaiah* affirms faithful people who withdraw from cities dominated by the powers of the earth-and-firmament space (*Asc. Isa.* 2.7-9; 4.1-13; 7.9-10), and put their trust in the knowledge and ultimate vindication that come from the higher heavens (*Asc. Isa.* 4.14-18; 5.13; 9.19-26).

Some apocalypses feature a cosmic tour in which the reader is assured that deviant, oppressive and destructive powers will themselves be suppressed or destroyed, because the means of their destruction already exists in the cosmos.¹⁴ Thus in the Book of Watchers the seer describes a fiery emptiness beyond the horizontal extremities of earth and sky, designated as the place and means by which rebellious angels will be punished and constrained, with no possibility of accessing the cosmos or exerting power within it (*1 En.* 18.11–19.1; 21.7-10. See also 10.4-6, 11-13). Versions of this idea are referred to in Mt. 25.41 and Lk. 8.31. For the communities that read *1 Enoch*, this

---

[12] Jonathan Ben-Dov argues that the Astronomical Book originally posited a 360-day year but was redacted to include an intercalary day in each quarter of the year. The additional four days bring the calendar to 364 days and thus closer to the actual length of the solar year (365.24 days). This would have practical benefits as the calendar stays closer to the natural seasons but Ben-Dov argues that 'the additional days were included on ideological grounds, in order to give special importance to the fourfold division of the year'. Jonathan Ben-Dov, *Head of All Years: Astronomy and Calendars at Qumran in Their Ancient Context* (Leiden: Brill, 2008), 52.

[13] This is true of the Greek recension. The Slavonic hints that access to higher cosmic levels may be possible for the righteous dead.

[14] David Russell observes that 'the apocalyptists noted the created order … to relate cosmology and individual eschatology'. David M. Russell, *The New Heavens and New Earth: Hope for the Creation in Jewish Apocalyptic and the New Testament*, Studies in Biblical Apocalyptic Literature (Philadelphia: Visionary Press, 1996), 131. I suggest a further point, that they related cosmology with the eschatology of oppressive powers.

has significance for how life is lived in relation to the powers that may be experienced as oppressive and destructive[15] and felt to be deviations from the kosher cosmic order.[16]

Cosmic tours can further demonstrate that the creator God of Israelite tradition is ultimately great and holy, and the only reality worthy of worship. This is a key element in many apocalypses with cosmic journeys but is expressed particularly strongly in the *Apocalypse of Abraham*, which first establishes the central motif of idolatry versus monolatry (*Apoc. Abr.* 1–9) and only then has the seer taken into the skies to observe that they are devoid of any other being worthy of worship (*Apoc. Abr.* 19.3). Similarly, the *Ascension of Isaiah* depicts an ascending series of seven heavens which serve no apparent purpose other than to intensify the greatness and holiness of the creator God on the seventh.[17]

Far from mere esoteric speculation, these cosmic tours and cosmological descriptions serve particular purposes, calling the reader to awe before the one creator God of Israelite tradition, to a life ordered by certain organizing principles and to perseverance in these practices in spite of the oppressive, destructive and deviant forces that dominate human existence.[18] In comparison to *1 Enoch*, *2 Enoch* and *3 Baruch*, Revelation has a lesser emphasis on cosmological description, and narration of the seer's movements through the cosmos is briefer in comparison to these works or to the cosmic journey narratives of the *Apocalypse of Abraham* or the *Ascension of Isaiah*. Nevertheless, I will show that Revelation's narrative operates in a cosmic story-space with ideological import in ways both similar and distinct from related ancient works.

In different ways the symbolic or ideological significance of Revelation's universe has been recognized by Elizabeth Schüssler Fiorenza, Steven J. Friesen, Ryan Leif Hansen and David deSilva, and I discuss their work below. Further to the existing scholarship, I consider the ideological significance of the tiered cosmic structure in which Revelation's narrative operates, in particular the complementary roles played by the sky-heaven and the hyper-heaven. I will argue that the conflicted sky-heaven exposes pagan imperial culture as draconian, thus demanding non-participation in its social and economic practices, while the hyper-heaven makes such non-participation a viable option.[19] Not only is hyper-heaven the source of positive change but its existence, in contradistinction to the mere human-proximate cosmos of earth and sky-heaven,

---

[15] George W. E. Nickelsburg, *1 Enoch 1: A Commentary on the Book of 1 Enoch*, Hermeneia (Minneapolis: Fortress Press, 2001), 5.

[16] David J. Bryan, *Cosmos, Chaos and the Kosher Mentality* (London: Sheffield Academic Press, 1995), 170, 184.

[17] Although the picture is modified by the presence of the Christ and the angel of the Holy Spirit in this distinctly Christian text.

[18] The forces that dominate human existence, and the apocalyptic response, are explored in Anathea. E. Portier-Young, *Apocalypse against Empire: Theologies of Resistance in Early Judaism* (Grand Rapids: Eerdmans, 2011).

[19] *Note:* The term 'pagan' is not used pejoratively. Rather, I refer to 'pagan empire' in acknowledgement of the role that the gods played in Roman imperial ideology. This ideology was expressed particularly in the imperial cults, which were felt to be an appropriate response to Roman presence in Asia Minor. Wei Hsien Wan, *The Contest for Time and Space in the Roman Imperial Cults and 1 Peter: Reconfiguring the Universe*, Library of New Testament Studies (London: T&T Clark, 2020), 52. Steven Friesen explains that imperial cults were 'an imperialist elaboration within Greco-Roman polytheism'. Friesen, *Imperial Cults*, 4.

is a present cosmic guarantee of the final cosmic transformation that creates a new space for human life exclusive of draconian elements. This gives a different context to present decisions.

1.2 Scholarship on cosmology in Revelation

1.2.1 Structural cosmology

Revelation's cosmology has been considered from different perspectives which can broadly be characterized as structural, dynamic and rhetorical. By 'structural', I mean the cosmic structure: the shape of the earth, the shape of the firmament, the material composition of the firmament, the number of heavens, the location of the abyss either below the earth or in the heavens, the location of the shaft of the abyss and related considerations. Almost all commentators assume in Revelation a three-tiered cosmos of heaven, earth and a level below the earth consisting of Hades and/or the abyss.[20] Friesen writes of 'three levels of spatial reality: heaven, earth, and the underworld (5:3)'.[21] Similarly, Ryan concludes, 'the cosmological frame of the Apocalypse is thus an archaic, three-level cosmos: a single heavenly tier at the top, a central zone divided into earth and sea, and an underworld realm that interacts with the realm above'.[22]

A tiered cosmos is a cosmos characterized by absolute verticality, meaning that 'up' has an absolute meaning at the cosmic scale, and not merely in relation to limited human experience. This is not the case in a de-centred modern cosmology or even in the cosmological speculations of Anaximander, who posited a drum-shaped earth with an inhabited antipode.[23] Within this broad agreement, scholars have differed on some aspects of the three-tier construction, such as the shape and material composition of the firmament/heaven, whether the earth is a disc or a square, what kind of distinction to make between Hades and the abyss, and the structural relationship between the abyss and the earthly seas.

---

[20] R. H. Charles, *A Critical and Exegetical Commentary on the Revelation of St. John*, vol. 1, *The International Critical Commentary* (Edinburgh: T&T Clark, 1920), 108. David E. Aune, *Revelation 1–5, Word Biblical Commentary*, vol. 52A (Nashville: Thomas Nelson, 1997), 347–9. David E. Aune, 'Apocalypse Renewed: An Intertextual Reading of the Apocalypse of John', in *The Reality of the Apocalypse: Rhetoric and Politics in the Book of Revelation*, ed. David L Barr (Atlanta: SBL, 2006), 51–2. Craig R. Koester, *Revelation: A New Translation with Introduction and Commentary, The Anchor Yale Bible*, vol. 38A (New Haven: Yale University Press, 2014), 119–20. David L. Barr, *Tales of the End: A Narrative Commentary on the Book of Revelation* (Santa Rosa: Polebridge Press, 1998), 115.

[21] Friesen, *Imperial Cults*, 152. He adds,

> Middle heaven might also be considered a separate region because it is an intermediate zone between heaven and earth where flying beings deliver divine announcements (8:13; 14:6; 19:17). Because middle heaven is inhabited mostly by birds and is subject to the sorts of events that also occur in the human realm, one might more appropriately categorize it as one part of the earthly realm that has a distinct mediating function.

Friesen, *Imperial Cults*, 155.

[22] Sean Michael Ryan, *Hearing at the Boundaries of Vision: Education Informing Cosmology in Revelation 9* (London: T&T Clark, 2012), 62.

[23] Hippolytus, *Refutations* 1.5

Heaven or sky or firmament

Where the shape of the firmament/heaven is considered, it is usually assumed to be domed,[24] with its edge resting on the edge of the earth, although Adela Yarbro Collins's work provides room to question that assumption. She explores the probable influence of Babylonian cosmology on Jewish and Christian apocalypses and from this perspective challenges the assumption that heavens are always spherical, domed or curved in some way.[25] While *3 Baruch* appears to have a flat earth of human habitation and a domed 'firmament (heaven) resting on the ends of the earth',[26] in other cosmological conceptions the sky/firmament is a broad sheet.[27] In fact, Revelation gives little hint as to whether its sky is domed or a broad sheet, and if the latter, how it remains in place above the earth. While the existence of a solid firmament is sometimes acknowledged,[28] its material construction is rarely considered. McDonough suggests that it is suspended water or ice.[29] Collins does not discuss the material composition of Revelation's firmament but does connect the expanses in the *Apocalypse of Abraham* with Babylonian and Hebrew concepts of something 'pulled out tightly' or 'spread out broadly', such as 'a strip of beaten metal'.[30]

While there is agreement that heaven is the upper tier, there is uncertainty among scholars as to which parts of the upper cosmos should be called 'heaven'. Sean M. McDonough describes a firmament called οὐρανός with God's throne room sitting atop this also called οὐρανός.[31] I argue that this description of the cosmic structure is correct. Revelation makes no *linguistic* distinction between a firmament and the visible sky at its underside and the throne room above; the simple term οὐρανός can denote any part of the upper cosmos.[32] This contributes to disagreement and uncertainty as

---

[24] McDonough, 'Revelation', 181. Frederick J. Murphy, *Fallen is Babylon: The Revelation to John* (Harrisburg: Trinity Press International, 1998), 170.
[25] Adela Yarbro Collins, *Cosmology and Eschatology in Jewish and Christian Apocalypticism*, Supplements to the Journal for the study of Judaism (Leiden: Brill, 1996), 36.
[26] Yarbro Collins, *Cosmology*, 44.
[27] Yarbro Collins, *Cosmology*, 36.
[28] Murphy, *Fallen*, 170.
[29] McDonough, 'Revelation'. Franz Boll wrote, 'Der Himmel ist die kristallene Halbkugel'. Franz Boll, *Aus der Offenbarung Johannis. Hellenistische Studien zum Weltbild der Apokalypse* (Leipzig: B. G. Teubner, 1914), 16–17.
[30] Yarbro Collins, *Cosmology*, 36.
[31] McDonough, 'Revelation', 181.
[32] It should not be surprising that an ancient text uses οὐρανός in more than one sense, even in relation to spatial reality and the structure of the cosmos. Aristotle explains that he uses the word in three senses:

> Let us first state what we say it is to be a heaven and in how many ways, in order that what we are inquiring into will become clearer to us. In one way, then, [1] we say that the substance belonging to the outermost revolution of the universe is heaven, or the natural body that is on the outermost revolution of the universe, since more than anything else it is the last upper region that we usually call heaven, the one in which we say that everything divine also has its seat. In another way, [2] it is the body that is continuous with the outermost revolution of the universe, in which we find the moon, the sun, and some of the stars, since we say that these bodies too are in heaven. Further, [3] we say that the body that is encompassed by the outermost revolution is heaven, since we are accustomed to say that the whole and the universe is heaven. Heaven is said, then, in three ways.

Aristotle, *De Caelo*, 278b10-20. Translation C. D. C. Reeve, *De Caelo* (Indianapolis: Hackett, 2020).

to which part of the cosmos is really 'heaven', or which parts of Revelation are really speaking of 'heaven' rather than 'just the sky'.

It is a common view that Revelation exhibits some tension in its presentation of the heaven on which God is enthroned, presenting it as the dwelling of God while also allowing some discordant elements within it. But there is often an assumed distinction between οὐρανός as the physical sky above the earth and οὐρανός as a spiritual realm distinct from spatial reality. Thus in 1878 Gebhardt wrote that the seer sometimes refers to the heaven that is perceptible to the senses 'with its sun and moon, vi. 12, and stars … and birds xix. 17' but more frequently means 'heaven in the peculiar, tropical, higher, and spiritual sense of the word', a 'region of being beyond time and space'.[33] Notably, the verses cited for stars in the visible sky are those in which the stars may be seen as mere lights (Rev. 6.13; 8.12), and not those which suggest that the stars are actors or personages (Rev. 9.1; 12.4).[34] This choice emphasizes the idea of an οὐρανός that is 'just the sky' in a sense consistent with modern science.

In 1966 Caird described three referents for οὐρανός. The first is the physical sky, the second is 'the uncreated realm which is the eternal dwelling of God' referred to in Rev. 3.12 and 21.1 and the third is the οὐρανός that is actually seen in John's visions. Even though these visions include God sitting on the Throne, this third οὐρανός cannot be the eternal dwelling of God because these visions also include symbols of the world's evil (Rev. 12.7). In Caird's estimation, the οὐρανός that is the scene of John's visions is neither the eternal dwelling of God nor the physical sky, but still 'part of the created universe' – not a part that sits atop the sky/firmament as described by McDonough, but 'a part which is entered by the opening of the spiritual eye'.[35]

In 2013 Gert Jordaan also assumed the distinction between οὐρανός as the physical sky above the earth and οὐρανός as a spiritual realm distinct from spatial reality. He wrote that because the stars of Rev. 12.4 are a figurative reference to (fallen) angels, the οὐρανός in which they are seen is not just the physical sky above but also becomes a metaphor for the dwelling place of God.[36] The assumption is that angels or similar beings do not dwell in the sky; instead, such beings dwell in some other place or some other realm of being, a 'spiritual dimension'[37] or 'divine point above time and history'.[38]

---

[33] Hermann Gebhardt, *The Doctrine of the Apocalypse and its Relation to the Doctrine of the Gospel and Epistles of John*, trans. John Jefferson, Clark's Foreign Theological Library, vol. 58 (Edinburgh: T&T Clark, 1878), 43, 50.

[34] Gebhardt actually cites 8.13, but this verse does not speak of stars at all and the citation was probably a typographical error. Based on context, I believe he intended to cite 6.13 and/or 8.12. Gebhardt, *Doctrine*, 43

[35] G. B. Caird, *A Commentary on the Revelation of St. John the Divine*, 2nd edn, Black's New Testament Commentaries (London: A&C Black, 1966), 62. Most scholars have not adopted Caird's distinction between the place where God is seen enthroned and another 'eternal dwelling of God', but he was followed by Harrington in 1993. Wilfrid J. Harrington, *Revelation*, Sacra Pagina Series, vol. 16 (Collegeville: Liturgical Press, 1993), 78.

[36] Gert J. C. Jordaan, 'Cosmology in the Book of Revelation/Kosmologie in die boek van Openbaring', *In die Skriflig*, 47/2 (2013): 3.

[37] G. K. Beale, *The Book of Revelation: A Commentary on the Greek Text*, The New International Greek Testament Commentary (Grand Rapids: Eerdmans, 1999), 319.

[38] Jordaan, 'Cosmology', 1.

So for Jordaan, where Revelation speaks of an οὐρανός of angels or other powerful sky-beings, this must be an οὐρανός that is figuratively 'higher' than the sky.

From Gebhardt to Jordaan, this way of distinguishing between the sky above the earth and the heaven of supernatural beings results from approaching Revelation from a modern mindset, which assumes a clear distinction between a 'natural' sky and a 'supernatural' heaven. Here I try to approach 'the heavens' from a perspective more aligned with ancient assumptions, that is, by recognizing that the visible sky may be a dynamic space within the cosmos, inhabited by powerful beings that impact human life on earth[39] but at the same time may not be the special realm of God's Throne and the awesome, holy attendants. Indeed, I will show that in Revelation's cosmic story-space this is precisely the case and is the reason why I speak not of 'sky' and 'heaven' but of 'sky-heaven' and 'hyper-heaven': at the underside of the firmament is a dynamic, conflicted space worthy of the name 'sky-heaven', while above the firmament is a dynamic, symphonic space worthy of the name 'hyper-heaven'.

Earth

The middle level of the three-tiered cosmos is generally called 'earth' but recognized as including both earth and sea.[40] This is accurate in terms of the tiered cosmic structure in which earth and sea are on the same plane and together constitute the space in which humans live and move, even though the sea can sometimes connote deep primordial chaos.[41] To the best of my knowledge, scholars have not commented on whether Revelation's sea roughly equates to the Mediterranean Sea or has a broader meaning even on the earthly plane. The exception is Sean Michael Ryan, who writes that Revelation's θάλασσα is not the Mediterranean Sea but an encircling ocean-river akin to the Ὠκεανός of Homeric literature.[42]

---

[39] Philo of Alexandria wrote,

> Those beings, whom other philosophers call demons [δαίμων], Moses usually calls angels [ἄγγελος]; and they are souls hovering in the air. And let no one suppose, that what is here stated is a fable, for it is necessarily true that the universe [κόσμος] must be filled with living things in all its parts, since every one of its primary and elementary portions contains its appropriate animals [ζῷον] and such as are consistent with its nature: the earth containing terrestrial animals, the sea and the rivers containing aquatic animals, and the fire such as are born in the fire (but it is said, that such as these last are found chiefly in Macedonia), and the heaven [οὐρανός] containing the stars [ἀστήρ]: for these also are entire souls [ψυχή, soul/being/person]. (*De gigantibus* 6–8)

> Translation C. D. Yonge, *The Works of Philo Judaeus, the Contemporary of Josephus* (London: H. G. Bohn, 1854).

[40] Gebhardt, *Doctrine*, 60. Aune, *Revelation 1–5*, 366. Koester, *Revelation*, 119.

[41] Gert Jordaan, while advocating a 'metaphorical' understanding of Revelation's cosmology, assumes that in a 'literal' reading the sea would refer to the lower cosmic depths. Jordaan, 'Cosmology', 3. See also Grant R. Osborne, *Revelation*, Baker Exegetical Commentary on the New Testament (Grand Rapids: Baker Academic, 2002), 264. McDonough recognizes that the sea is linked with earth as part of the good creation of God yet can also connote deep primordial chaos. McDonough, 'Revelation', 183–4.

[42] Ryan, *Hearing*, 68–9, 90. I find this unlikely and reach the opposite conclusion: Revelation's sea is the Mediterranean (including the Aegean). In ancient sources the sea is surrounded by land, and the land is surrounded by the ocean-river. Plato comments, 'The earth is very large, and we live around the sea in a small portion of it between Phasis and the Pillars of Heracles, like ants or frogs around a

Sean Michael Ryan also provides a distinctive description of the shape of the earth. Some scholars take the 'four corners' of Rev. 7.1 to mean that earth is actually a square,[43] while others suggest that the 'four corners' refer to the four compass points, which would allow for a disc-shaped earth.[44] Ryan depicts a square earth surrounded by an encircling ocean such that 'earth and sea' as a whole is circular,[45] a 'terrestrial disc'.[46]

Two further cosmic regions are sometimes identified by scholars and described as part of 'earth', broadly understood. The first is the μεσουράνημα (Rev. 8.16; 14.6; 19.17), when understood as a cosmic level at the midpoint between earth and sky. Friesen writes that γῆ is 'composed of earth in the limited sense (i.e., "dry land"), the sea, and middle heaven'. In this understanding, mid-heaven is appropriately categorized as part of the earthly realm because it is 'inhabited mostly by birds and is subject to the sorts of events that also occur in the human realm'.[47] I broadly agree with this understanding of mid-heaven, but I will argue that there is a higher sky-heaven that is also, in an important sense, part of the human realm. Ryan Leif Hansen holds a similar view with a different nuance, describing mid-heaven as one of the 'middle spaces that serve as the site of transversals across the boundaries'.[48] While I share the broad perspective of Friesen and Hansen that the μεσουράνημα is a kind of half-level at the midpoint between οὐρανός and γῆ, it should be noted that scholars more commonly read μεσουράνημα as the cosmic apex at the midpoint between east and west,[49] or a central section of the starry sky in Greek and Babylonian astrological systems.[50]

In addition to these considerations, Koester suggests that earth-space also includes some spaces just beneath the ground, the dwelling place of ordinary creatures that praise God with the rest of creation (Rev. 5.13) and quite distinct from the ominous cosmic region further below, the dwelling places of demons and of the human dead.[51] This suggestion is plausible, and it resolves a tension in Revelation's portrayal of underworld beings but is difficult to assess.[52] If such a space exists in Revelation, it plays no discernible role in the narrative.

swamp' (Plato, *Phaedo* 109b). The sea is a 'hollow', while Okeanos is a great river that flows around the outside of the earth (Plato, *Phaedo* 112e). See also Virgil, *Aeneid* 1.236-237.

[43] Yarbro Collins, *Cosmology*, 107. Charles, *Revelation*, vol. 1, 203. J. Massyngberde Ford, *Revelation*, 1st edn, *The Anchor Bible*, vol. 38 (Garden City: Doubleday, 1975), 115. Harrington, *Revelation*, 98. Aune describes τὰς τέσσαρας γωνίας τῆς γῆς as the four quarters of the compass yet also states that earth is here conceived of as a flat, square shape. David E. Aune, *Revelation 6–16*, Word Biblical Commentary, vol. 52B (Nashville: Thomas Nelson, 1998), 450.

[44] Philip Edgcumbe Hughes, *The Book of the Revelation: A Commentary* (Leicester: Inter-Varsity Press, 1990), 93. Beale, *Revelation*, 406. Koester, *Revelation*, 414.

[45] Ryan, *Hearing*, 68–70.

[46] Ryan, *Hearing*, 84.

[47] Friesen, *Imperial Cults*, 155.

[48] Ryan Leif Hansen, *Silence and Praise: Rhetorical Cosmology and Political Theology in the Book of Revelation* (Minneapolis: Fortress Press, 2014), 38.

[49] Henry Barclay Swete, *The Apocalypse of St. John*, 3rd edn (London: Macmillan, 1906), 111. Charles, *Revelation*, vol. 1, 237. Ford, *Revelation*, 139–40. Koester, *Revelation*, 451.

[50] Malina and Pilch, *Social-Science*, 86.

[51] Koester, *Revelation*, 119–20.

[52] McDonough, 'Revelation', 184. The beings of the abyss are usually understood as the kinds of beings that do not worship God. Some suggest that Rev. 5.13 includes *unwilling* recognition of God's glory (Beale, *Revelation*, 365), while others emphasize that this is a *rhetorical* picture of the whole cosmos recognizing God. David Arthur DeSilva, *Seeing Things John's Way: The Rhetoric of the*

Below earth

In the tiered cosmic framework Hades and the abyss are both located on the lowest tier. Friesen maintains a distinction between the abyss as 'a prison for evil creatures … in line with the usage of the term in Luke 8:31 and *1 Enoch* 18:10' and Hades as 'the abode of dead humans', a distinction shared by Swete, Charles and Koester.[53] On the other hand, Sean Michael Ryan treats Hades and the abyss as essentially synonymous.[54] Malina and Pilch also assume that Hades and the abyss are synonymous, even as they locate the abyss/Hades in a non-tiered cosmic schema (see further below).[55] In Chapter 5 I argue that Hades and the abyss have distinct characteristics in the narrative and should not be treated as synonymous.[56]

Additionally, it is sometimes argued that the abyss is synonymous with the sea, or structurally connected with the sea.[57] The reasons for this include Revelation's use of ἄβυσσος for a deep, chaotic, threatening place, recalling its use in the Septuagint for the chaotic, threatening, watery cosmic deep (see Gen. 1.2; 7.11; Deut. 8.7; Job 41.23-24), and Revelation's use of θάλασσα with similar connotations (Rev. 13.1; 21.1). The parallel between Rev. 11.7 and Rev. 13.1 is another significant factor suggesting an association between ἄβυσσος and θάλασσα.[58]

Sean Michael Ryan argues that in Revelation's cosmos there is a structural connection between the abyss and the terrestrial waters.[59] In doing so, Ryan identifies Revelation's θάλασσα with the encircling Ὠκεανός of Homeric literature, and the μέγας ποταμός of *1 En.* 17.6.[60] Ryan's Hearer-Construct One (a hypothetical hearer-construct with a low level of Greek education) understands the shaft of the abyss to open up in the Ὠκεανός/θάλασσα at the north-west extremity of the 'terrestrial disc'.[61] In Chapter 5 I argue that Revelation's implied hearer has a broader knowledge base than Ryan's hearer-construct and can therefore see the abyss opening up onto any part of the earth. I argue that Revelation is ambivalent as to a connection between the abyss and the sea, but it is not correct to identify its sea with an encircling ocean-river. In ancient conceptions the land is not surrounded by the sea; rather, the sea is surrounded by land (Virgil, *Aeneid* 1.236-237), which in turn is surrounded by the ocean-river.

Book of Revelation (Louisville: Westminster John Knox Press, 2009), 262.). Charles understood πᾶν κτίσμα … ὑποκάτω τῆς γῆς to mean deceased humans in Hades, showing the 'progress that theology has made from O.T. times, when no praise of God was conceived of as possible in Sheol'. Charles, *Revelation*, vol. 1, 150.

[53] Friesen, *Imperial Cults*, 156. Swete, *Apocalypse*, 112. Charles, *Revelation*, vol. 1, 239-40. Koester, *Revelation*, 120.
[54] Ryan, *Hearing*, 70-1, 87-8.
[55] Malina and Pilch, *Social-Science*, 129-30.
[56] See Sec. 5.2.5.
[57] Bousset argued that the abyss is synonymous with the sea. W. Bousset, *Die Offenbarung Johannes* (Göttingen: Vandenhoeck and Ruprecht, 1966), 358.
[58] 'The abyss from which he ascends is intended to be identical with the sea from which the beast emerges in 13:1.' Aune, *Revelation 6-16*, 616.
[59] Ryan, *Hearing*, 85.
[60] Ryan, *Hearing*, 68-9, 88-90.
[61] Ryan, *Hearing*, 110.

Spherical cosmos

In contrast to the tiered cosmos described above, Malina and Pilch propose a spherical cosmic structure.[62] This differs from the tiered cosmos in several key respects:

- the earth is a sphere and thus has a southern hemisphere, although it is not clear whether their southern hemisphere is inhabited (whether by people or by ordinary animals or by extra-ordinary beings);
- the sky/firmament is a sphere and is not attached to the earth and does not need to be held up by a structural connection with the earth or in any other way; and
- the concepts of 'up' and 'down' require a little more nuance, and yet there is a sense in which the northern hemisphere and its sky is 'up', while the sky of the southern hemisphere is 'down'. The abyss/Hades is located in the sky of the southern hemisphere (or perhaps in the sky of the northern hemisphere, but in the southern section of this sky; they are unclear on this point).[63]

Their assertion of a spherical cosmic structure derives from their premise that the intended audience is a group of astral prophets who would be up-to-date with the latest cosmology.[64] Hence, they map John's journey and the things he sees onto the cosmos known from the most up-to-date developments in Greek cosmological theorizing and the most detailed astrological observations and categorization of the skies. I am unpersuaded by this premise because Revelation's intended primary audience appears to be the congregations of Asia Minor (Rev. 1.4) as Revelation is read out to them (Rev. 1.3; 22.18). Indeed, 'it is as if the author of the book knows that the text would be read in a particular setting, within a community … and sought to differentiate it from those Jewish apocalyptic writings that were usually read in private'.[65] Additionally, they do not provide specific evidence that early Christian prophecy included prophetic circles with these specific characteristics, that is, educated not only in common astrological lore but also in elite Greek cosmological theories, and practiced in interpreting heavenly visions through this lens. We may note that the *Ascension of Isaiah* implies the existence of a Christian prophetic circle that withdrew from urban life and saw visions of the heavens (*Asc. Isa.* 3.31), but this text exhibits no discernible influence from the cosmological theories discussed among highly educated Greeks.

Further, this cosmic construction cannot be the story-space in which the narrative operates. In subsequent chapters I will show that it does not accord with the narrative moves made in the text; rather, the narrative operates in a tiered cosmic story-space. Note, for example, the star having fallen *to earth* to open the shaft of the abyss (Rev. 9.1) makes little sense in the proposed cosmology of Malina and Pilch, in which the abyss is located in the sky.[66]

---

[62] Malina and Pilch, *Social-Science*, 77–81.
[63] Malina and Pilch, *Social-Science*, 129–30, 33–4.
[64] Malina and Pilch, *Social-Science*, 12–13, 19, 77.
[65] Lourdes García Ureña, *Narrative and Drama in the Book of Revelation*, trans. Donald Murphy, Society for New Testament Studies Monograph Series, vol. 175 (Cambridge: Cambridge University Press, 2019), 9–10.
[66] Malina and Pilch, *Social-Science*, 129.

In a sense, the approach of Malina and Pilch is fruitfully modified by Sean Michael Ryan in his use of Hearer-Construct Two, a hypothetical hearer-construct with a high level of Greek education who maps Revelation's narrative onto his existing cosmic schema. This hearer-construct adopts an allegorical method of interpretation similar to that of Philo and thus equates the abyss with the celestial sea in the sky of the southern hemisphere.[67] But Ryan does not suggest that this hearer-construct closely resembles the primary intended real audience in the way that Malina and Pilch would have it.

Still, I do see value in attempting to map the journey and locate the sights in the cosmos. Where Malina and Pilch map the journey and sights onto sections of the sky (the southern part of the sky, the line of the ecliptic and so on), I will show that there is value in locating the sights and events by their *height* in the cosmos, that is, whether an event described in the οὐρανός occurs below or above the firmament.

1.2.2 Dynamic cosmology

Contrasting with structural cosmology, another perspective on Revelation's cosmology is 'dynamic cosmology'. In using this term I refer primarily to the work of Walter Wink and of Anthony Gwyther, who consider the nature of 'heaven' and its relationship with the more plainly visible aspects of the human world.

Walter Wink's 'Powers' trilogy lays out a way of understanding the New Testament's language and concepts of power with a focus on those entities and realms of the Bible that tend to be labelled as 'supernatural'. His attempt to understand the function of angels, demons and 'heaven' is worth consideration. Wink laboriously examines each of the New Testament's terms related to power in the contexts in which they are used, asking what kind of power it is—an office, an incumbent or a dominion—and always asking if the term is used in reference to a good or bad power, and a 'material' or 'spiritual' power. He concludes, 'The Powers are simultaneously the outer and inner aspects of one and the same indivisible concretion of power … Nothing less than insistence on this unity makes sense of the unexplained ambiguity in the usage of the New Testament language of power.'[68] 'Heaven' is 'the realm of "withinness", the metaphorical "place" in which the spirituality of everything is "located", … the habitat of angels, spirits, cherubim, and seraphim, but also of demons and the devil and all the Powers "in the heavenly places".'[69] For Wink, beings in heaven have counterparts on earth, and vice versa, and neither can exist without the other because they are the two aspects of the same reality.[70] This is most obviously the case for the 'angels of the nations' (Deut. 32.8-9; Dan. 10.13, 20-21),[71] which finds expression in Michael, the dragon and the beasts of Revelation 12, 13 and 17,[72] and for the 'angels of the churches'

---

[67] Ryan, *Hearing*, 150.
[68] Walter Wink, *Naming the Powers: The Language of Power in the New Testament* (Philadelphia: Fortress Press, 1984), 107.
[69] Wink, *Naming*, 119.
[70] Wink, *Naming*, 134.
[71] Wink, *Naming*, 126–7.
[72] Wink, *Naming*, 34.

in Revelation 1–3.[73] In this way heaven and earth function in dyadic relationship, and seeing an earthly entity in its heavenly aspect can create a clearer picture of its true nature. Thus for Wink, heaven functions as a 'place' of conflict inextricably bound to earthly conflict.[74]

I find Wink's interpretation of heaven helpful and persuasive but limited in two respects.[75] Firstly, this almost consistent description of heaven is in tension with Wink's important comment that heaven is also 'where God is enthroned' and 'the source of the transformative possibilities that God presents to every actual entity'.[76] Wink's work does not address this tension. Secondly, I do not believe it gives due consideration to the 'upness' of heaven in ancient cosmological conceptions and in Revelation's narrative movements.

Anthony Gwyther also considers the nature of 'heaven' and its relationship with the more plainly visible aspects of the human world, but from a different perspective. His doctoral dissertation applies a 'socio-literary reading methodology' which 'attempts to take seriously both the literary world of the text and the socio-historical world for which the text was written'.[77] In Gwyther's analysis, '"Earth" is the perspective of empire. "Heaven" is the perspective of God.'[78] His subsequent book written with Wes Howard-Brook adds, 'John's look behind the veil gave him a sense that reality was *bifurcated* … The world defined by those with power represents one branch … The world where God lives and reigns is the other branch … Revelation calls these realities "heaven" and "earth"' (emphasis in the original).[79] The argument is that since heaven is co-present with earth, Revelation's constant appeal to heaven is an appeal for its hearers to live their lives on earth in accordance with the heavenly narrative and not with the imperial narrative that underpinned Roman order.[80]

As helpful as this is, Gwyther's understanding of the relationship between 'heaven' and 'earth' is in significant tension with Wink's portrayal of a conflicted heaven existing as another dimension of earthly conflict. A limitation in Gwyther's work is that his description of οὐρανός as 'wherever the truth of God is believed and practised'[81] leads

---

[73] Walter Wink, *Unmasking the Powers: The Invisible Forces that Determine Human Existence* (Philadelphia: Fortress Press, 1986), 69–71.

[74] Sweet made the similar comment, 'Heaven represents not a different world so much as the inward and spiritual behind the outward and physical … heaven contains the spiritual powers behind all things in our world, both evil and good.' J. P. M. Sweet, *Revelation*, Westminster Pelican Commentaries (Philadelphia: Westminster Press, 1979), 16.

[75] Wink's work has helped inspire Christian movements for justice and nonviolence, and has earned its respected place in that context.

[76] Wink, *Naming*, 119.

[77] Anthony Gwyther, 'New Jerusalem Versus Babylon' (Queensland, Australia: Griffith University, 1999), ii, http://www4.gu.edu.au:8080/adt-root/uploads/approved/adt-QGU20030226.092450/public/01Front.pdf.

[78] Gwyther, 'New Jerusalem Versus Babylon', 48.

[79] Wes Howard-Brook and Anthony Gwyther, *Unveiling Empire: Reading Revelation Then and Now* (Maryknoll: Orbis, 1999), 121–2.

[80] Howard-Brook and Gwyther, *Unveiling*, 153. Howard-Brook and Gwyther further suggest to their contemporary Christian readers that 'where and/or how' they think of 'heaven' as existing may affect how they live day to day. And indeed, their work has sometimes been used by contemporary Christians seeking an anti-imperial or post-colonial praxis.

[81] Gwyther, 'New Jerusalem Versus Babylon', 48.

to difficulties dealing with visions of οὐρανός as a site of conflict (Rev. 12, and see also 2 Macc. 5.1-4),[82] or with approving descriptions of οὐρανός coming to an end (Rev. 6.14; 20.11; 21.1). Gwyther's work also exhibits an inner tension similar to that of Wink, but in reverse. While persistently speaking of heaven as 'the world where God lives and reigns', he once states that 'heaven was a battleground in which competing claims were played out', yet this tension does not appear to be noted, still less resolved.[83] We find a similar situation in 'Cosmology in the Book of Revelation'/'Kosmologie in Die Boek Van Openbaring', by Gert Jordaan. He describes the 'heaven' of Rev. 12.1-9, in which the dragon attempts to eat the male child and then battles the angelic army, as 'a metaphor for the dwelling place of God', and later describes heaven as 'a qualitative reference to a situation where all and everyone live in God's presence, in ceaseless praise, worship and obedience to him as Lord'.[84] Jordaan notes the contradiction but makes no attempt to resolve it. This unresolved tension is also reflected in the comments of a number of commentators on Revelation.[85] I will argue that in fact Revelation does not exhibit tension in its depiction of heaven, between heaven as a site of conflict and heaven as the realm in which God truly reigns, and that the work of both Gwyther and Wink can be brought into fruitful conversation with structural cosmology.

Related to this, I offer the same critique of Gwyther that I made of Wink; I do not believe his work gives due consideration to the 'upness' of heaven in ancient cosmological conceptions, and also in Revelation's narrative movements. Howard-Brook and Gwyther attempt to address this question by writing that scholars

> often demur on the question of where heaven is, finding themselves caught between what they sometimes think is the ancient sense of heaven as literally in the sky and their own scientifically informed knowledge of the physical universe', concluding that this view fails 'to be true to both a close reading of Revelation and to an understanding of how ancient people understood reality.[86]

Contrary to Howard-Brook and Gwyther, it does not follow from accepting a dynamic understanding of heaven that the ancients did not also hold quasi-scientific concepts

---

[82] Wink, *Naming*, 130, n. 23.
[83] Gwyther, 'New Jerusalem Versus Babylon', 50. Rather than speaking of 'heaven' versus 'earth', Minear speaks of the 'first heaven-and-earth' and the 'new heaven-and-earth' as the conflicting realities throughout Revelation. Paul S. Minear, 'The Cosmology of the Apocalypse', in *Current Issues in New Testament Interpretation*, ed. William Klassen and Graydon F. Snyder (London: SCM Press, 1962), 33. This framing avoids the tension present in Gwyther's work. On the other hand, Gwyther's framing provides a more straightforward accounting for Revelation's negative references to 'earth-dwellers'.
[84] Jordaan, 'Cosmology', 3, 5.
[85] As seen, for example, in the comment, 'While there are indications in 12.7-12 of primordial struggles in heaven, and of the erstwhile presence of Satan as accuser in the heavenly throne room, for the most part heaven serves as the place, as in the Lord's Prayer, where God's will is done.' McDonough, 'Revelation', 182. Similar observations have been made for some time. In 1878 Gebhardt described heaven and the 'heavenly state' in terms of worship and homage to God in contrast to earth where Satan rages and makes war. In this vein he wrote, 'We see that it is in heaven as it should be on earth', and yet a few sentences later he also commented that heaven is the place of Michael's struggle with the dragon. Gebhardt, *Doctrine*, 50–1.
[86] Howard-Brook and Gwyther, *Unveiling*, 120, 121.

of heaven. Several apocalypses and Greek cosmological writings show that in fact they did.[87] Further, I will show that in a close reading of Revelation's narrative movements, there is a real 'upness' to its sky-heaven and hyper-heaven; this is part of Revelation's dynamic cosmic story-space that carries ideological import for the hearer.

1.2.3 Rhetorical cosmology

Other work on Revelation focusses on its 'symbolic universe', 'worldview' or 'rhetorical cosmology'. While Wink and Gwyther also develop the ideological implications of their work, their approach is distinctive in its focus on the nature of heavenly reality in relation to earthly reality, and so considered together in the previous section. Another approach to Revelation's cosmology is more directly rhetorical.

Elizabeth Schüssler Fiorenza did much of the early work on the rhetorical interpretation of Revelation. In her analysis, John addresses the socio-political 'rhetorical situation' of his communities not by simply writing a letter of exhortation but by creating a new 'plausibility structure' and 'symbolic universe'. As Jewish communities and the pagan empire both came to view Christians as separate from the Jewish community, Christians lost the tolerance afforded to Jewish communities in Roman Asia Minor and the difficulty of living as a Christian in the pagan empire intensified. With accommodation to pagan empire an increasingly attractive option, John writes rhetorically in that he seeks to persuade and motivate people 'to act right', but does so by 'constructing a "symbolic universe" that invites imaginative participation'.[88] So, for example, in the context of this symbolic universe, the group of 144,000 in Rev. 14.1-5 is the empirical Christian community seen on 'a cosmic plane and made majestically independent of the vicissitudes of individual existence'.[89] By imaginatively participating in this symbolic universe the individual Christian is enabled to face the terror of suffering and death, and so enabled to act rightly according to John's prophetic view of the situation.

David deSilva also offers a rhetorical-critical reading of Revelation, using the classical categories of ethos, pathos and logos to illuminate the ways in which John works to influence his hearers. His chapter on 'the cosmic order' concerns itself with 'John's evocations of particular configurations of symbols and formulation of the "general order of existence", and the ways in which these evocations and formulations impact the congregations' experience of, evaluation of, and orientation toward their everyday situations'.[90] By expanding the cosmic map to include heaven and its hosts, all worshipping God on the Throne, the situation for Christians is reversed. No longer are they the deviant minority refusing to worship the gods, rather, those who participate in pagan imperial worship are the deviant minority who worship idols and fail to participate in the universal worship of God on the Throne. In a perspective that

---

[87] See Sec. 3.4.
[88] Elisabeth Schüssler Fiorenza, *The Book of Revelation: Justice and Judgment*, 2nd edn (Minneapolis: Fortress Press, 1998), 187.
[89] Schüssler Fiorenza, *Revelation*, 197.
[90] DeSilva, *Seeing*, 96.

would be counterintuitive for most in this society, the participants in the pagan empire are 'out of order' in relation to the greater cosmic order.[91] This becomes one way in which Revelation 'problematizes peaceful coexistence with, even prosperity within, the surrounding society' and so the hearers of Revelation are moved to distance themselves from pagan imperial practices.[92]

From the perspective of this expanded cosmic map, specific realities in the 'everyday world' are reinterpreted, in particular Roman imperialism and the Roman emperor. In this 'de-imperialization of the local Christians' worldview' the emperor no longer represents divine peace and order, but monstrous violence and chaos.[93] Contrary to the 'Roman peace', John portrays a cosmos at war, evoking an attitude of resistance in his hearers.[94] The genre of apocalypse enables greater rhetorical effect than, for example a pastoral letter, because 'the voyeuristic experience of entering into John's encounter with the unseen world – and looking back from there upon the landscape of the visible world' is an experience that facilitates a change in perspective against the emperor, *Roma Aeterna*, imperial economics and accommodation to them.[95]

The work of Steven Friesen is also worth considering here, as its description of Roman imperial religion includes the aspect of its cosmology as a point of comparison with Revelation. Through examination of literature, inscriptions, coins, sculpture and architecture, Friesen shows that 'imperial cult institutions defined how space and time were to be experienced'.[96] In the experience of space, Rome became the centre of meaningful geography. In the experience of time, the empire and emperors formed the beginning of the eternal age of peace, the basis of the calendar, and were recognized in rhythms of work, rest and celebration. Further, the eternal age of Roman peace was validated by association with divinity. Ultimately, the 'discourse of imperial cults was committed to preventing the imagination from imagining the end of this world',[97] from imagining that the world could be different or should be different. In this context, Revelation is a radical exercise of an alternative mythic imagination.

Friesen describes the way Revelation centres spatial and temporal existence in contrast to the dominant imperial discourse. While to some extent it eludes systematization, there is still a 'relatively coherent imagined geography in the visionary's world', and this involves 'at least three levels of spatial reality: heaven, earth, and the underworld'.[98] Heaven is the most definitive stratum in Revelation's universe, and heaven is spatially and functionally centred around the Throne. In this way John 'tried to disabuse his audience of the notion that Jerusalem, Rome, or any earthly city could function as the geographic center of reality'.[99] Rather, all other space is given meaning

---

[91] DeSilva, *Seeing*, 100.
[92] DeSilva, *Seeing*, 30.
[93] DeSilva, *Seeing*, 104–5.
[94] DeSilva, *Seeing*, 107.
[95] DeSilva, *Seeing*, 116.
[96] Friesen, *Imperial Cults*, 3, 124. Wei Hsien Wan fruitfully applies this approach to 1 Peter, showing how the construal of space and time in 1 Peter differs from that of the imperial cults of Anatolia, and has an ideological character that helps define the relationship between Christians and the empire. Wan, *Contest*.
[97] Friesen, *Imperial Cults*, 130.
[98] Friesen, *Imperial Cults*, 152.
[99] Friesen, *Imperial Cults*, 165.

in relation to God's Throne. Rejecting the ways that Roman imperial cult defined time and space, John 'fashioned instead a more dangerous definition of reality'[100] in which it became possible to worship God to the exclusion of Roman emperors, and to imagine the end of that world.

Ryan Leif Hansen's work is influenced by Friesen, deSilva and Schüssler Fiorenza, but he develops his 'rhetorical cosmology' in a particular way, arguing that it is something more than only a 'symbolic' universe or 'worldview'.[101] One can also see the influence of the socio-rhetorical interpretation of Vernon K. Robbins[102] and others when Hansen writes that he approaches Revelation as an example of the 'apocalyptic rheterolect',[103] with elements of 'rhetology' (rational argumentation), but especially of 'rhetography' (pictorial argumentation).[104] Hansen regards Revelation's cosmology as symbolic, but also more than symbolic, as socially and mythologically constructed, but also material. John engages in an ideological 'war of worldcraft',[105] and yet 'the cosmos John evokes is not solely a construction; it also seems to be a participation in something that is already there. John does expect the world order of Rome to end, not simply as a subjective experience in the minds of his audience, but in a way that those inside and outside his community will experience somehow objectively'.[106]

In Hansen's estimation, John's rhetorical cosmology calls his hearers to non-participation in the present cosmos centred on Rome, and therefore to participation in its unmaking. They were to withdraw from participation in the Roman imperial cult and economy: 'Trade through Roman coinage was a key way in which Rome extended its own cosmological discourse … In John's view, to participate and flourish in the Roman economy through trade meant to participate in the cosmology crafted by the cult.'[107] John's rhetorical cosmology is also a call to worship God and therefore participate in the re-making the cosmos.[108]

Work on rhetorical cosmology has described a 'universe' created by Revelation and shown how this is meaningful for hearers of Revelation in late-first-century Asia Minor, particularly with regard to life in a social context infused with pagan imperialism. Some of the work on rhetorical cosmology has contrasted the universe created by Revelation with the conceptions and experience of time and space created by imperial ideology and practices, that is, the experience of time and space in which Rome is the eternal, functional centre of reality. I agree with Hansen that 'John does expect the world order of Rome to end, not simply as a subjective experience in the minds of his audience, but in a way that those inside and outside his community will

---

[100] Friesen, *Imperial Cults*, 166.
[101] Hansen, *Silence*, 4.
[102] See Vernon K. Robbins, *The Tapestry of Early Christian Discourse: Rhetoric, Society, and Ideology* (London: Routledge, 1996). Vernon K. Robbins, 'Rhetography: A New Way of Seeing the Familiar Text', in *Words Well Spoken: George Kennedy's Rhetoric of the New Testament*, ed. C. Clifton Black and Duane Frederick Watson (Waco: Baylor University Press, 2008), 81–106.
[103] Hansen, *Silence*, 26.
[104] Hansen, *Silence*, 30–1.
[105] Hansen, *Silence*, 49.
[106] Hansen, *Silence*, 6.
[107] Hansen, *Silence*, 50.
[108] Hansen, *Silence*, 10.

experience somehow objectively'.¹⁰⁹ That is, the virtual experience of Revelation's cosmic-story space is meant to shift the hearer's perception of the real cosmos. I argue that our understanding of rhetorical cosmology can be developed further through closer attention to structural cosmology.

1.3 Conclusion: Apocalypse and cosmos

While Revelation does not describe its cosmos with the same complexity as *1 Enoch*, *2 Enoch* or *3 Baruch*, its cosmic story-space carries just as much theological significance as the cosmological assertions of the other apocalypses. These descriptions and explanations of the cosmos and its workings are not just abstract speculation. Rather, they promote particular ways of understanding the world and living in it – from giving order to the normal life of the community to negotiating existence alongside oppressive power structures. Likewise, Revelation's cosmology has significance in its social, political and economic setting.

In this chapter I examined the scholarship on cosmology in Revelation using the categories of structural, dynamic and rhetorical cosmology. Scholarship on structural cosmology is limited. Almost all commentators assume in Revelation 'an archaic, three-level cosmos: a single heavenly tier at the top, a central zone divided into earth and sea, and an underworld realm that interacts with the realm above'.¹¹⁰ The variation in views is almost entirely within that framework, but Malina and Pilch assume a spherical schema, with a spherical sky surrounding a spherical earth.¹¹¹ I argue that the spherical schema does not accord with Revelation's narrative moves and, further, that a careful reading of the narrative in fact shows a four-level cosmos.

The dynamic cosmologies of Wink and Gwyther are persuasive and insightful but also contain the unresolved tension between heaven as a metaphorical 'place' of conflict, an 'inner dimension' of earthly conflict and heaven as the realm in which God truly reigns and all beings respond in worship. I argue that this tension is resolved when their dynamic cosmology is brought into conversation with a four-level structural cosmology that distinguishes between sky-heaven and hyper-heaven.

Schüssler Fiorenza, deSilva, Friesen and Hansen have shown that Revelation's cosmology – or 'symbolic universe' or 'worldview' – has ideological import, as have Wink and Gwyther in their distinctive ways.¹¹² While these studies have given little attention to the specifics of Revelation's cosmic structure, I will demonstrate below how the ideological dimension of Revelation's cosmology can be further explored through

---

[109] Hansen, *Silence*, 6.
[110] Ryan, *Hearing*, 62. Exegetical commentaries express this view: Charles, *Revelation*, vol. 1, 108. Aune, *Revelation 1–5*, 347–9. Koester, *Revelation*, 119–20. See also Friesen, *Imperial Cults*, 152.
[111] Malina and Pilch, *Social-Science*, 77–81.
[112] Jon Newton has also written about 'the Revelation worldview' but means something different. He considers modern and post-modern paradigms of what is real and how we know, especially in relation to God/gods, 'the spirit world' and the validity of meta-narratives. Revelation's most basic assumptions are considered in relation to these. Jon K. Newton, *The Revelation Worldview: Apocalyptic Thinking in a Postmodern World* (Eugene: Wipf and Stock, 2015).

more careful consideration of Revelation's cosmic structure, the nature of the spaces within that structure and the ways in which they relate to each other. Specifically, my argument is that Revelation's narrative operates in a four-tiered cosmic structure, defining a hyper-heaven space and a sky-heaven space above the earth and abyssal depths, and that this particular spatial construction has particular ideological import.

In the following chapters I show that Revelation's implied hearer experiences a four-tiered spatial structure; then in Chapters 7 and 8 I explore how the experience of this four-tiered cosmic story-space relates to the hearer's understanding of the real cosmos and to appropriate action in cosmic context. I argue that sky-heaven and hyper-heaven play complementary roles, with the conflicted sky-heaven exposing pagan imperial culture as draconian, thus demanding non-participation in its social and economic practices, while the hyper-heaven makes such non-participation a viable option. Adopting part of Friesen's methodology, I contrast the understanding/experience of spatial reality that Revelation creates for its hearer with the understanding/experience of spatial reality that pagan empire creates for its subjects and participants.

2

Methodology

This study considers Revelation's cosmos through the story of John's cosmic journey and the hearers' experience of a virtual visionary journey very similar to, but not identical with, that of the character John. It follows their movements through the cosmos, their location in the cosmos as events unfold and how they see events from their current location.

As a consideration of visionary narrative, this approach is inspired in part by the growing scholarly interest in vision and envisionment in the Bible and its world.[1] A form of visual exegesis has emerged from the socio-rhetorical interpretation developed by Vernon K. Robbins and others,[2] while other forms have been fruitfully applied by scholars including Harry O. Maier, Robyn Whitaker and Brigitte Kahl.[3] In *Reading Second Peter with New Eyes*, Dennis D. Sylva discusses the possibility of reading and describing a biblical text with 'language like one finds in cinematography',[4] a notion with visual and narrative aspects that has resonated with my experience of reading novels and 'seeing' the imaginary worlds they create. In a sense, this has become my response to the challenge posed by Malina and Pilch, to take seriously the experience of a journey into the sky, considering *what* is seen and *where* it is seen. I have found the narratological concept of 'focalizer' useful in this regard,[5] and so the approach taken here is ultimately narratological, considering *what* is seen and *where* it is seen

---

[1] The EABS/SBL International Conference in Helsinki, August 2018, included the program unit Vision and Envisionment in the Bible and its World.

[2] See Robbins, *Tapestry*. Robbins, 'Rhetography'.

[3] H. O. Maier, *Picturing Paul in Empire: Imperial Image, Text and Persuasion in Colossians, Ephesians and the Pastoral Epistles* (London: Bloomsbury, 2013). Robyn J. Whitaker, *Ekphrasis, Vision, and Persuasion in the Book of Revelation*, Wissenschaftliche Untersuchungen zum Neuen Testament (Tübingen: Mohr Siebeck, 2015). Brigitte Kahl, *Galatians Re-Imagined: Reading with the Eyes of the Vanquished* (Minneapolis: Fortress Press, 2010). Davina C. Lopez, *Apostle to the Conquered: Reimagining Paul's Mission* (Minneapolis: Fortress Press, 2008).

[4] Dennis D. Sylva, 'A Unified Field Picture of Second Peter 1.3-15: Making Rhetorical Sense Out of Individual Images', in *Reading Second Peter with New Eyes: Methodological Reassessments of the Letter of Second Peter*, ed. Robert L. Webb and Duane Frederick Watson (London: T&T Clark, 2010), 94, citing correspondence with Vernon K. Robbins.

[5] In narratology, the focalizer is one of the 'agents' in a narrative, alongside actor, narrator, implied author and implied reader. Narratology uses the concept of a focalizing agent, or focalizer, to understand the perspective from which a scene is described. The concept, and its use in this study, is explained further below (see Sec. 2.2).

in the virtual visionary experience of the hearer as the text is read out, with the visual perspective supplied by the focalizer.

2.1 Hearer assumptions

The 'hearer' is the 'implied reader' of narrative theory, a construction of the text.[6] This imagined hearer has real significance because the experience of the imagined audience is the experience towards which Revelation pulls its real audience.[7] No real hearer will have an experience identical to that of another real hearer or identical to that of the implied hearer, but the experience of the implied hearer is the experience towards which Revelation pulls its real hearers. As Revelation's narrative operates in its cosmic story-space, this story-space is recreated in the imagination of the hearers; the spatial recreations of the intended hearers are pulled towards that of the implied hearer.

Working with the implied hearer is a different approach to that of Sean Michael Ryan, who uses a particular hearer-construct, a plausible historical reconstruction of an early real hearer.[8] His approach is fruitful, showing how a historically plausible real hearer could have understood the cosmological references in Revelation 9, particularly the location of the abyss in the cosmic schema. It is notable that Ryan briefly describes Revelation's own cosmic schema before showing how it would be appropriated by the historically plausible real hearer.[9] I suggest that if it is worthwhile to describe Revelation's own cosmic schema then it is also worth investigation, and this can be achieved by using the implied hearer.

This does not remove the necessity of historically plausible reconstruction. While a construction of the text, Revelation's implied hearer has knowledge and assumptions not explicitly described and explained in the text itself. It is, for example, familiar with the tales of Nero's return and must be so in order to understand Revelation's allusions.[10]

---

[6] The implied hearer is an agent within the text. While Barr writes, 'The churches of Asia Minor constitute the implied audience of this story', it would be more accurate to say that the churches of Asia Minor are *identified with* the implied hearer, which is an agent within the text. Barr, *Tales*, 89. In a similar way, the narrator is usually identified with the character John, but the two are not the same.

[7] Barr, *Tales*, 26. Leif Hongisto discusses the connection between the internal narratee and external narratee. Leif Hongisto, *Experiencing the Apocalypse at the Limits of Alterity* (Leiden: Brill, 2010), 187–91. De Waal also found implied author and implied hearer/reader to be useful constructs for analysing select texts in Revelation. Kayle B. de Waal, *A Socio-Rhetorical Interpretation of the Seven Trumpets of Revelation: The Apocalyptic Challenge to Earthly Empire* (Lewiston: Edwin Mellen Press, 2012), 174.

[8] Ryan, *Hearing*.

[9] Ryan, *Hearing*, 60–2, 68–72.

[10] While the implied reader is within the text, the historical study of the real world remains part of a narratological reading. It must, because the reader implied by a biblical text has knowledge that may not be known to a modern real reader. As Powell notes, unlike many modern readers the implied reader of Matthew surely knows that a talent is worth more than a denarius. Mark Allan Powell, *What is Narrative Criticism?*, Guides to Biblical Scholarship. New Testament Series (Minneapolis: Fortress Press, 1990), 20. Similarly, the implied reader of Mark may know that the temple curtain is a tapestry displaying the heavens, which would be significant for a cosmological reading. This isn't always accepted. J. L. Resseguie's narrative-critical commentary on Revelation avoids tying the narrative to historical realities or going beyond the text to ask what historical realities the implied reader is aware of. James L. Resseguie, *Revelation Unsealed: A Narrative Critical Approach to John's Apocalypse*, Biblical Interpretation, vol. 32 (Leiden: Brill, 1998). On the other hand, in David L. Barr's

It also has familiarity with other texts; as Barr notes, the implied hearer is familiar with Daniel and Ezekiel,[11] and much of the Hebrew scriptures or their Greek-language equivalents. Crucially, the implied hearer has basic starting assumptions regarding many aspects of life, including basic cosmological concepts. Revelation aims to change the perspectives of its audience but, as in all communication, it must work with assumptions even as it seeks to change them.

The importance of this point can be explained by analogy with modern narratives that feature journeys to the stars. When the science-fiction author describes a character leaving a planet in a space-craft, the implied reader has the starting assumption that a planet is a large sphere similar to earth (which is also a large sphere), that it revolves around a sun and that leaving the planet involves passing through a region of air (atmosphere). The science-fiction author does not need to explain that the character was able to pass through the sky because the sky is just a region of air and not a physical barrier; this is already the starting assumption of the implied reader. On the other hand, if the science-fiction author wishes the reader to understand that this planet is *not* a sphere and it *does* have a solid sky-structure acting as a ceiling over it, the author works to shift the reader from their assumed picture to a new conception, describing the structure and explaining how it is possible.[12]

The implied reader of a science-fiction novel begins with modern cosmological concepts; the implied hearer of Revelation begins with very different cosmological concepts. Certain conceptions that would require careful development for a modern reader, Revelation introduces briefly and moves on with casual assurance that its reader has understood. To approach the experience of Revelation's implied hearer, we shift our starting assumptions to concepts that may plausibly be the basic starting assumptions of this implied hearer. As Lourdes García Ureña writes, 'The reader must approach the text with the right attitude in order for their reading to be effective and correspond to what the text really transmits.'[13]

The shift in our starting assumptions will influence, for example, our reading of the θύρα ἐν τῷ οὐρανῷ in Rev. 4.1. A modern real reader begins with the assumption that the sky is a gaseous region above the earth, beyond which is empty space. As Revelation does not work to shift its reader from this assumption to a different conception, this general cosmic concept is likely to remain in place for the modern real reader. In this context the θύρα ἐν τῷ οὐρανῷ cannot have a material component and makes no sense in terms of the cosmic structure, and is therefore assumed to have a purely non-material, non-structural meaning. Thus the modern real reader is likely to read the θύρα ἐν τῷ οὐρανῷ as a purely symbolic image, perhaps conveying the idea of 'an invitation into a new spiritual experience'.[14] When we shift our starting assumptions

---

narrative-critical commentary on Revelation he makes explicit use of historical knowledge. Barr, *Tales*. My approach is closer to Barr's.

[11] Barr, *Tales*, 25.
[12] Terry Pratchett does exactly this in his novel *Strata*. Terry Pratchett, *Strata* (Gerrard's Cross: Colin Smythe, 1981).
[13] Ureña, *Narrative and Drama*, 2.
[14] A meaning suggested to me in oral communication. In a somewhat similar manner, Aune describes the motif of an opening door as part of the epiphanic experience. Aune, *Revelation 1–5*, 281. Koester comments, 'The open door signals that revelation is about to be given.' Koester, *Revelation*, 367.

to concepts that may plausibly be those of the implied hearer, then Revelation's brief mention of a θύρα ἐν τῷ οὐρανῷ can easily have meaning in terms of the cosmic structure. If we should finally judge that it *does not* have meaning in terms of the cosmic structure, it will not be because it *can not*.

My sources for plausible basic assumptions include the Hebrew scriptures (or their Greek-language equivalents), Greek cultural stories and cosmological theorizing, apocalypses and literary sky-journeys and ideas present in the early Christian movement as evidenced by writings prior to or roughly contemporaneous with Revelation (the first century and the first quarter of the second century). While most of the first real hearers would have been partially familiar with at least some of these sources, few, if any, would have been fully versed in all these sources. Whatever the differing levels of knowledge in the first real hearers, I argue that the literary construct that is Revelation's implied hearer is familiar with these sources. For example, Revelation makes many biblical allusions, and so the implied hearer is familiar with much of the Hebrew scriptures or their Greek-language equivalents.[15] These are part of the existing repertoire of ideas shared between implied author and implied hearer. Cosmological concepts from these writings are plausibly part of the basic starting assumptions of the implied hearer. I will show, for example, that in all these sources the 'sky' is primarily imagined as a material construction, perhaps of metal or crystal or a material akin to animal skins, rather than an expanse of mere gases. It is most plausible then that the implied hearer will hear 'sky' as a reference to a material construction, unless Revelation does the work of shifting the hearer from this assumption. I will show further basic starting assumptions, and cosmological concepts regarding the shape and nature of the earth and skies, that are plausibly part of the existing repertoire of ideas shared between the implied author and implied hearer, which Revelation can use or modify or put aside in its own construction of cosmic space. The way in which it does so is through the hearer's experience of a virtual visionary journey, the real hearer's experience pulled towards that of the implied hearer.

2.2 Visionary narrative

Ruth Anne Reese has argued that narrative criticism has often focussed too narrowly on events to the point of disregarding description,[16] and here I develop a greater emphasis on the visual element of the narrative through renewed attention to the role of the focalizer.[17] Along with the implied author, implied reader, narrator and narratee,

---

[15] Swete, *Apocalypse*, cxxxv. Steve Moyise, *The Old Testament in the Book of Revelation*, Journal for the Study of the New Testament Supplement Series, vol. 115 (Sheffield: Sheffield Academic Press, 1995). G. K. Beale, *John's Use of the Old Testament in Revelation*, Journal for the Study of the New Testament Supplement series, vol. 166 (Sheffield: Sheffield Academic, 1998). Koester, *Revelation*, 123.

[16] Ruth Anne Reese, 'Narrative Method and the Letter of Second Peter', in *Reading Second Peter with New Eyes: Methodological Reassessments of the Letter of Second Peter*, ed. Robert L. Webb and Duane Frederick Watson (London: T&T Clark, 2010), 143. Ryan Leif Hansen's study of 'rhetorical cosmology' also draws explicitly from both narrative criticism and from the visual approach developed by Vernon K. Robbins. Hansen, *Silence*.

[17] The role of the focalizer is often underdeveloped in biblical narrative criticism, especially the visual focalizer. Barr mentions the concept in his narrative commentary on Revelation but doesn't develop

identified by narratology as agents in the narrative, the focalizer is a function of the text. While the narrator provides the words, the focalizer provides the point of view, including the visual point of view. It has long been recognized that a verbal narrative creates images in the mind of the reader; indeed, the reality of descriptive words leading an image 'under the eye' was recognized by ancient writers under the name ἔκφρασις.[18] Aelius Theon, roughly contemporaneous with John of Patmos, wrote school textbooks (προγυμνάσματα) on rhetoric and the use of ekphrasis, citing passages from the Iliad as examples to be emulated. As described by ancient writers, the subjects of ekphrasis include not only 'people, places, things', but also such events as 'earthquakes, war and peace, storms, famines, or plagues'.[19] Similarly, Longinus wrote, 'Do you observe, my friend, how he leads you in imagination through the region and makes you see what you hear?'[20] In modern narratology consideration has been given to the point from which a scene is described; that point is described as an agent within the text and given the name of focalizer. Anticipating the suggestion that we read and describe a biblical text with 'language like one finds in cinematography',[21] Seymour Chatman discusses the function of the focalizer and the creation of story-space by analogy with cinema. He comments, 'Story-space in cinema is "literal", that is, objects, dimensions and relations are analogous, at least two-dimensionally, to those in the real world. In verbal narrative it is abstract, requiring a reconstruction in the mind. Thus, a discussion of story-space begins most conveniently with the cinema.'[22] The 'eye which surveys the scene', now called the focalizer, is analogous to the camera, as recognized by the use of the term 'camera eye' in literary criticism.[23] While 'the "camera eye" names a convention ... which pretends that the events just "happened" in the presence of a neutral recorder',[24] the camera eye may also be identified with a character and/or narrator. As Labahn points out, 'Wie in einem Film durch die Kameraführung zu einem neuen Spielort hinüber geleitet wird, so berichtet der Seher den Lesern, Leserinnen sein Erleben.'[25] The point from which the elements are viewed 'can lie with a character ... or outside it',[26] that is, the focalizer may or may not be coincident with a character at any moment

---

it. Barr, *Tales*, 48. Similarly, Powell discusses the rhetorical device known as the *evaluative point of view*, but this is not the same concept as the *visual point of view*. Powell, *Narrative Criticism*, 53. However, Ureña's literary analysis of Revelation considers focalization along with other literary elements and makes some observations about the visual point of view. Ureña, *Narrative and Drama*, 125.

[18] '(Ekphrasis): a vivid description that leads the subject before the hearers' eyes. Described in the rhetorical handbooks and other theoretical literature, and utilized in speeches and novels from the Classical and Hellenistic eras, ekphrasis uses words to lead an image "under the eyes".' Whitaker, *Ekphrasis*, 5-6.

[19] Whitaker, *Ekphrasis*, 41-2.

[20] Longinus, *Peri Hypsous*, cited in Hongisto, *Experiencing*, 192.

[21] Sylva, 'A Unified Field Picture of Second Peter 1.3-15', 94. citing correspondence with Vernon K. Robbins.

[22] Chatman, *Story*, 97.

[23] W. J. Harvey, *Character and the Novel* (Ithaca: Cornell University Press, 1965), 95.

[24] Chatman, *Story*, 154.

[25] Michael Labahn, '"Apokalyptische" Geographie: Einführende Uberiegungen zu einer Toponomie der Johannesoffenbarung', in *Imagery in the Book of Revelation*, ed. Michael Labahn and Outi Lehtipuu, *Contributions to Biblical Exegesis and Theology* (Leuven: Peeters, 2011), 114.

[26] Mieke Bal, *Narratology: Introduction to the Theory of Narrative*, trans. Christine Van Boheemen (Toronto: University of Toronto Press, 1985), 104.

in the narrative. Bal shows that a switch between these two states can even occur from one sentence to the next.²⁷ By definition then, the hearer always views the unfolding scenes from the visual perspective of the focalizer. The hearer may also view a scene from the visual perspective of a character or narrator, but only so long as the character or narrator is coincident with the focalizer.

In Revelation's narrative, the focalizer is always coincident with the narrator, with one brief exception (Rev. 11.12).²⁸ The narrator may speak as an anonymous unbound narrator and say 'the twenty-four elders fell on their faces' (Rev. 11.16) or 'the ark of his covenant became visible in his temple' (Rev. 11.19) while at another moment the narrator may be coincident with the character John and say, 'I heard a loud voice' (Rev. 12.10), but in each case the narrator is coincident with the focalizer. The narrator does not say 'John heard a loud voice' or 'John saw something that seemed to him to be like a sea of glass'. In that case the character and focalizer would be coincident with each other, but not with the narrator. But this doesn't happen.²⁹ While the focalizer is always coincident with the narrator, simultaneously it is very often coincident with the character John, but not always, and this will be important for understanding how the hearer views the scene – sometimes in ways that would not be possible for the character John. This in turn affects the development of story-space.

It is a notable feature of Revelation that its real author, implied author, narrator and central character share a significant degree of identification. The real author, implied author and central character are all identified as 'John'. The narrator is often coincident with the character John, and while coincident uses first-person verbs and pronouns.³⁰ But if we are lured into an over-identification of these agents and collapse them into one, then at times we will be unable to perceive how the narrative is functioning, specifically the ways in which the hearer's experience shares the perspective of the narrator-focalizer and is sometimes slightly different to the experience of the character John. Genette's observation that 'the narrator almost always "knows" more than the hero, even if he himself is the hero' holds true for Revelation and influences the hearer's experience.³¹

---

[27] Bal, *Narratology*, 105.

[28] The two witnesses experience the voice from their limited perspective. Some manuscripts do not have this exception, with ἤκουσα standing in place of ἤκουσαν (most notably 𝔓⁴⁷). Ureña's analysis of the verbs of seeing and hearing can be extended to show that Rev. 11.9 and 18.9 are not exceptions. When the hearer is invited to share John's experience, the verbs used are εἶδον and ἤκουσα. By contrast, βλέπω describes the behaviour of John as actor. So, in Rev. 1.11 he is instructed to write down what he is going to see; the verb is not part of the creation of a scene. Similarly, in Rev. 1.12 βλέπειν indicates John's intention to look but the sight is introduced by εἶδον. The third and final occurrence of βλέπω with John as subject (Rev. 22.8) refers back to John's act of witnessing. Similarly, in Rev. 11.9 and 18.9 βλέπω is used to indicate the characters' act of looking, while the focalizer is outside the characters, seeing them look. Ureña, *Narrative and Drama*, 51–5.

[29] Within the narrative proper (Rev. 1.9–22.5) John's experiences or actions are never spoken of with third-person verbs or pronouns. It is only Rev. 1.1-3, which functions as a prologue or extended title for the work, that uses third-person language for John. Ureña, *Narrative and Drama*, 7.

[30] The narrator is never coincident with any other character. When using first-person language it is coincident with the character John.

[31] Gérard Genette, *Narrative Discourse: An Essay in Method* (Ithaca: Cornell University Press, 1980), 194. The places where John explains how he knows something that he could not visually perceive (Rev. 7.4; 9.16) contrast with the many places where the narrator 'just knows'. Michaels identifies John as the narrator and identifies passages where he knows more than what he sees, writing,

We must, of course, acknowledge what Lourdes García Ureña has convincingly demonstrated, that Revelation identifies the narrator as John and presents the narrative as 'what John saw and heard'.[32] However, it remains true that the narrator is a distinct agent in the text, and at times Revelation 'colours outside the lines' of the identification of the narrator with the character John. There is consistency in the nominal identification of the narrator but not in the functional coincidence of narrator and character. The use of εἶδον and ἤκουσα 'reflects the narrator's desire to present himself as the visual and auditory witness of the revelation',[33] but at times Revelation leads the hearer into a virtual visionary experience that differs from the experience of the character John.

2.3 Time

As we engage with this narrative text, we consider the relationship between the story and the telling of the story. We may speak of 'narrative' as the discourse that conveys events and 'story' as the series of events conveyed by the narrative.[34] Any narrative text has the facet called story and the facet called narrative, discourse or presentation. In Revelation, we may say that John's experience is the story, and the way that Revelation relates John's experience is the narrative presentation of that story. In this case, the order of events in the narrative is the same as the order of events in the story. Revelation first tells what happens to John first and next tells what happens to John next; the order of presentation is the same as the natural logic of the story.[35] As Friesen notes, 'The oral enactment of Revelation in the churches approximated the revelatory experience.'[36]

However, Revelation has another layer to it, and we could alternatively define what happens in the cosmos as the story and what John sees concerning the cosmos as the narrative presentation to John.[37] Looked at this way, John's experience is not the story

---

> In all these passages there is a distinction between things that John presumably could see in his visions, and things he could not actually see but about which he had some kind of higher knowledge, so that he could identify or explain them to his readers ... Because he is a prophet as well as a seer, John is granted divine insight into the meaning of certain of his visions.
>
> J. Ramsey Michaels, *Interpreting the Book of Revelation*, Guides to New Testament Exegesis (Grand Rapids: Baker Academic, 1998), 99–100. Similarly, Ureña notes that Rev. 15.2 includes information that 'could not result from visual perception, but only from the seer's own knowledge'. Ureña, *Narrative and Drama*, 100. I am not entirely persuaded that this is the best way of framing the issue, as Revelation frequently presents the character John as limited in knowledge. I suggest that from a literary perspective, we can acknowledge that even while narrator and character are coincident, the narrator knows more than the character.

[32] Ureña, *Narrative and Drama*, 6, 52.
[33] Ureña, *Narrative and Drama*, 51.
[34] Genette, *Narrative*, 27.
[35] Chatman, *Story*, 43. One exception to this occurs in Rev. 21, and I argue below for seeing here a repetitive anachrony.
[36] Friesen, *Imperial Cults*, 158.
[37] Michaels shows partial recognition of the reality of the two levels, although he frames it differently: 'A distinctive feature of a prophetic book such as Revelation is that John also is a kind of reader. He is trying to "read" his own visions, just as we are reading what he writes.' Michaels, *Interpreting*, 97.

but the narrative presentation of the cosmic story. We now note differences between story-sequence and narrative-sequence, as each subsequent vision does not necessarily present the chronologically subsequent event in the cosmos.[38] While noting this as necessary, the focus of this study is on the *story* of John's experience and the *narrative* that relates John's experience to the hearer.

2.4 Space

Just as we investigate the relationship between narrative and time, so too we investigate the relationship between narrative and space. Bal describes it as 'self-evident' that a narrative text creates space, and yet the way in which it does so is worthy of investigation.[39] 'In principle, places can be mapped out, in the same way that the topological position of a city or river can be indicated on a map.'[40] We note with Bal that in the narrative process places are linked to certain points of perception. 'These places seen *in relation to their perception* are called space. The point of perception may be a character, which is situated in a space, observes it, and reacts to it. An anonymous point of perception may also dominate the presentation of certain places' (emphasis in the original).[41] Put another way, the point of perception is the focalizer, which may be coincident with a character or separate from any character.

A scene is described from a certain perspective, and this shows different places in relation to each other and creates the space. In cinema, Chatman notes, 'Each existent is situated (a) in the vertical and horizontal dimension of the frame, and (b) in relation to other existents within the frame, at a certain angle from the camera: head on or from the rear, relatively high or low, to the left or to the right.'[42] Following the analogy between the camera in cinema and the visual focalizer in verbal narratives, we note that all objects/places exist in spatial relation to other objects/places, and at a certain angle from the visual focalizer. The point of perception (the location of the focalizer) exists in spatial relationship with the perceived object or place. A character standing on a high mountain gazes forward and diagonally downward to view the city; the spatial relationship between the city and the top of the mountain is closely related to the angle of the gaze (Rev. 21.9–22.5).

---

[38] Barr writes, 'John's three dramatic actions do not constitute a sequential, unified action. One does not happen before or after the other. They represent alternative tellings of the story of Jesus.' Barr, *Tales*, 24. Also David L. Barr, 'The Story John Told: Reading Revelation for its Plots', in *Reading the Book of Revelation: A Resource for Students*, ed. David L. Barr (Atlanta: Society of Biblical Literature, 2003), 18. Here Barr is considering Revelation at the level in which the story is what happens in the cosmos (or perhaps, the story of Jesus in the cosmos). At this level Barr is absolutely correct that Revelation is not a straightforward, sequential chronology. By contrast, I primarily consider Revelation at the level in which the story is John's experience (or the reader's experience) and at this level Revelation does have a straightforward, sequential chronology.
[39] Bal, *Narratology*, 93.
[40] Bal, *Narratology*, 93.
[41] Bal, *Narratology*, 93.
[42] Chatman, *Story*, 97.

In addition to sight, we follow Bal in recognizing that sounds also contribute to the presentation of space.[43]

> If a character hears a low buzz, it is probably still at a certain distance from the speakers. If it can understand word for word what is being said, then it is situated much nearer, in the same room, for instance, or behind a thin screen. A church clock sounding in the distance increases the space; suddenly perceived whispering points to the proximity of the whisperer.[44]

As we read Revelation we will note in particular the manner in which the character John hears noises and voices ἐκ τοῦ οὐρανοῦ, and how this contributes to an understanding of space.

2.5 Movement, events and narrative inferences

Chatman writes that there is value in becoming 'conscious of how scenes change, characters get from one spot to another, and so on'.[45] As Revelation's story-space opens to the hearer through the virtual visionary journey, we maintain this consciousness of how the scenes change and how characters, John in particular, move from one spot to another. As in other cosmic journey narratives, Revelation's seer is not only taken into the sky but also returned to earth and moved to different locations at various stages of the journey.[46] Some of these movements are the clear implication of the narrative (Rev. 4.2), some are narrated explicitly (Rev. 17.3; 21.10) while other changes in location are discerned through the audiovisual perspective of the focalizer where the focalizer is coincident with the character John (Rev. 10.1; 15.2). While Ureña writes that there are 'many points in the narrative where the listener/reader is not sure where John is',[47] in fact when we allow that the focalizer is not always coincident with John, then his location is discernible at each stage in the journey.[48]

The location and movements of John and other characters are discernible through close attention not only to the aural and visual elements within the narrative but also to the logic of narrative development. A story contains events that lead to subsequent events; the prior event may either *enable* or *cause* the subsequent event.[49] When the narrator relates two events in sequence, the implied hearer assumes a causal relationship between them. Thus, when the narrator relates the release of the four angels who were bound at the great river Euphrates, and then the appearance of terrifying destructive

---

[43] Bal, *Narratology*, 94.
[44] Bal, *Narratology*, 94.
[45] Chatman, *Story*, 105.
[46] *Apoc. Ab.* 30.1; *T. Levi* 5.3; *Asc. Isa.* 11.35; *3 Bar.* 17.2; *1 En.* 81.5; *2 En.* 38.1-3;
[47] Ureña, *Narrative and Drama*, 37.
[48] For example, it is not John who may perhaps have 'left heaven to witness first-hand what is taking place on earth' in Rev. 6.12-17 but the focalizer. Ureña, *Narrative and Drama*, 37.
[49] Powell, *Narrative Criticism*, 40-2.

cavalry (Rev. 9.13-19), the hearer assumes a causal link between these events, even as the nature of that causal link is not explained in the narration. As Chatman describes it, 'The drawing of narrative inferences by the reader is a low-level kind of interpretation ... This narrative filling-in is all too easily forgotten or assumed to be of no interest, a mere reflex action of the reading mind. But to neglect it is a critical mistake.'[50] As we read Revelation we pay attention to causality and 'narrative filling-in'. We note how events lead to subsequent events, and pay attention to how and why a character moves from one spot to another, and how this develops the story-space in which these things happen.

2.6 Ideological comparison

There has been growing awareness that the human perception and experience of space is socially constructed, shaped by practices and conceptions regarding the physical/social order.[51] Steven Friesen and Wei Hsien Wan have aptly shown that in Asia Minor and neighbouring Roman provinces the imperial cults played a significant role in shaping the experience of space, through modification of physical spaces and social practices.[52] Given the reciprocal relationship between ideas about cosmology and ideas about the social order, this perception and experience of space reinforced pagan imperial practices and conceptions.[53]

For the hearer, a reading of Revelation becomes an alternative experience of space, experienced virtually in the story-space of the narrative and yet shaping an alternative perception and experience of the world beyond the text.[54] This study explores key aspects of this story-space not previously considered in Revelation scholarship, including aspects of the structure and the nature of particular spaces within the larger cosmic construction. Setting this cosmic construction against a pagan imperial cosmic construction, we see how Revelation shapes a cosmological understanding that reinforces alternative practices and conceptions. The ideological import of Revelation's cosmos is seen in the way its spatial conception shapes the hearer's understanding of the human-proximate cosmos in relation to the greater cosmos, their place within that reality and appropriate action in cosmic context.

---

[50] Chatman, *Story*, 31.
[51] Early work on this was done by Henri Lefebvre. Henri Lefebvre, *La production de l'espace* (Paris: Éditions Anthropos, 1974). English translation: Henri Lefebvre, *The Production of Space* (Oxford: Blackwell Publishing, 1991). See also Rob Kitchin and Phil Hubbard, eds, *Key Thinkers on Space and Place* (London: Sage, 2010).
[52] Friesen, *Imperial Cults*, 124–7. Wan, *Contest*, 131–55.
[53] Wan, *Contest*, 26. '*Weltbild* and *Weltanschauung* are inextricably and substantially intertwined'. Jonathan T. Pennington, and Sean M. McDonough, *Cosmology and New Testament Theology*, ed. Jonathan T. Pennington and Sean M. McDonough (London: T&T Clark, 2008), 4.
[54] Hansen writes, 'John ... is not talking about some other cosmos besides the one in which the Philadelphians and Laodiceans live ... he is not talking about a reality completely severed from the real world of the people of Smyrna and Pergamum'. Hansen, *Silence*, 8.

2.7 Conclusion: A visual-narrative reading

The methodology used here has a narratological framework and within that a particular focus on the descriptive and visual elements of the narrative with a renewed focus on the role of the focalizer – leading to 'language like one finds in cinematography'. This methodology could be called narrative-criticism, although with a much greater emphasis on the role of the visual focalizer than is typical in biblical narrative-criticism. A visual-narrative reading of Revelation shows how the hearer is drawn into the apocalyptic narrative, leading to a virtual visionary experience of the cosmos that it creates.[55] As the narrator describes a scene through the visual perspective of the focalizer, the hearers participate in the perspective of the focalizer. Their position within story-space and the angle of their gaze determine the spatial relationship of objects or locations within story-space. As a character moves through story-space from one location to another, the hearer has a sense of the direction of travel and thus the spatial relationship between those locations.[56] A visual-narrative reading of key passages shows how each part of story-space is created and then built upon – how each new part of story-space is spatially related to the locations and structures that have already been created, leading to a complete picture of the cosmic structure and its nature and functional patterns. As the hearers are developing a sense of the spatial relations in the narrative, they are likewise developing a sense of the cosmic template,[57] Revelation's 'relatively coherent' imagined cosmography.[58]

Finally, setting this cosmic construction against pagan imperial cosmic construction, the ideological import is explored. We shall see how this alternate perception and experience of space reinforces alternate perceptions of social order and appropriate practices in cosmic context.

---

[55] As this methodology is distinct from the narrative-criticism practiced by biblical scholars, so too is it distinct from narratology as described by Seymour Chatman, who writes, 'Literary theory is the study of the nature of literature. It is not concerned with the evaluation or description of any particular literary work for its own sake.' Chatman, *Story*, 18. By contrast, this study is very much concerned with the evaluation and description of the book of Revelation for its own sake.

[56] In her ekphrastic reading of some apocalyptic 'tours of hell', Meghan Henning comments, 'One of the analogies used to describe *ekphrasis* is that of a "journey" or *periëgēsis* in which the speaker is a tour guide leading the audience around the site that is being described', and in this there are 'directional markers connecting one place to the next'. Meghan Henning, 'Eternal Punishment as Paideia: The Ekphrasis of Hell in the Apocalypse of Peter and the Apocalypse of Paul', *Biblical Research*, 58 (2014): 36, 42.

[57] As Labahn comments,

'Der Text entwickelt durch Präsentation und Selektion von geographischen Angaben einen gegliederten Raum, in dem sich einzelne Handlungen abspielen. Mittels der Qualifizierung dieser Räume durch den Erzähler entsteht ein sinngefüllter Raum, der Deutungshorizonte für seine impliziten Leser und Leserinnen eröffnet. Für die Hermeneutik jeglichen literarischen Werkes ist es also von einschneidender Bedeutung, dass jeder Text einen qualifizierten „Sinnatlas" seiner textuellen Welt entwirft. Die Strukturierung eines Textes in seiner Geographie und Räumlichkeit verhilft ihm zu einer eigenen Realität, die im Verständnis der Rezipienten erzeugt wird. So hat die narrative Geographie ihren produktiven Anteil am narrativen Sinnbildungspotential eines Textes.'

Labahn, '"Apokalyptische" Geographie: Einführende Uberiegungen zu einer Toponomie der Johannesoffenbarung' in *Imagery in the Book of Revelation*, 107–43.

[58] Friesen describes in Revelation a 'relatively coherent imagined geography', by which he means the entire cosmic schema. Friesen, *Imperial Cults*, 152.

3

Assumptions and existing conceptions

3.1 The sources

This chapter describes a range of cosmological conceptions that are part of the shared knowledge between Revelation's implied author and implied hearer. These cosmological conceptions are drawn from the cultural milieu in which Revelation's implied author and implied hearer participate, specifically, from broadly defined sources with which they show familiarity. As the implied author and/or implied hearer show familiarity with Greek culture, with much of the Hebrew scriptures or their Greek-language equivalents, with apocalypses and sky-journeys, and with ideas present in Christian circles, cosmological conceptions that recur across these sources are a reasonable approximation of the initial assumptions shared between the author and the hearer of Revelation's cosmic-journey narrative. We consider texts that were composed prior to Revelation or roughly contemporaneous with Revelation, that is, no later than the first quarter of the second century. Specifically, we consider: the Hebrew (and Aramaic) scriptures that comprise the Old Testament; the Septuagint; the apocalypses; the works that record and retell Greek cultural stories; the Greek works that propose theories about the structure and workings of the earth and skies; and the early Christian writings, including those that comprise the New Testament.[1]

The familiarity with these sources is well documented. Swete wrote in 1906 that, 'of the 404 verses of the Apocalypse there are 278 which contain references to the Jewish Scriptures'.[2] Recent studies show that Revelation has clearly drawn on Samuel, Kings, Job, Psalms, Proverbs, Isaiah, Jeremiah, Ezekiel, Daniel, Hosea, Joel, Amos, Micah, Nahum, Zephaniah and Zechariah.[3] Shared familiarity with these writings enables communication between implied author and implied hearer[4] and effects 'a sense of continuity along with change in the activity of God'.[5]

---

[1] Included in this is *2 Enoch*. While this text has undergone significant revision over subsequent centuries, its earliest forms are roughly contemporaneous with Revelation. F. I. Andersen, '2 (Slavonic Apocalypse of) Enoch', in *The Old Testament Pseudepigrapha*, ed. James H. Charlesworth, vol. 1 (Garden City: Doubleday, 1983), 94. Hahne, *Corruption*, 83. It is considered with appropriate caution.
[2] Swete, *Apocalypse*, cxxxv.
[3] Koester, *Revelation*, 123. See also Beale, *John's*. Moyise, *Old Testament*.
[4] Barr, *Tales*, 26.
[5] Koester, *Revelation*, 125.

Though less extensive, shared familiarity with Greek culture is also apparent. Adela Yarbro Collins showed that in narrating the attack of a serpentine dragon on a pregnant woman and her offspring (Rev. 12.1-6, 13-17), Revelation allows the reader to feel resonances with familiar stories, in particular the Greek story of Python's pursuit of Leto and her unborn twins Apollo and Artemis.[6] Terms and images reminiscent of the Apollo cult are not limited to Revelation 12 but found throughout Revelation. Rev. 19.16 recalls the inscription on Apollo's thigh, a known image from story and statuary; hopes expressed in connection with Apollo are in fact fulfilled in Jesus Christ.[7] Revelation also engages with Greek culture in more adversarial ways. Steven Friesen argues that Revelation 13 alienates its audience from mainstream society by inverting the mythology of the imperial cults which themselves reused Greek mythology.[8]

Revelation shows in various ways that its implied author and implied hearer share familiarity with many of the ideas present in early Christian circles. The epistolary form shows influence from the Pauline writings, while the narratee is identified with Christian churches (Rev. 1.4).[9] Many comments on the work of Christ are references to existing knowledge, even if they give it a particular slant (Rev. 1.5-7; 5.6-10; 12.1-13),[10] and the messages to the seven churches assume knowledge of intra-Christian debates (Rev. 2.2, 6, 14-15, 20-24).

Familiarity with cosmic-journey narratives is shown by Revelation's use of that form and the easy assurance that the hearer will understand what is happening with very little explanation. Rev. 4.1-2 uses the 'conventional theme' of a door opened in heaven, here indicating the heavenly ascent common in apocalypses, assuming that the hearer will understand even without explicit narration of the ascent.[11] The 'open door' and John becoming 'in the spirit' suggest how such an ascent is possible but only to those already familiar with sky-journeys.[12]

In this way Revelation shows confidence in its implied hearer to understand sky-journeys and its use of such an implied hearer is not unreasonable. Given that knowledge of apocalypses and sky-journeys was not uncommon among first-century Christians, it is reasonable to think that many of the first real hearers would have sufficient understanding to participate in the experience of the implied hearer. We see this knowledge of apocalypses and sky-journeys not only in Jude, which makes explicit reference to Enochic material in v. 14, but also in several other early Christian writings

---

[6] Adela Yarbro Collins, *The Combat Myth in the Book of Revelation* (Missoula: Scholars Press, 1976).
[7] James R. Edwards, 'The Rider on the White Horse, the Thigh Inscription, and Apollo: Revelation 19:16', *JBL*, 137/2 (2018): 519–36.
[8] Steven J. Friesen, 'Myth and Symbolic Resistance in Revelation 13', *JBL*, 123/2 (2004): 281, 289, 309.
[9] Koester, *Revelation*, 110. 'Both the *incipit* and the salutation bear a great similarity to the way in which NT letters usually begin.' Ureña, *Narrative and Drama*, 12.
[10] 'Readers are expected to know that the slain Lamb is Jesus, though his name is not used, and that Jesus suffered death by crucifixion (Rev 1:5, 18; 2:8; 11:8).' Koester, *Revelation*, 386.
[11] Jonathan Knight, *Revelation, Readings: A New Biblical Commentary* (Sheffield: Sheffield Academic Press, 1999), 58–9.
[12] Note *Asc. Isa* 6.10-14; 2 Cor. 12.2-4.

arguably influenced by *1 Enoch*.[13] Further, 2 Cor. 12.1-7 speaks of the author's sky-journey in somewhat uneasy terms but with the assumption that such events are not unheard of and the *Ascension of Isaiah* is itself an early Christian text detailing a sky-journey and implying that such experiences were known in the circle that produced this text (*Asc. Isa.* 3.30-31).[14]

Early Christians commonly had knowledge of sky-journeys and of apocalyptic texts that narrate sky-journeys, as do Revelation's implied author and hearer. Even if we cannot define specific texts as part of the shared knowledge between implied author and implied hearer, some knowledge of some of this material is assumed. Cosmological concepts that recur across this material and the other sources are a reasonable approximation of the implied hearer's initial assumptions.

We certainly cannot say that the implied author and/or implied hearer is familiar with every Hebrew scripture, every apocalyptic text, every story from Greek culture and every idea present in Christian circles. But we can say that they have at least some familiarity with each of these sources. It follows from this that the cosmological conceptions that are common in these sources can be used as a reasonable approximation of the range of cosmological conceptions with which the implied hearer is already familiar.

3.2 Earth

The earth is a key defining reality in ancient cosmologies; in most cases the cosmos is co-extensive with the earth on the horizontal axis.[15] When discussing an ancient cosmological conception we are either talking about the earth itself or a region defined

---

[13] Edgar J. Goodspeed, 'Some Greek Notes: IV. Enoch in 1 Peter 3:19', *Journal of Biblical Literature* (1954): 91. W. J. Dalton, *Christ's Proclamation to the Spirits: A Study of 1 Peter 3:18-4:6* (Rome: Pontifical Biblical Institute, 1965), 163-76. Svere Aalen, 'St. Luke's Gospel and the Last Chapters of 1 Enoch', *New Testament Studies*, 13 (1966). Birger A. Pearson, 'A Reminiscence of Classical Myth at 2 Peter 2:4', *Greek, Roman, and Byzantine Studies*, 10 (1969): 71-80. J. Theisohn, *Der auserwählte Richter: Untersuchungen z. traditionsgeschichtl. Ort d. Menschensohngestalt d. Bilderreden d. Äthiopischen Henoch* (Vandenhoeck und Ruprecht, 1975). George W. E. Nickelsburg, 'Enoch, Levi, and Peter: Recipients of Revelation in Upper Galilee', *Journal of Biblical Literature*, 100 (1981): 575-600. Pieter G. R. de Villiers, ed., *Studies in 1 Enoch and the New Testament* (Stellenbosch: University of Stellenbosch Press, 1983). James C. VanderKam, '1 Enoch, Enochic Motifs, and Enoch in Early Christian Literature', in *The Jewish Apocalyptic Heritage in Early Christianity*, ed. James C. VanderKam and William Adler (Minneapolis: Fortress Press, 1995) 33-101. George W. E. Nickelsburg, 'Revisiting the Rich and the Poor in 1 Enoch 92-105 and the Gospel According to Luke', *Society of Biblical Literature Seminar Papers*, 134/37 (1998): 579-605. Nickelsburg, *1 Enoch 1*, 82-108. Loren T. Struckenbruck and Gabriele Boccaccini, eds., *Enoch and the Synoptic Gospels: Reminiscences, Allusions, Intertextuality, Early Judaism and Its Literature* (Atlanta: SBL Press, 2016).

[14] Jonathan Knight, *The Ascension of Isaiah. Guides to Apocrypha and Pseudepigrapha* (Sheffield: Sheffield Academic Press, 1995), 9-10. Robert G. Hall, 'The Ascension of Isaiah: Community Situation, Date, and Place in Early Christianity', *Journal of Biblical Literature*, 109/2 (1990): 294.

[15] Job 28.24; Isa. 13.5; *1 En.* 33.1; *3 Baruch* 2.1. See also M. R. Wright, *Cosmology in Antiquity* (London; New York: Routledge, 1995), 7, 38. Edward Adams, 'Graeco-Roman and Ancient Jewish Cosmology', in *Cosmology and New Testament Theology*, ed. Jonathan T. Pennington and Sean M. McDonough (London: T&T Clark, 2008), 7.

in relation to the earth, especially the regions above the earth and the regions below.[16] But these are only broad categories, and many cosmic schemata have multiple sky-layers as distinct from each other as they are from the earth.

In most cases, the assumption is that the earth stretches from east to west, and north to south, reaching an end at these distant extremities. Very rarely is it considered that the earth of human habitation may be the curved surface of a sphere or that in some other manner the earth may have a three-dimensional shape with significance for the cosmos as a whole.[17]

Thus the Hebrew scriptures speak of the whole earth 'from one end to the other', giving 'the ends of the earth' the same meaning as 'the ends of the skies' (Deut. 4.32; 13.7; 28.49, 64; 33.17; Job 28.24; Isa. 13.5). At other times they refer to the extremities of the earth with the term כַּנְפוֹת (Isa. 11.12; Job 37.3; 38.13), translated as πτέρυγας in the Septuagint (LXX).[18] In cosmic journey texts the seer may be taken to observe the extremities of the earth, at one or all points of the compass (*1 En.* 18.1–36.4; *3 Bar.* 2.1). From a sufficient vantage point an observer may see the whole earth (*1 En.* 83.11; Mt. 4.8; Lk. 4.5).[19]

It is sometimes unclear whether the earth is imagined as a square or circle. The compass directions in *1 Enoch* are sometimes understood to indicate a square earth with corners,[20] but in attempting to draw *1 Enoch*'s earth, first Grelot then Milik and then Bautch all drew it circular.[21] In the Hebrew scriptures (Job 37.3; 38.13; Isa. 11.12; 24.16) the earth is said to have כַּנְפוֹת. The term is traditionally translated as 'corners', although it commonly refers to wings or to the edges of a garment and is consistently translated in the Septuagint (LXX) as πτέρυγες rather than γωνία. The specification in one verse (Isa. 11.12) that the earth has four of these could suggest a square shape for the earth or could simply be a way of referring to the entire earth extending out to the extremities in all four directions.[22] When the Hebrew scriptures speak of an object that has actual corners, different words are used. Ezek. 41.22 speaks of the מִקְצֹעוֹת (literally means 'corners') of the altar (LXX κέρας), and Ezek. 46.21-22 speaks of the four מְקֻצָעוֹת of the court (LXX μέρος and κλίτος).[23] A reference to corners certainly does not

---

[16] Commenting on the book of Revelation, Franz Boll wrote, 'Himmel und Erde sind eine große Einheit, ein Paar, in dem der "Himmel" in Wahrheit nur von der Größe der Erde aus vorgestellt und in seiner Ausdehnung bestimmt wird.' Franz Boll, *Aus der Offenbarung Johannis*, 16. Occasionally we may speak of a region beyond the horizontal extremities of the earth/cosmos (*1 En.* 18.12; 21.1).

[17] Hippolytus, *Refutations* 1.5; Plato, *Phaedo* 108e-109a.

[18] Similarly, the *Testament of Asher* speaks of τὰς τέσσαρας γωνίας τῆς γῆς (*T. Ash.* 7.2).

[19] Matthew and Luke indicate the whole inhabited earth. Even if one posits a spherical, cubic or cylindrical earth any proposed southern hemisphere or antipode is not the kind of space in which humans live.

[20] Charles, *Revelation*, vol. 1, 204. Harrington, *Revelation*, 98.

[21] Pierre J. Grelot, 'La géographie mythique d'Hénoch et ses sources orientales', *Revue Biblique*, 65/1 (1958): 46. Józef T Milik, *Dead Sea Scrolls Study: The Book of Enoch Aramaic fragments, Qumran Cave 4* (Oxford: Oxford Clarendon Press, 1976), 40. Kelley Coblentz Bautch, *A Study of the Geography of 1 Enoch 17–19: No One Has Seen What I Have Seen*, vol. 81 (Brill, 2003), 185.

[22] Jeremiah 25.36 refers to the four extremities of the skies. This is often translated as the 'four corners' but neither the Hebrew word (קָצָה) nor the LXX Greek (ἄκρον) indicate corners or angles, instead simply indicating ends, borders, outskirts or extremities.

[23] Ezek. 43.20 and 45.19 speak of the four פִּנּוֹת ('faces') of the ledge of the altar. In the LXX this is translated as τέσσαρας γωνίας and is almost always translated into English as 'four corners', although 'four sides' might be better (so CEB).

remove the possibility that the earth is imagined as a circle or in some cases even a sphere; Ptolemy's *Tetrabiblos* refers to the τόπων καὶ γωνιῶν at the four cardinal compass points (Ptolemy, *Tetrabiblos* 1.10) while affirming that the earth is spherical.

Comments regarding the earth's construction suggest something analogous to a floor, mat or platform, reinforcing the picture of an earth laid out across the horizontal plane. 1 Sam. 2.8 proclaims, 'The pillars [מָצוּק] of the earth are the LORD'S, and on them he has set the world', and Ps. 75.3 (75.4 Hebrew), 'When the earth totters, and all its inhabitants, it is I who keep steady its pillars [עַמּוּד].' In a broadly similar vein, Ps. 104.5 reports, 'You set the earth on its foundations [מָכוֹן], so that it shall never be shaken.'[24] This gives the impression that the construction of the earth in some ways resembles a human structure of wood and stone – although if pillars hold up the earth it is not clear what holds up the pillars or what other firm foundation they rest upon. A different impression is given by Isa. 42.5; 44.24 and Ps. 136.6 in which the earth is 'spread out' (רקע) as one would spread out a substance such as soft metal or mud – or indeed, in the way that the רָקִיעַ is spread out.[25] In the last of these verses the earth is spread out on the waters as if it were some kind of mat floating on the sea.[26] A similar picture may be suggested in Ps. 24.1-2, Prov. 8.27 and also in *2 En.* 47.3.[27]

The exceptions to this conception of the earth are found in Greek cosmological theorizing. Some Greek thinkers, including Anaximenes, Anaxagoras and Democritus, maintained a disc-shaped earth capped by a dome-shaped sky and provided theoretical justification for this model (Aristotle, *De Caelo* 294b13-21; Hippolytus, *Refutations* 1.6).[28] Increasingly, however, the models were of a spherical cosmos, the earth at its centre being in one case cylindrical with an inhabited antipode (Hippolytus, *Refutations* 1.5) but more commonly spherical. In these models the earth remains in place without need of anything to hold it up (Hippolytus, *Refutations* 1.5; Plato, *Phaedo* 108e–109a).

While the spherical model existed, it appears to have had little influence beyond the higher education of elite Greeks and Romans.[29] It has not influenced Greek cultural stories of gods and heroes, and nor does this model recur in Hebrew scriptures, early Christian writings or in written accounts of cosmic journeys. One possible exception is the J recension of *2 Enoch* 23–38. Its spherical cosmos, with skies that are concentric crystalline spheres, is derived from the Greek spherical models and possibly implies a spherical earth at its centre. However, with the difficulty in dating *2 Enoch*, and the

---

[24] מָכוֹן is used in relation to a structure in Ezra 2.68 – 'made freewill offerings for the house of God, to erect it on its *site*' (emphasis mine).

[25] See 2 Sam. 22.43 – 'I crushed them and *stamped them down* like the mire of the streets' (emphasis mine).

[26] Thus I disagree with Kyle Greenwood's assertion that 'unlike Israel's neighbours, there is no indication that the Hebrews thought of the earth as floating on the cosmic sea'. Kyle Greenwood, *Scripture and Cosmology: Reading the Bible Between the Ancient World and Modern Science* (Downers Grove: IVP Academic, 2015), 79. But I acknowledge that there is more evidence for the Hebrews thinking of the earth as set on foundations or pillars.

[27] According to Aristotle, the Greek thinker Thales held that the earth floats on water 'like a log'. Aristotle, *De Caelo* 294a28-34.

[28] Wright, *Cosmology*, 42.

[29] Ryan, *Hearing*, 72–4.

evidence of extensive editing, this section may have been written several centuries after Revelation.[30] It also conflicts with other parts of *2 Enoch*.[31]

Across all these sources, the conception that strongly predominates is an earth that stretches from east to west, north to south, reaching an end at these extremities. I have avoided the term 'flat'; it seems inappropriate where mountains can be cosmological features reaching up to the heavens (*1 En.* 17.2). Using the term 'flat' would also call to mind 'spherical' as an alternative, whereas in most of these sources the broad earth stretching from east to west was an assumption without an alternative.

3.3 Below the earth

With the earth assumed to stretch out across a horizontal plane, these sources frequently describe regions beneath the earth that are beyond the ordinary experience of a living human being. There are two broad concepts that recur throughout these sources: a dwelling place for whatever remains of the human person following death and a region associated with a powerful threat to the cosmic order. These are quite distinct concepts, as one relates to the ordinary cycle of human life and death that is expected as part of the cosmic order, while the other is a threat to the cosmic order, but they are both located below the earth and there is sometimes a structural or poetic connection between them.

3.3.1 The two regions

In speaking of human death, the Hebrew scriptures make frequent reference to שְׁאוֹל (Sheol), often in connection with ירד (go down).[32] A consistent picture emerges of Sheol as a region deep beneath the land, vertically opposite the heavens high above (Amos 9.2), and probably cavernous like chambers or rooms (חֲדָרִים, Prov. 7.27). In the Hebrew scriptures Sheol is the space appropriate to the shadowy semi-existence of all humans following death.

The potential threat to cosmic order is the subterranean, and sub-Mediterranean, cosmic waters. While the Genesis cosmogony divided the primal waters and named the lower waters 'sea', the Hebrew scriptures sometimes give the sense that beneath

---

[30] Józef T. Milik, *The Books of Enoch: Aramaic Fragments of Qumran Cave 4* (Oxford: Clarendon Press, 1976), 109, 112. James H. Charlesworth, ed., *The Pseudepigrapha and Modern Research, With a Supplement* (Chico: Scholars Press, 1981), 104.

[31] In *2 Enoch* 1–22 the seer journeys through the skies, the journey showing a cosmos with a flat earth as the lowest cosmic layer, with seven (A recension) or ten (J recension) sky-layers above. In *2 Enoch* 23–38 God speaks to the seer, explaining his acts of creation, and in the J recension this cosmic explanation depicts a cosmos composed of seven concentric crystalline sky-spheres each with a planet attached to it as in the theoretical speculations of Anaximander, Plato, and Aristotle. In *2 Enoch* 39–73 the seer relates his experiences to the members of his household and in this retelling the cosmos features a flat earth with a hell below and a paradise in the skies above.

[32] Verses with שְׁאוֹל in connection with ירד: Gen. 37.35; 42.38; 44.29, 31; Num. 16.30, 33; 1 Sam. 2.6; 1 Kgs. 2.6, 9; Isa. 5.14; 14.11, 15; 38.18; Ezek. 31.15-17; 32.21, 27; Amos 9.2; Ps. 30.4; 55.16; Job 7.9; 17.16; Prov. 1.12; 5.5; 7.27.

the earth and terranean sea there still exists a deeper, wilder, more threatening, primal cosmic sea. It is this that bursts up through the springs of the earth in Genesis 7, combining with the upper cosmic waters to flood the entire earth and partially unmake the cosmos.[33] Sometimes Sheol and the primal watery deep are associated with each other, at least poetically, as in Job 2.1-5.[34]

Greek sources tell of the subterranean dwelling-place of deceased humans – the 'realm of Hades' or simply 'Hades' (ᾅδης). It has similarities with the Sheol of the Hebrew scriptures but its characteristics are more explicitly developed. It is a cavernous region beneath the earth (Homer, *Odyssey* 10.560; 24.204; *Iliad* 23.51), and while it can potentially be accessed through certain openings in the ground[35] it is not the appropriate space for a living human being; it is the appropriate space for the shadowy semi-existence of all humans after death (Homer, *Odyssey* 11).

The deepest, darkest part of the cosmos is Tartaros (Hesiod, *Theogony* 720),[36] sometimes used as a prison for powerful beings that emerged in the early stages of the cosmogonic process, and who could potentially threaten the cosmic order that developed (Hesiod, *Theogony* 617–720, 820–868; Apollodorus, *Library* 1.1.2. See also Josephus, *Apion* 2.240). In rare cases Tartaros and/or Hades may be a place of punishment for especially noteworthy humans guilty of archetypal crimes (Homer, *Odyssey* 11.582-600; Apollodorus, *Library* 1.9.2).[37] Sources differ as to the relationship between Tartaros and Hades. Tartaros may be far beneath Hades (Homer, *Iliad* 8.13-16)[38] or described as an especially deep and gloomy place *within* the realm of Hades (Apollodorus, *Library* 1.1.2).[39]

The two underworld concepts recur in apocalypses and early Christian writings, which demonstrate both Hebrew and Greek influence, with blending and development

---

[33] Note also Exod. 20.4.
[34] It is a great overstatement to say, as Beale does, 'The "abyss" is synonymous with the concept of Hades.' Beale, *Revelation*, 493.
[35] As it was in the story by Heracles and Orpheus, and in ritual by the participants at the Hierapolis ploutonion. Strabo, *Geographica* 5.4.5; 14.1.11. Keith Dyer, 'The Four Horsemen of the Apocalypse and the Consequences of War (Revelation 6.1-11)', in *Ecological Aspects of War: Engagements with Biblical Texts*, ed. Anne Elvey and Deborah Guess (London: T&T Clark, 2017), 138–40.
[36] 'As far beneath the earth as heaven is above earth; for so far is it from earth to Tartarus. For a brazen anvil falling down from heaven nine nights and days would reach the earth upon the tenth: and again, a brazen anvil falling from earth nine nights and days would reach Tartarus upon the tenth.' Hesiod, *Theogony*, 720. Translation, Hugh G. Evelyn-White, *Hesiod, the Homeric Hymns, and Homerica*, The Loeb Classical Library (London: Heinemann, 1914).
[37] Alan E. Bernstein, *The Formation of Hell: Death and Retribution in the Ancient and Early Christian Worlds* (Ithaca: Cornell University Press, 1993), 38. Like many Greek heroes, Tantalos has some divine parentage but is a mortal/human. Plato (*Gorgias* 523b) suggests that Tartaros could be a place of 'requital and penance' for significant numbers of impious humans, but this idea seems to be less common.
[38] 'I shall take him and dash him down to the murk of Tartaros (Tartarus), far below, where the uttermost depth of the pit lies under earth, where there are gates of iron and a brazen doorstone, as far beneath the house of Aides as from earth the sky lies.' Homer, *Iliad* 8.13-16. Translation, Richmond Lattimore, *The Iliad of Homer*, ed. Richard Martin (Chicago: University of Chicago Press, 2011).
[39] 'But then Sky bound and cast into Tartarus, a gloomy place in Hades as far distant from earth as earth is distant from the sky.' Apollodorus, *Library*, 1.1.2. Translation, James George Frazer, *Apollodorus, The Library* (London: Heinemann, 1921).

of concepts and varying use of terminology. In some cases traditionally underworld locations are relocated to the skies.

In the LXX the Hebrew שְׁאוֹל is translated with the Greek ᾅδης and early Christian writings in the Greek language use this term to refer to a concept apparently identical with Sheol, that is, an under-earth region simply connected with death and loss (Mt. 11.23; Lk. 10.15; Acts 2.27, 31). While the LXX uses the term ἄβυσσος for the other under-earth concept (the deep, primordial waters that potentially threaten cosmic order), Romans 10.6-7 apparently uses the term in much the same way that Matthew, Luke and Acts use ᾅδης.[40]

There is a distinctly different picture in Lk. 16.23, where ᾅδης denotes a place for the dead that includes post-mortem torment of the unrighteous. While Hades' position within the cosmos is not specified, if the parable is read in the context of Luke then the reader must picture it beneath the earth (Lk. 10.15).[41] While Hades is the location for the rich man's post-mortem experience, the poor man's location is unclear. I suggest that the rich man and the poor man both go down to Hades, one to a negative experience in Hades and one to a positive experience in Hades. Much as the Hebrew scriptures speak of a patriarch 'descending to the grave/Sheol' as synonymous with being 'gathered to his people' or 'lying with his fathers' (Gen. 25.8; 37.35; 42.38; 44.29; 47.30; 49.29; Deut. 31.16; 1 Kgs 2.10), so the poor man is not left to be eaten by the dogs but is instead carried to Hades by angels,[42] where he is gathered to his ancestors (εἰς τὸν κόλπον Ἀβραάμ). Obviously the rich man is not left to be eaten by dogs, having the privilege of a proper burial and a proper entrance into Hades. But he discovers that he has not been gathered to his ancestors and is instead subjected to fiery punishment in a different part of Hades. This shares similarities with the Book of Watchers, whose equivalent of Hades/Sheol is a set of four cavities in a mountain at the edge of the earth. Three of these are dark, but the fourth is bright with a spring of water, and this one is reserved for the righteous (*1 En.* 22.1-14). The different experience in Hades has a strong parallel in the beliefs that Josephus ascribes to Pharisees, writing, 'They also believe that souls have an immortal vigor in them, and that under the earth there will be rewards or punishments, according as they have lived virtuously or viciously in this life.'[43] Luke may not be advocating the actual existence of a fiery section in Hades, as this occurrence is within a parable[44] and in all other instances Luke-Acts uses ᾅδης

---

[40] In Romans ἄβυσσος either refers to the subterranean realm of the dead or to the subterranean regions of the cosmos *including* the realm of the dead. Kim Gary Papaioannou, 'Places of Punishment in the Synoptic Gospels' (Durham: University of Durham, 2004), 169.

[41] 'The transgression of the boundary between narrative levels, whereby the outer story told by Luke penetrates the embedded stories told by Jesus, a procedure known as metalepsis, constitutes one of the main communicative factors at work in the Third Gospel.' Sławomir Szkredka, 'Postmortem Punishment in the Parable of Lazarus and the Rich Man (Luke 16: 19-31): Between Coherence and Indeterminacy of Luke's Eschatology', *Verbum Vitae*, 36 (2019): 124.

[42] Similarly, *4 Ezra* speaks of the souls of the righteous being gathered into subterranean chambers and guarded by angels (*4 Ezra* 7.32, 95). Plato posits that upon death, every human soul is led by its spirit guide to an appropriate under-earth location (Plato, *Phaedo* 107d-e; 113d).

[43] Josephus, *Ant.* 18.14.

[44] It is not only a parable but also a hyperbolic parable; the best that a mortal ordinarily hopes for is a proper burial, but the poor man receives the special honour of being carried into Hades by angels. Though differing from my reading in some ways, Marlene Yu Yap makes a similar point, arguing, 'This parable is not meant to give a description of what heaven and hell look like, and neither is

simply in relation to death, loss and the grave.[45] Nevertheless, it shows familiarity with the concept.

Matthew (and to a lesser extent Mark, Luke and James) speaks of something called γέεννα, associated with fire and punishment for humans who choose the wrong path.[46] It is a genuine question whether γέεννα in these writings should be thought of cosmologically or historically, that is, as a place beneath the earth or in some other extraordinary place in the cosmos, in which the unrighteous dead are tormented/destroyed, or as a more ordinary place on the earth where Roman armies will shamefully treat the corpses of their enemies when they put down the military rebellion in Jerusalem.[47] In *4 Ezra* 7.36 Gehenna is clearly a place in which the unrighteous dead are tormented and some commentators take that as evidence that it should be so understood in the early Christian writings as well.[48] In *4 Ezra* it is an extra-ordinary place that opens up in the earth in the future cosmos.

The second underworld concept occurs in a few places. Reflecting LXX usage, where ἄβυσσος is used for the deep, watery place associated with a potential threat to cosmic order,[49] Lk. 8.21 uses ἄβυσσος for a threatening place beneath the earth that is the proper abode of demons. It is unclear whether the *watery* sense of ἄβυσσος carries through into its usage in Luke.[50] Jude and 2 Peter speak of deep, dark places of captivity

---

Hades a place where the good and the bad await judgement. The description just provides necessary imagery ... Honor reversal occurs in this parable, where the one who was shamed on earth is now honored in heaven.' Marlene Yu Yap, 'Three Parables of Jesus Through the Shame-Honor Lens', *Asian Journal of Pentecostal Studies*, 19/2 (2016): 221.

[45] 'The author of Luke-Acts does not make clear how these different eschatological expectations are related to one another.' Outi Lehtipuu, *The Afterlife Imagery in Luke's Story of the Rich Man and Lazarus*, Supplements to Novum Testamentum, vol. 123 (Leiden: Brill, 2007), 297.

[46] Mt. 5.22, 29; 10.28; 18.9; 23.15, 33; Mk 9.43; Lk. 12.5; Jas 3.6.

[47] Andrew Perriman, *The Coming of the Son of Man: New Testament Eschatology for an Emerging Church* (Eugene: Wipf and Stock, 2012), 16-37, 91-4. Mark 9, the only chapter in Mark that mentions Gehenna, speaks of it as the place 'where their worm does not die and the fire is not quenched'. This is a direct quote from Isa. 66.24, 'And they shall go out and look on the dead bodies of the men who have rebelled against me. For their worm shall not die, their fire shall not be quenched, and they shall be an abhorrence to all flesh.' The Isaiah text speaks about human corpses that are not given a proper burial but left to rot (worm) and burn (fire). This is closely paralleled in Jer. 7.32-33,

> Therefore, behold, the days are coming, declares the LORD, when it will no more be called Topheth, or the Valley of the Son of Hinnom, but the Valley of Slaughter; for they will bury in Topheth, because there is no room elsewhere. And the dead bodies of this people will be food for the birds of the air, and for the beasts of the earth, and none will frighten them away.

> The corpses remain, left to worms or to carrion birds, and the fire continues to burn, as a sign to all people. The 'Valley of (the Son of) Hinnom' is גֵּי־הִנֹּם or in Greek γέεννα. Craig Evans suggests that Jesus' use of scripture shows familiarity with the Aramaic paraphrase, noting, 'In the Isaiah Targum, which in its extant form, of course, post-dates Jesus, the verse reads "And they shall go forth and look on the bodies of the sinful men who have rebelled against my Memra; for their breaths will not die and their fire shall not be quenched, and the wicked shall be judged in Gehinnom ..."'. Craig A. Evans, *Mark 8:27-16:20*. Word Biblical Commentary, vol. 34B (Nashville: Thomas Nelson, 2001), 72.

[48] Donald Alfred Hagner, *Matthew 1-13*, Word Biblical Commentary, vol. 33A (Dallas: Word Books, 1993), 116.

[49] Gen. 1.2; 7.11; Deut. 8.7; Ps. 148.7.

[50] We may view it as ironic that the demons want to avoid the abyss, the great deep primordial sea, and end up in the Sea of Galilee. But Luke here calls it the *Lake* of Galilee and it is not clear whether the abyss is still conceived of as watery.

for deviant stars and rebellious angels, with 2 Pet. 2.4 showing Greek influence in using the verb ταρταρόω, literally 'cast into Tartaros'.

The dwelling place for whatever remains of the human person following death occurs throughout the apocalypses. *2 Baruch* speaks of ܐܝܘܠ (Sheol, *2 Bar.* 11.6) and assumes that the dead are in or under the earth (*2 Bar.* 21.24; 50.2). *4 Ezra* also speaks of ܐܝܘܠ in the Syriac and *infernus* in the Latin, which simply indicates a lower world.[51] There is relative consistency throughout *4 Ezra* if this is understood as a more or less neutral realm of the dead (in distinction from the fiery *clibanus gehennae* that opens up in the future cosmos, in *4 Ezra* 7.36). But while it has appeared that Sheol is the neutral dwelling of all the dead as they await the final judgement (and possible consignment to the *clibanus gehennae*), 7.75-101 paint a modified picture. Sheol is now portrayed as a safe, contented, restful waiting-place, the current dwelling place of the righteous dead.[52] These 'chambers of the souls' in *4 Ezra* 4.35 are explained in 4.41 as the chambers in Sheol. The righteous souls rest in chambers in the earth until 'the earth shall give up those who are asleep in it, and the dust those who rest there in silence; and the chambers shall give up the souls that have been committed to them' (*4 Ezra* 7.32 NRSV)[53]; then they shall receive the harvest of their reward (*4 Ezra* 4.35). By contrast, the unrighteous dead have no home but are left to wander like restless ghosts, tormented by regrets and anxiety until their condemnation and punishment at the final judgement. This is similar to the picture in *1 Enoch*, with its set of four cavities serving as the dwelling-place of the human dead as they await either vindication or condemnation at the coming judgement (*1 En.* 22.4). These souls are less than their living selves and the righteous souls seek justice, yet even now there is a separation of the righteous and unrighteous, as three of the four cavities are dark.

The concept of an under-earth region associated with a powerful threat to the cosmic order also occurs in the apocalypses, with significant variation. Also at the western edge of the cosmos, the Book of Watchers has two such places; a non-place beyond the edge of the cosmos with neither sky above nor earth below, where seven deviant stars are imprisoned (*1 En.* 18.12-15; 21.1-6),[54] and a great fiery cleft extending down into the abyss (ἄβυσσος), which is the prison of angels (*1 En.* 18.11; 21.7-10). It is not clear whether this ἄβυσσος is watery as in the LXX.

---

[51] Despite the temptation for an English-speaker to link it with such words as 'infernal' and 'inferno'.

[52] J. Edward Wright is incorrect to say that the righteous soul immediately ascends to heavenly habitations. These 'chambers of the souls' in 4.35 are explained in 4.41 as the chambers in Sheol. J. Edward Wright, *The Early History of Heaven* (Oxford: Oxford University Press, 2000), 132.

[53] New Revised Standard Version.

[54] As there are seven such stars it is tempting to consider these the seven 'wandering stars' of ancient cosmology: Saturn, Jupiter, Mars, Sun, Venus, Mercury and Moon. Yet while these all deviate relative to the 'fixed' stars, Sun and Moon cannot be considered deviant for moving across the sky. In addition, an observer of the sky would see that all seven are still in the sky following their individual courses, not bound in a prison. And yet perhaps in some settings the concept of the seven wandering stars became unstuck from actual observations and developed into the concept of the seven deviant stars. Contra Ryan (Ryan, *Hearing*, 50.) these seven deviant stars cannot be identified with angels/watchers; *1 Enoch* defines these as two distinct categories of powerful sky-beings, each punished in their own time. Stars stand in for angels/watchers only in the thoroughly allegorical Animal Apocalypse (*1 En.* 85–90).

In the *Ascension of Isaiah* we hear that beneath the earth is Sheol (ሲኦል), and beneath that Perdition/Destruction (ሐጕል, *Asc. Isa.* 10.8). If interpreted in connection with the first half of the *Ascension of Isaiah*, the Perdition/Destruction may be seen as identical to the Gehenna of 1.3 and 4.14, and therefore as a place of punishment/ imprisonment for powerful beings.

Throughout these sources we have seen two distinct under-earth regions. The first is the dwelling place for whatever remains of the human person following death. This is usually a neutral or slightly sad place for all the human dead, but sometimes a distinction is introduced between the post-mortem experiences of the righteous and the unrighteous. The second under-earth region is associated with a powerful threat to the cosmic order. The Hebrew scriptures assume a watery deep that threatens to burst forth and destroy the creational divisions between sea, land and sky, but the threat more commonly comes from the powerful beings that are found within it. In some texts these powerful beings are native to this space, while in others texts they have been imprisoned there by the forces of cosmic order. These two regions usually coexist within the cosmic schema, remaining distinct both functionally and spatially even as they share the under-earth cosmic tier. While distinct, the two spaces sometimes share a structural connection or a poetic association.

3.3.2 Relocation

While *1 Enoch* has a distinctive location for the human dead (inside a mountain at the western extremity of the earth), some apocalypses have taken the radical step of relocating this under-earth space into the skies. This occurs where the broader cosmological schema has shifted such that the earth is the lowest part of the cosmos.

3 Baruch has places in the skies for categories of deceased humans, including a place called Hades which is the undesirable destination of the vast majority of the unrighteous humans (*3 Bar.* 4.2; 5.3). The righteous dead have a separate dwelling in the skies (*3 Bar.* 10.5). Although different terminology is used, the same is true of *2 Enoch* 1–22 (*2 En.* 8.1–10.6).[55] Just as there is no place below the earth for the human dead, so there is no subterranean Tartaros or abyss or any other under-earth region associated with a powerful threat to the cosmic order. Instead, *2 Enoch* has such a place located in the skies; specifically, a prison for the rebellious sky-beings known in the Enochic traditions, those who threatened the cosmic order by descending to earth live in the manner of earth-beings (*2 En.* 7.1-5; 18.3).[56] Under-earth spaces are not relocated to the skies individually,

---

[55] As noted above, other parts of *2 Enoch* present conflicting cosmologies.

[56] While *2 En.* 18.7 says that they were sentenced under the earth, this 'simply does not fit the cosmography of the rest of the book, and even contradicts this very ch., which locates the other fallen angels in the second heaven'. M. A. Knibb, 'The Martyrdom and Ascension of Isaiah', in *The Old Testament Pseudepigrapha*, ed. James H. Charlesworth, vol. 2 (Garden City: Doubleday, 1985), 132.

There is a chronological difficulty at this point. Genesis 5 implies that 869 years (187 + 182 + 500) passed between the time that Enoch became a father and the time that sky-beings went down to earth to procreate with human women. But only 300 years passed between the time that Enoch became a father and the time he was taken by God. So the rebellious angels should not have been condemned and imprisoned in the second sky until centuries after Enoch's ascent through the skies.

but only as part of a cosmic remodelling in which any and all under-earth spaces are relocated to the skies and the earth becomes the lowest space. We will return to this point when considering the location of Hades within Revelation's cosmic schema.

3.4 Skies

This section will show several key recurring concepts relating to the skies. These are: a sky/firmament that is a material structure like a ceiling high above the earth, often with openings that allow passage through this structure; a significant space at the underside of the sky-structure; a significant space above the sky-structure; a 'God-space' at or above the highest sky, and not part of the human-proximate cosmos, sometimes not accessible to humans at all, even after death or in an extra-ordinary experience; a conflicted space in the lower skies or firmament, distinct from the higher God-space; powerful beings that populate the skies, including the bright living beings that are visible from earth in the ordinary cosmic rhythms of day and night.

In these sources, there are several recurring concepts regarding the nature of the skies, with variation within a certain range. The cosmos almost always contains at least one 'sky' that is a material structure above the earth, like a great ceiling. There is variation in its supposed material composition with options ranging through metal, stone, crystal, ice or something like cloth or leather, but in almost every case it is a solid structure. This sky-structure may be a broad, flat plane high above the broad, flat earth, or it may be dome-shaped with its edges resting on the edges of the earth. Even when dome-shaped the high/central part of this sky is treated as a horizontal layer, high above the horizontal earth-layer. Often above this first sky there are additional skies that are also solid horizontal structures, making it a multi-layered cosmos.

3.4.1 The sky-structure

The concept of a sky/firmament that is a material structure is found consistently throughout our sources with only a few partial exceptions. The material-structural nature of this sky is shown by explanations of its structure, including how it was constructed, how it remains in place above the earth, the openings that allow beings to move between higher and lower cosmic layers and the openings that allow the meteorological functioning of the cosmos. This is sometimes accompanied by discussion of its material composition.

In the Hebrew scriptures we find a sky-structure called רָקִיעַ and associated with שָׁמַיִם. The cosmogony of Genesis 1 describes primordial waters that are divided into upper and lower waters by the creation of a רָקִיעַ, that is, an expanse, a surface or something stretched out perhaps in the way metal is stretched out when beaten with a hammer.[57] Adela Yarbro Collins describes it as literally 'a strip of beaten

---

[57] *Brown-Driver-Briggs Hebrew and English Lexicon* (*BDB*). Wenham makes the רָקִיעַ consistent with modern scientific cosmology by describing it as the air between the sea and the clouds. Gordon J. Wenham, *Genesis 1–15. Word Biblical Commentary* (Waco: Word Books, 1987), 20. As well as avoiding the straightforward sense of רָקִיעַ in Genesis 1, this reading cannot make sense of Gen.

metal'.[58] It is certainly 'eine feste und starke Platte mit Tragkraft',[59] because it serves as a barrier to divide the primordial waters and keep the upper portion separate from the lower portion.[60] The upper portion (now associated with the term שָׁמַיִם) presumably remains in a normal watery form resembling the seas (יַמִּים) below, so requiring the 'Platte mit Tragkraft'.[61] If holes should open in the רָקִיעַ / שָׁמַיִם then upper waters would come down to rejoin the waters below, covering the earth and at least partially unmaking the cosmos (Gen. 7.11. See also *1 En.* 54.7-9). רָקִיעַ is usually translated as 'firmament' or 'expanse', and occasionally as 'dome' (NRSV, CEB),[62] although there is no explicit indication in Genesis that the רָקִיעַ is curved.[63]

This cosmic picture recurs throughout the Hebrew scriptures with some variation. Sometimes the שָׁמַיִם are said to have been 'stretched out', perhaps like a curtain or like the cloth/leather of a tent as it is being erected.[64] In these places the verb is not רקע,

---

1.14-18 where God puts lights (sun, moon and stars) in the רָקִיעַ. If the רָקִיעַ is the space between land/sea and clouds, then placing the sun and stars in the רָקִיעַ would place them below the clouds. Any ancient person could see that the sun and stars are *above* the clouds, not below, so this is simply not a plausible ancient cosmology.

Note the verbal forms in connection with metal in Exod. 39.3; Num. 16.38-39; Isa. 40.19, and with mud/earth in 2 Sam. 22.43; Isa. 42.5; 44.24; Jer. 10.9; Ps. 136.6. It is used without a substance and translated 'stamped your feet' in Ezek. 6.11; 25.6. In Job 37.18 it is used in connection with the sky/skies and put in poetic parallel with metal: 'Can you, like him, *spread out* the skies, hard as a molten mirror?' (NRSV; emphasis mine). While רָקִיעַ occurs 17 times in the Hebrew Bible, שָׁמַיִם occurs 421 and appears to have a slightly broader meaning than רָקִיעַ.

[58] Yarbro Collins, *Cosmology*, 36.
[59] C. Houtman, *Der Himmel im Alten Testament: Israels Weltbild und Weltanschauung*, Oudtestamentische studiën (Leiden Brill, 1993), 222–3.
[60] 'It is necessary that the firmament be *firm* ... if the waters of the heavenly sea are to remain separated from the earth' (emphasis original). Jonathan Moo, 'The Sea That Is No More: Rev 21:1 and the Function of Sea Imagery in the Apocalypse of John', *Novum Testamentum*, 51 (2009).
[61] 'The second fiat calls into existence a *firmament*, whose function is to divide the primaeval waters into an upper and lower ocean' (emphasis in the original). John Skinner, *A Critical and Exegetical Commentary on Genesis*, 2nd edn, International Critical Commentary on the Holy Scriptures of the Old and New Testaments (Edinburgh: T&T Clark, 1930), 21. This is paralleled in other ancient cosmologies. 'To the Egyptians, the universe consisted of a limitless ocean (Nun) above the sky, paralleled by waters under the earth.' John H. Walton, *Genesis 1 as Ancient Cosmology* (Winona Lake: Eisenbrauns, 2011), 35.
[62] Common English Bible.
[63] Gerhard von Rad writes, 'The second day brings the creation of the firmament, which the ancients imagined as a gigantic hemispherical and ponderous bell.' Gerhard von Rad, *Genesis: A Commentary*, Rev. ed., Old Testament Library (London: SCM Press, 1972), 53. However, while he explains that רָקִיעַ indicates something that is 'firmly hammered', he does not explain how the shape is known. Skinner writes, 'The "firmament" is the dome of heaven, which to the ancients was no optical illusion, but a material structure.' Skinner, *Critical*, 21. It appears that Skinner gets the shape from his own observation that the sky looks like a dome and combines this with ancient descriptions of a solid sky to get the concept of a solid dome. Westermann, citing O. Brocksch, notes that 'מרקע is found in Phoenician for a hammered out bowl', which may support a dome shape, but only very tangentially. Claus Westermann, *Genesis 1–11: A Commentary*, trans. John J. Scullion (Minneapolis: Augsburg, 1984), 117. More directly, Job 37.18 compares the sky to a hammered out metal mirror, which presumably is flat. Kyle Greenwood comments that רָקִיעַ is treated in the Septuagint and Vulgate as referring to a hard dome. Greenwood, *Scripture*, 84. This is not completely true. They certainly treat it as a solid structure but neither the Greek στερέωμα nor the Latin *firmamentum* specifically convey a curved shape.
[64] This finds a parallel in the *Enuma Elish*. When Marduk constructs the sky from the corpse of Tiamat, the process is described as erecting a tent. See Greenwood, *Scripture*, 57.

which would suggest spreading out metal by beating it with a hammer, but verbs more appropriate to cloth/leather, such as נטה (Isa. 40.22; 42.5; 44.24; 45.12; 51.13; Jer. 10.12; 51.15; Zech. 12.1; Ps. 104.2; Job 9.8). When Isa. 34.4 speaks of the שָׁמַיִם 'rolling up like a scroll' this also evokes an image of the sky as something more like cloth/leather than like the beaten metal implied in Genesis.

Some kind of רָקִיעַ is also mentioned in Ezek. 1. The seer describes a fiery storm cloud coming from the north (or possibly down from the sky)[65] with extra-ordinary beings in it. He then sees something like a רָקִיעַ 'like glittering ice stretched out over their heads' (Ezek. 1.22 CEB). William Brownlee calls this a 'double entendre' because it represents both the 'platform' that is carried around by these beings, on which the divine throne rests, and the 'firmament of the sky'.[66] Although the vision primarily concerns a moving platform/chariot, it also suggests a picture of the sky as a firm icy substance,[67] with the throne of God atop it.[68]

Some Hebrew texts reinforce the concept of a material sky-structure with hints of how it remains in place. The sky is pictured as co-extensive with the earth (see Isa. 13.5), with suggestions that the edges of the sky are held up at the edges of the earth. Job 26 speaks of the earth having 'pillars' (עַמּוּד). 2 Sam. 22.8 speaks of the foundations (מוֹסָדָה) of the skies (שָׁמַיִם) and of these foundations shaking together with the earth, implying that these foundations are set on the earth.[69] Amos 9.6 speaks of God who 'builds his upper chambers in the heavens and founds his vault (אֲגֻדָּה) upon the earth'. The difficulty there is that אֲגֻדָּה only occurs four times in the Hebrew scriptures, but it appears to suggest something tied together, perhaps a bunch of hyssop (Exod. 12.22) or in this context perhaps 'the tent of the heavens'. If this reading is correct then the sky is depicted as constructed upon the earth in some way, probably fixed at the edges of the earth. Among those texts that speak of a רָקִיעַ, implying a solid sky-structure of beaten metal, none give any clues as to how it remains in place. If we imagine the רָקִיעַ as dome-shaped, then its edges could rest on the edges of the earth, which would not work for a sky material analogous to cloth/leather. It should be remembered, however, that it is never specified that the רָקִיעַ is curved.

A similar picture emerges from Greek cultural stories. Summarizing the *Iliad* and the *Odyssey*, the ancient Greek oral narratives that became written texts in around 540 BCE, M. R. Wright concludes, 'The cosmic structure assumed in these poems was a simple one of earth as a circular disk ... the hemisphere of the vault of the sky was above.'[70]

---

[65] צָפוֹן may be used this way in Job 26.7.
[66] William Hugh Brownlee, *Ezekiel 1–19. Word Biblical Commentary*, vol. 28 (Waco: Word Books, 1986), 34.
[67] 'Dazzling, ice-like expanse borne above their heads and outspread wings.' Moshe Greenberg, *Ezekiel 1–20: A New Translation with Introduction and Commentary*, 1st edn (Garden City: Doubleday, 1983), 52. For the substance of which it is composed, *Tg. Ezek.* 1.22 uses גְּלִיד (ice, frost).
[68] Interestingly, the apparently crystalline רָקִיעַ is described as 'stretched out' (נטה). This verb is often used in connection with שָׁמַיִם when viewed as analogous to cloth or animal skin, but it is somewhat surprising to see it used with רָקִיעַ, especially when described as crystalline.
[69] Isa. 13.13 and Joel 2.10 also speak of the sky and the earth shaking together, perhaps suggesting that they are part of the same structure, although this could also be read as simply making a poetic parallel between earth and sky.
[70] Wright, *Cosmology*, 16. *Iliad* 5.504; 17.425; *Odyssey* 15.329. See Adams, 'Graeco-Roman', 7.

In this cosmic structure, the hemispherical sky is composed of bronze or iron, with its edges resting on the edges of the earth (*Iliad* 5.504; 17.425; 18.607; *Odyssey* 15.329).[71] This picture is congruent with some of the Hebrew texts described above. Alternatively, the Homeric cosmos could be modelled as 'a round house with the earth as its circular floor, the sky as a disc of comparable size above it, and the two held apart by pillars' (*Odyssey* 1.52-54; *Theogony* 519–521).[72] Again, this picture is paralleled in some of the Hebrew texts described above, with their mention of sky-pillars and the suggestion of an earth-and-sky cosmic structure analogous to a human-made structure.

This disc earth and dome sky was affirmed by some Greek theoreticians (Anaximenes, Anaxagoras, Democritus), while others proposed alternative cosmic models of a spherical cosmos with the skies as concentric spheres around the earth at the centre (Anaximander, Plato, Aristotle, Ptolemy). In these models the sky does not need to be held up and is not attached to the earth in any way. There is no structural connection between the earth and skies (such as sky-pillars) but even here the skies are structures composed of a material substance, likely crystalline.[73]

A writing from the early Christian movement hints at an assumed conception of the sky, showing similarity with those parts of the Hebrew scriptures that suggest a material akin to cloth or animal skins stretched out like a tent or like an opened scroll. In this narrative the skies (τοὺς οὐρανούς) are seen tearing open (Mk 1.10), which can be seen in parallel with the tearing of the temple curtain (Mk 15.38).[74] As Josephus notes, this curtain was a tapestry showing 'the panorama of the heavens' and together Mark 1 and 15 suggest a picture of the sky (or skies) as something like a vast stretch of cloth.[75]

The apocalypses and literary sky journeys frequently describe sky-structures in detail, suggesting a material structure that divides the space below from the space above. This is especially explicit in *3 Baruch* which details the seer's journey through multiple layered sky-structures, explaining the distances between each sky-structure and the thickness of each (*3 Bar.* 2.5). Related to that, it details how long it takes to pass through the door/passageway that leads upward through the sky-structure, to emerge onto its upper surface (*3 Bar.* 2.2; 3.2; 4.2).[76]

---

[71] Wright, *Cosmology*, 38. Adams, 'Graeco-Roman', 7.

[72] Wright, *Cosmology*, 38, referencing *Odyssey* 1.52-4.

[73] Pseudo-Plutarch, *Placita Philosophorum* 2.11.2; 2.13.11; 2.14.3. Dirk Couprie shows that, at least in some texts, the sky-sphere is clearly a physical structure and not merely a geometric representation. In one model, the sun spirals around an imaginary cylinder, but its movements are limited by a real crystalline sky-sphere. Dirk L. Couprie, 'The Spiral Movement of the Sun on an Imaginary Cylinder According to Empedocles and Anaximander', *Philologia Classic*, 15/1 (2020): 9–10. Among classical scholars it has long been recognized that Aristotle's spheres constitute a physical/mechanical model of the cosmos. T. L. Heath, *Aristarchus of Samos: the Ancient Greek Copernicus* (Oxford: Clarendon Press, 1913), 217. J. L. E. Dreyer, *A History of Astronomy from Thales to Kepler* (New York: DoverPublications, 1953), 122.

[74] See Michael F. Bird, 'Tearing the Heavens and Shaking the Heavenlies: Mark's Cosmology in its Apocalyptic Context', in *Cosmology and New Testament Theology*, ed. Jonathan T. Pennington and Sean M. McDonough (London: T&T Clark, 2008), 45–59.

[75] Josephus, *War* 5.212-214.

[76] *3 Bar.* 4.2 reads καὶ εἶπέν μοι ἄγγελος· Δεῦρο διέλθωμεν μετὰ τοῦ ἀγγέλου ἀπὸ τοῦ τόπου ἐκείνου ὡσεὶ πορείας ἡμερῶν ἑκατὸν ὀγδοήκοντα πέντε, which would translate, 'And the angel said to me, "Come, let us go through with the angel from that place like a journey of 185 days."' As it stands it is confusing and the second part would read better if it were the speech of the narrating character, in

In *3 Baruch* each sky-structure functions as the ceiling of the world below and the floor of the world above.[77] Each sky-structure is exponentially higher and thicker than the last. They are vast in breadth, and the plains that are their upper surface can be treated as flat. Still, there appears to be some curve to them such that the edge of the first sky rests on the edge of the earth.[78] This structure accords with the suggestions for its material composition. *3 Baruch* is undecided as to whether the sky is made of clay, glass, iron or copper/brass/bronze, but any one of these materials would allow for a curved sky whose edges rest on the edges of the earth.[79] *1 Enoch*'s single sky-layer is structured in the same way – as a dome whose edges rest on the edges of the earth (*1 En.* 33.1).[80] *2 Enoch* is remarkably similar to *3 Baruch*. Although it exhibits conflicting cosmologies,[81] it does show consistency in depicting layered sky-structures that are solid enough to stand on and composed of a material substance.[82]

Not all literary sky-journeys are as clear as these aforementioned texts. The *Ascension of Isaiah*, for example, speaks of multiple sky-layers but gives little hint as to the possible structure and materiality of its skies. The *Apocalypse of Abraham* presents an ambivalent picture; its upper sky-layers are somewhat solid and somewhat airy, but substantially opaque.[83] Despite the vagueness of the *Ascension*

---

parallel to 3.2 and 2.2. A scribal omission due to homoeoteleuton may have occurred if the earlier text read καὶ εἶπέν μοι ἄγγελος· Δεῦρο διέλθωμεν. Καὶ διῆλθον μετὰ τοῦ ἀγγέλου ἀπὸ τοῦ τόπου ἐκείνου ὡσεὶ πορείας ἡμερῶν ἑκατὸν ὀγδοήκοντα πέντε. It then translates, 'And the angel said to me, "Come, let us go through", and I went through with the angel from that place like a journey of 185 days.' The parallel with 3.2 and 2.2 suggests that they are going through a door in the next sky.

[77] See *3 Bar.* 2.2-3; 3.1-2. Baruch and his angelic guide fly upwards (ἀναπτερόω) through a cosmic ceiling, with the door as something like a man-hole, and when they emerge they see the plains of the next sky. While Kulik suggests as a possibility that the journey is 'not a literal ascent but a horizontal motion between the gates at the lower "ends of heavens"', the movement does appear to be upwards. Alexander Kulik, *3 Baruch: Greek-Slavonic Apocalypse of Baruch* (Berlin: Walter de Gruyter, 2010), 55.

[78] The angelic guide takes Baruch to where the sky is securely set in place, where there is an uncrossable river (*3 Bar.* 2.1). An uncrossable river implies not the Jordan or the Euphrates but something more like the Ὠκεανός, the great river that encircles the earth. Thus the reader sees Baruch on the edge of the earth and the sky secured there, presumably secured to the earth in some way. There is no mention of enormous mountains or pillars reaching up to the sky to hold it in place; the implication is instead that the edge of the sky rests on the edge of the earth.

[79] *3 Bar.* 3.7. The second sky is the place of cursed existence for those who planned the tower of war against God (the tower of Babel, *3 Bar.* 2.7) and planned to take an auger to bore the sky, to test if it is made of clay or copper/brass/bronze or iron (Greek), or of stone or glass or copper (Slavonic).

[80] 'At the eastern edge of the earth's disk, where the heavenly canopy rests like an inverted cup on a saucer of the same diameter, Enoch views the gates from which the stars begin their celestial journey.' Nickelsburg, *1 Enoch 1*, 330. This is somewhat obscured in Isaac's translation: 'I saw the ultimate ends of the earth which rests on the heaven.' Isaac, '1 (Ethiopic Apocalypse of) Enoch', 590. Nickelsburg translates, 'To the east of these beasts I saw the ends of the earth, on which the heaven rests, and the gates of heaven open.' Nickelsburg, *1 Enoch 1*, 329.

[81] As noted above, each section of *2 Enoch* (1–22; 23–38; 39–73) has its own cosmological schema. The first has multiple layers with earth as the lowest layer. The second has a cosmos of concentric sky-spheres (J recension). The third has multiple layers including a layer beneath the earth.

[82] *2 Enoch* 27 (J recension) speaks of a crystalline composition for the skies. *2 Enoch* 47 speaks of God spreading out the skies in a way reminiscent of the רָקִיעַ of the Hebrew scriptures. *2 Enoch* 25–26 speaks of a ceiling of solidified light marking the upper extremity of the cosmos and a foundation of solidified darkness marking the lower extremity of the cosmos, although these are distinct from the skies.

[83] Opaque: see *Apoc. Abr.* 19.1-9. Unusually in apocalyptic literature, the narrating character standing on a sky-layer cannot see downward to a lower sky-layer or to the Earth. Abraham cannot see lower

of Isaiah and the ambivalence of the *Apocalypse of Abraham*, apocalypses and literary sky-journeys show considerable consistency in the depiction of material sky-structures.

A sky that is a material structure may allow a being to move along its upper surface, or others to attach to its lower surface, while hindering movement between cosmic layers. A recurring concept in these cosmic schemata is the openings in the sky-structure that allow beings to move between higher and lower layers and openings that allow the astronomical and meteorological functioning of the cosmos.

While Gen. 7.11 speaks of 'the windows of the heavens' opening to allow water through as part of a cataclysmic event (see also Isa. 24.18; *2 En.* 73.4), other texts including the Book of Watchers (*1 En.* 1-36), the Astronomical Book (*1 En.* 72-82), *2 Enoch* and *3 Baruch* describe openings that allow the daily, monthly and yearly functioning of the cosmos.[84] Daily, the sun passes through an opening at the eastern edge of the cosmos so that it is then able to travel across the visible sky before passing out through a matching opening at the western edge of the cosmos at the conclusion of daylight hours (*1 En.* 72.2-73.37; *2 En.* 13.1-15.4; *3 Bar.* 6.1-8.5). There are in fact several sun-gates at each edge of the cosmos, the sun passing through the opening that is appropriate to the season, that is, to the sun's varying course across the sky throughout the year.[85] Likewise, the moon (*1 En.* 72.3; 74.1-9; 78.1-79.6; *2 En.* 16.1-8) and the stars (*1 En.* 33.2-4; 36.2-3; 72.3; 75.1-6) enter the visible sky each day/night cycle through their appropriate openings in the eastern extremity of the sky, traveling their appropriate course and exiting through matching gates in the west. Stars may use

---

cosmic layers unless the intervening layers move aside to allow a clear line of sight, or unless an image of them appears on the uppermost surface as if on screen or horizontal tapestry (*Apoc. Abr.* 21.1-2).

Solid or airy: see *Apoc. Abr.* 15.4-5; 17.3-5; 18.1; 19.4. Abraham, as narrating character, tells that he wanted to prostrate himself, to 'fall face down on the earth', but he is now standing on a 'place of highness' where there is 'no ground to which I could fall prostrate'. The place on which Abraham stands is presumably 'the air', understood as some kind of surface from 15.5. Still, 'the air' is not an entirely solid surface but somewhat fluid, as indicated by Abraham being unable to fall prostrate on it. In addition, it is described as 'now stopping on high, now rolling down low'.

The tension between the seventh sky as a moving airy surface and something more like a solid floor perhaps supports the suggestion that we see this surface as a cosmic temple curtain. Andrei Orlov notes similarities between this account and the later works of *3 Enoch* and the Hekhalot literature. Notable is the role of the pargod, 'a portentous celestial boundary, which like the veil in the terrestrial sanctuary intends to separate the holy abode of the Deity from the profane realm of the rest of creation'. Orlov suggests that in the *Apocalypse of Abraham* we see a 'horizontal spatial arrangement of the macrocosmic "veil"', carrying both cultic and cosmological significance, such that the lower layers of the cosmos 'can be understood as exterior chambers of the temple of the universe'. Andrei A. Orlov, *Heavenly Priesthood in the Apocalypse of Abraham* (New York: Cambridge University Press, 2013), 160, 175. As in the later work *3 Enoch*, this surface can be seen as something like an embroidered curtain or horizontal tapestry that becomes a 'screen' showing 'a motion picture film depicting the history of Israel'. George W. MacRae, 'Some Elements of Jewish Apocalyptic and Mystical Tradition: And Their Relation to Gnostic Literature' (Cambridge, MA: Andover-Harvard Theological Library, 1981), 68.

[84] Note also Ps. 78.23-24.

[85] The same observation, that the sun's course varies throughout the year, was explained by some Greek thinkers as the sun spiralling around an imaginary cylinder. The spiralling motion moved the sun gradually northward until the summer solstice, and then southward until the winter solstice. Couprie, 'The Spiral Movement of the Sun', 10.

the same gates as the sun or their own smaller gates (*1 En.* 3.2-3). As wind, rain, snow and hail come to earth from storerooms/reservoirs in the skies (*1 En.* 18.1; 41.4; 60.11-23; 69.24; *2 En.* 5.1–6.1; 40.10; *2 Bar.* 10.11; *3 Bar.* 10.6-9), openings in the primary sky-structure allow these objects to enter into the space between the primary sky-structure and the earth (*1 En.* 34.2; 36.1; 60.12; 76.1-14) to become part of the human experience.[86]

Beings that move between upper and lower cosmic levels often need openings in the sky-structures in order to pass through. Stars, of course, are understood to be powerful sky-beings who move across the cosmos of their own volition (*1 En.* 18.13-15; 21.3-6; 43.1; 69.21; 72.1-3; 75.1; 79.1–80.8; *2 En.* 11.3; *Apoc. Abr.* 19.9),[87] though under orders and punished if they deviate from the correct path and formation (*1 En.* 18.13-15; 21.3-6; Jude 13). They often have their own gates in the sky-structure. Other beings, those that move vertically between the earth and higher cosmic layers, sometimes use other openings that enable this movement (*3 Bar.* 2.2; 3.1; 4.2; 11.1-6; *3 Macc.* 6.18; *T. Levi* 2.6; 5.1).[88]

These descriptions of the sky show a near universal assumption that the sky that is seen high above the earth is a material construction. This assumption is shown in descriptions of how it was created, how it remains in place above the earth, its material composition and how beings and meteorological phenomena move through openings within it. It is sometimes spoken of as something akin to cloth or animal skin, stretched out above the earth, with mountains at the edges of the earth acting as tent-poles. In other conceptions it is composed of something like metal or crystal, held up by pillars, or dome-shaped, so that its edges rest on the edges of the earth. Certain Greek thinkers and *2 Enoch* sometimes describe a crystalline sphere that surrounds the earth and remains in place without need for support. It may be transparent or opaque. Stars may move freely at its underside or be affixed to its underside. There may be the one sky above the earth or there may be several layered skies. But almost always the shared assumption is a material sky-structure like a ceiling high above the earth, dividing what is below from what is above.

---

[86] 'Storehouses must have doors through which their contents are brought out.' George W. E. Nickelsburg and James C. VanderKam, *1 Enoch 2: A Commentary on the Book of 1 Enoch*, Hermeneia (Minneapolis: Fortress Press, 2012), 229.

[87] The Animal Apocalypse (*1 En.* 85–90) is excluded from this list as it is entirely allegorical; just as its cows are actually humans, its 'stars' are angels/watchers and not truly stars.

[88] In the context of the sky-journey narrative, *T. Levi* 5.1 indicates an opening to allow access from the second sky into the third sky and ultimate sky (although some recensions have seven skies). Adela Yarbro Collins, 'The Seven Heavens in Jewish and Christian Apocalypses', in *Death, Ecstasy, and Other Worldly Journeys*, ed. John J. Collins and Michael A. Fishbane (Albany: State University of New York Press, 1995), 63.

The *Ascension of Isaiah* also has gates at each sky-layer, but the narrative treats these more like customs stations than as necessary structural openings (*Asc. Isa.* 10.24-27).

3.4.2 Spaces above and below the sky-structure

In these cosmic schemata, a sky-structure forms the border of a cosmically significant space and the beginning of another, the space above the sky-structure having different characteristics than the space below with different inhabitants as appropriate to the different nature of each space. This plays out differently depending on whether the cosmos has a single sky-structure or several layers.

The *Ascension of Isaiah* shows each sky-layer dividing the space below from a differently characterized space above. It depicts the underside of the first sky as characterized by evil and filled with rebellious beings, in that sense a mirror image to earth, while the space above this sky is holy and in harmony with God (*Asc. Isa.* 7.9-17). Each subsequent sky-space is still more holy and awesome than the last, reaching a culmination on the upper side of the seventh sky-layer.[89] In *3 Baruch* each stage of the seer's journey takes him through the next sky-structure onto its upper surface, there to see different features of the cosmos. His journey stops just before the fifth sky-layer, because from here there is a shift in the nature of the spaces, such that human entry is not possible (*3 Bar.* 2.2; 3.1; 4.2; 11.1-2; 14.1).[90] Similarly, the *Apocalypse of Abraham* depicts each of the higher sky-layers filled with powerful beings, but with differing levels of power and authority appropriate to the space in which they exist. On the fifth sky-layer are the hosts of stars, these powerful beings having power over the elements of the earth below, but under orders from the beings in higher spaces. On the sixth sky-layer the space is filled with and defined by the 'spiritual angels', who obey the orders of the 'fiery angels' who exist in a higher space. On the seventh layer are the fiery beings and God's fiery throne (*Apoc. Abr.* 15.4-7; 18.1-3; 19.1-9).

This function of dividing two spaces is common to all these sky-structures, but sometimes this goes a step further: a sky-structure may also create a significant space at its immediate underside, distinct in character from the space further below. This occurs most frequently in the primary sky-structure or in cosmos schemata with a single sky-structure. We have already noted that the sky-structure in Genesis forms a barrier that holds back the upper cosmic waters. Set into this sky-structure, or moving through the space beneath it, are sun, moon, stars and birds (Gen. 1.14, 20), and so the space at the underside of the barrier is different in character from the region above – and different again from the earth-space far below, which is defined by the growth of plants (Gen. 1.11-12) and filled with inhabitants appropriate to that space (Gen. 1.24-25).[91]

The single sky-structure in the Book of Watchers divides the space above, which is the awesome place of the divine palace with God's throne room at the centre[92] and the

---

[89] The penultimate region is the underside of the seventh sky-layer called 'the air of the seventh' (*Asc. Isa.* 9.1; compare 8.1), while the ultimate space is above the seventh sky-layer (*Asc. Isa.* 9.6).
[90] Fischer argues that the seer's journey originally took him through all sky-layers, culminating at the seventh and ultimate sky-layer. Ulrich Fischer, *Eschatologie unt Jenseitserwartung im hellenistischen Diasporajudentum*, vol. 44, BZNW (Berlin: de Gruyter, 1978), 79. But Harlow shows that this is unlikely. Daniel C. Harlow, *The Greek Apocalypse of Baruch (3 Baruch) in Hellenistic Judaism and Early Christianity*, Studia in Veteris Testamento pseudepigrapha v. 12 (Leiden: Brill, 1996), 34–76.
[91] Note also 1 Cor. 15.35-41; Plato, *Timaeus* 39e–40b.
[92] Philip Francis Esler, *God's Court and Courtiers in the Book of the Watchers: Re-Interpreting Heaven in 1 Enoch 1–36* (Eugene: Cascade, 2017).

native home of awesome beings called cherubim and watchers/angels, from the space below, where bright beings called stars move across the underside of the sky-structure in ordered ranks (*1 En.* 33.1-4).[93] In both spaces the beings obey God but when they disobey they do so in different ways. Beings from the space above rebel against the cosmic order by leaving this space and moving down to earth, to live in the manner of an earthly being (*1 En.* 6.1-8; 12.4; 15.1-7), while the beings that move across the underside of the sky-structure rebel against the cosmic order when their horizontal journey deviates from the set itinerary (*1 En.* 18.13-15; 21.3-6. See also Jude 14).[94]

The *Ascension of Isaiah* has multiple sky-layers, but its first has a significant space at its underside. This space has parallels with the earth-space to which it is linked, especially in terms of the evil that fills each yet is distinct in that it is not the habitation of humans but of beings far greater in power (*Asc. Isa.* 4.2; 7.9-12). Distinctively, its highest sky-layers also have significant spaces at their underside. The seer's upward journey takes him into ever more glorious spaces above each new sky-layer, but when he moves from the space immediately above the fifth sky-layer to the air at the underside of the sixth, this is described as a distinct space more glorious than the last. Thus the sixth sky-layer creates a glorious space at its underside and a still more glorious space above it, and the same is true of the seventh and final sky-layer (*Asc. Isa.* 8.1, 16; 9.1, 6).

Finally, we note some parallels in the writings of Plato, which describe stratified cosmic spaces, each with different characteristics and different inhabitants, as appropriate to the nature of each space. In a quasi-scientific portion of *Phaedo*, Plato paints a distinctive picture of stratified cosmic spaces created not by a dividing sky-structure, as in biblical and apocalyptic texts, but by the stratification of different substances (Plato, *Phaedo* 109b–111c). Plato proposes that Mediterranean civilizations live in a great basin containing water, air and ether. The water has settled in the lowest point of the basin, and this is the Mediterranean Sea. Various marine creatures live in the water and move about in it. The air has settled in the mid-level of the basin, and this is the space in which Plato and his readers live, clustered around the edge of the Mediterranean Sea but living slightly higher than it and moving about in the air. At the highest level in the basin is the ether. The ether-space is as different from the air-space as the air-space is from the water-space. In the ether-space are plants and precious stones (carnelian, jasper, and emerald) far more beautiful than those we see in the air-space and human beings who are superior in every way to those who live below. There are temples in which gods really live and speak to humans face-to-face. The dividing line between the ether-space and the air-space is as definite as the line between the air we breathe and the water of the Mediterranean Sea. In other writings Plato presents an expanded cosmic picture that includes layered sky-structures; the Myth of Er is a cosmic journey narrative in which this cosmic structure is observed (Plato, *Republic*

---

[93] Across cultures, stars were commonly conceived as living beings that dwell in the sky. When Aristotle describes the functioning of the cosmos, he assumes that stars are living beings. Aristotle, *De Caelo* 292a15-292b19.

[94] This cosmic schema, in which the skies consist of a single sky-structure with a space above and a space immediately below, may also be assumed by the *Gospel of Thomas* which speaks of 'this heaven and the one above it' (*Gos. Thom.* 11.1).

614–621). In *Phaedrus* Plato tells of gods ascending through the ultimate sky-structure to stand on its outer surface, the ὑπερουράνιος (Plato, *Phaedrus* 247b-c).

3.4.3 Conflicted spaces, human spaces and the God-space

As the sky-structures of biblical and apocalyptic texts create differently characterized spaces above and below, the nature of the spaces is frequently distinguished in particular ways. A space may be part of the ordinary experience of humans or accessible to humans only in special circumstances or completely inaccessible to humans. A space may be characterized by conflict/rebellion or it may be in harmony with God. Finally, a cosmic schema frequently has a God-space; the place where God dwells, with particular characteristics to reflect that and so distinguished from all other spaces.

The borders of the cosmos-of-ordinary-human-experience differ between cosmic schemata. The *Ascension of Isaiah* presents a close connection between the earth and the space at the underside of the first sky-layer: 'Then the voice of the Beloved will reprove in anger this heaven, and this earth, and the mountains, and the hills, and the cities, and the desert, and the trees, and the angel of the sun, and that of the moon, and everywhere that Beliar has appeared and acted openly in this world' (*Asc. Isa.* 4.18).[95] Its cosmos-of-ordinary-human-experience extends from the earth to the underside of the first sky-layer; it is not that humans ordinarily dwell in the sky or travel to the sky, but they may look upward to see the sun and the moon, and life on earth is strongly influenced by Beliar and the other rebellious powerful beings who dwell in that space. While living humans ordinarily cannot see or access the spaces above the first sky-layer, a spirit-journey may take a human into these spaces, even up to the God-space on the highest sky-layer (*Asc. Isa.* 7.13; 9.1, 6). Deceased righteous humans also dwell in this space (*Asc. Isa.* 9.7).

In *3 Baruch*, the cosmos-of-ordinary-human-experience extends into the fourth sky-structure, as humans can look up into these skies to see the sun and moon, and their crops receive water from them (*3 Bar.* 6.1; 10.1-9). These skies are also the dwelling places of humans following death; various categories of deceased humans dwell on the first, second, third and fourth sky-structure respectively (*3 Bar.* 2.1-7; 3.1-8; 4.2-5; 5.3; 10.1-5).[96] The first four skies are also open to extra-ordinary human experiences such as Baruch's. In *3 Baruch*'s cosmic schema, the upper (three?) skies are in no way open to human experience: they are not within the ordinary experience of living humans, nor open to extra-ordinary human experience,[97] nor are they the dwelling of deceased humans (righteous or otherwise). From the fifth sky-structure and beyond is the Kingdom of the Skies in which the God-space is

---

[95] Translation Knibb, 'The Martyrdom'.

[96] The presence on the third sky-structure of a Hades for the unrighteous dead is clear only in the Greek recension. The next sky-structure is labelled a 'third' in the Greek, but in the narrative of the seer's journey it is clear that this is actually the fourth.

[97] *3 Bar.* 11-17. Through this repeated opening and closing of the gate the narrative conveys that the fifth sky and all higher skies are not open to Baruch or to the reader. This established, the narrating character summarily reports that his angel guide returned him to where he was at the beginning, that is, to earth.

located. *3 Baruch*'s God-space is accessible only to the highest-ranking angels, never to humans, whether righteous or unrighteous, living or dead. Similar pictures emerge in other literary sky-journeys, including *1 Enoch*, *2 Enoch*[98] and the *Apocalypse of Abraham*.[99]

While there is variation in these cosmic schemata there are also remarkable consistencies. The God-space is at the highest cosmic level,[100] beyond the cosmos-of-ordinary-human-experience.[101] It may or may not be accessible to humans in special circumstances, but it is certainly not accessible to beings who are in a state of rebellion against God, nor to beings who are undergoing punishment for their former rebellion. For example, in *1 Enoch*, powerful beings who have rebelled against God and the cosmic order are imprisoned in a deep dark part of the earth (*1 En.* 10.4-5, 11-12; 14.5), or in a terrible non-place beyond the horizontal extremity of the cosmos (*1 En.* 18.10–19.1; 21.1-10). *2 Enoch* has them imprisoned on the second sky-layer (*2 En.* 7.1-5), far from the God-space on the seventh/tenth sky (*2 En.* 22.1).

While some have thought that the *Apocalypse of Abraham* has a place of punishment called a 'fiery Gehenna' on its highest sky-layer (see *Apoc. Abr.* 15.6-7), this is not the case. There are textual questions around the term 'fiery Gehenna'[102] and Kulik concludes that the Greek text underlying the Slavonic did not reference Gehenna.[103] Elsewhere in this apocalypse it is in the underworld that we find a place of fiery punishment (*Apoc. Abr.* 31.3). The fire on the seventh sky-layer is better understood as a holy fire filled with heavenly beings crying out words above human understanding, much like the fire which burns around the throne and its creatures (*Apoc. Abr.* 18.1-3).[104] This accords

---

[98] At the fifth sky there is a change in focus from the lower four realms that directly affect humans (including the sun and moon and the realms of the dead) to the upper three realms (A recension) less directly connected with human life. On the fifth sky are vast armies of human-like giants called Grigori. They are powerful sky-beings whose role it is to worship God. On the sixth sky are glorious beings, angels, phoenixes and cherubim, who sing in unison and ensure the proper running of the cosmic order.

[99] It is possible that the experience described in 2 Cor. 12.2-4 involved ascension to the God-space in the third and ultimate sky (as in some recensions of *T. Levi*). It is equally possible that he ascended only halfway through several sky-layers, coming to a paradise that is below and separate from the God-space (as in *3 Bar.*).

[100] See also *2 Bar.* 59.3: 'The heavens which are under the throne of the Mighty One.'

[101] In the Hebrew scriptures the location of God is a complex question. One paradigm suggests that God is present throughout the cosmos, while another has heaven as the space of God's dwelling; a third paradigm suggests that God is qualitatively different from the created heaven-and-earth cosmos, such that there is no need to locate God's dwelling-place within the cosmos. Konrad Schmid, 'Himmelsgott, Weltgott und Schöpfer', *Jahrbuch für Biblische Theologie*, 10 (2005): 111–48. M. G. Brett, *Locations of God: Political Theology in the Hebrew Bible* (New York: Oxford University Press, 2019), 129–30.

[102] R. Rubinkiewicz, 'Apocalypse of Abraham', in *The Old Testament Pseudepigrapha*, ed. James H. Charlesworth, vol. 1 (Garden City: Doubleday, 1983), 696.

[103] Alexander Kulik, *Retroverting Slavonic Pseudepigrapha: Toward the Original of the Apocalypse of Abraham* (Atlanta: Society of Biblical Literature, 2004), 60.

[104] Orlov writes that 'the patriarch beholds a vision of Gehenna while standing next to the divine throne … [he] is able to see the highest and lowest points of creation'. Orlov, *Heavenly Priesthood*, 158. If we follow Orlov in this, we retain a simple picture, consistent with this Apocalypse as a whole, of skies above the Earth and a fiery Gehenna below. While this is tempting, the narrative does not present this as a 'vision', or the fire as something below, but simply as what Abraham saw in front of him when he stood on the seventh sky. Later in the text a device is introduced to distinguish

with the translation preferred by Himmelfarb: 'By that light I saw a burning fire of people – many people, males all of them, changing their appearance and their form, running hither and thither as they changed their form, and worshipping and crying out in a language I did not know.'[105]

Just as the places of punishment for rebellion are separate from the God-space, so actively rebellious beings are separate from the God-space. The *Ascension of Isaiah* has its actively rebellious powerful beings in the space at the underside of the first sky-layer, very much separated from the God-space atop the seventh sky-layer. In *1 Enoch* the rebellious angels/watchers once had access to the space above the sky-structure, the same cosmic level where the God-space is located, but their act of rebellion was to leave this space, descending to earth to live as earthly beings. Having completed this act they no longer have access to the higher cosmic level (*1 En.* 14.5), so the God-space remains free of rebellion and rebellious beings. In Job's God-space there is a sky-satan who argues with God but this being is not in rebellion against God (Job 1.6–2.7).[106]

Lower sky-spaces are not the God-space but they are significant spaces within the cosmic schema, having distinct characteristics and inhabited by beings appropriate to the space (including the bright living beings that are visible from earth in the ordinary cosmic rhythms of day and night).[107] This is true of the spaces between sky-layers in those cosmic schemata with multiple skies and in notable instances it is also true of the space at the underside of the first/only sky-layer. Where conflict exists in the skies it exists in the lower sky-spaces, including the space at the underside of the first sky-layer, and never in the God-space on the ultimate sky.

This picture is consistent throughout the Hebrew scriptures, the early Christian writings and the apocalypses. It is only in the Greek stories of gods, monsters and heroes that a god-space can potentially be threatened. While Greek stories have gods throughout the cosmos the distinctive god-space is Olympos, which 'even in Homer was more often in some indefinite area of the sky than on the mountain in Thrace'.[108] Existing at the highest point in the cosmos, it would take a whole day, or even ten days, to fall from Olympos to earth (Homer, *Iliad* 1.590-594; Hesiod, *Theogony* 721–725). Home to the third-generation gods who established permanent rule and cosmic order, the space itself is not inherently exclusive of rebellion and threat but is always successfully defended by the ruling gods and their allies (Apollodorus, *Library* 1.6.1-3). Given the Greek stories we will be alert to a God-space that is potentially subject to threat and rebellion. Yet, in contrast, the opposite picture is found consistently throughout the Hebrew scriptures, early Christian writings and apocalypses. We therefore will be especially alert to a God-space exclusive of any rebellious elements and any possibility of threat.

---

between the two modes of seeing, reaffirming this early sight as straightforward seeing and forcing the reader to see the fire on the seventh sky and decide on its meaning.

[105] Martha Himmelfarb, *Ascent to Heaven in Jewish and Christian Apocalypses* (New York: Oxford University Press, 1993), 63. See also *1 En.* 71.1.
[106] Peggy Lynne Day, *An Adversary in Heaven: Satan in the Hebrew Bible*, Harvard Semitic Monographs, vol. 43 (Atlanta: Scholars Press, 1988).
[107] Note also Plato, *Laws*, 898d–899b; *Timaeus* 39e–40b; 1 Cor. 15.35-41.
[108] Wright, *Cosmology*, 38.

3.5 Cosmic disorder and existing means of repair

It is worth noting one more recurring theme in the apocalypses. While the cosmos currently has elements of disorder, there already exists in the cosmos the means of setting things right. One such means for setting things right is an existing cosmic location with the appropriate characteristics to permanently destroy the power and influence of a powerful being. Several examples of this can be found in the literature.

The *Ascension of Isaiah* has a place called Perdition/Destruction (ሕጕለ) at the lowest cosmic level, below earth and Sheol (*Asc. Isa.* 10.8). Read together with the first half of the *Ascension of Isaiah*, this Perdition can be identified with the Gehenna of *Asc. Isa.* 1.3 and 4.14.[109] Already existing in the cosmos, this place is ready to receive Beliar and his hosts in the eschaton. In this way the oppressive and disordered powers will be punished and permanently incapacitated, so that they can no longer dominate 'this heaven and this earth' (*Asc. Isa.* 4.18).

In the Book of Watchers the place to punish and incapacitate powerful beings is located just beyond the horizontal extremity of the cosmos. The powerful sky-beings who disrupted the cosmic order are currently held in a deep, dark part of the earth (*1 En.* 10.4-5, 12), but in the eschaton they will be cast into another place (*1 En.* 10.6, 13). This ultimate destination is a place of absolute enduring imprisonment; it effects permanent destruction of their power and permanent removal of their ability to access and influence the cosmos proper. It already exists for Enoch to see it and thus be assured that the cosmos will be set back in order (*1 En.* 18.11–19.1; 21.7-10). Mt. 25.41 portrays a similar concept when it speaks of 'the eternal fire prepared for the devil and his angels'.

In addition to powerful beings, the existing means of repairing disorder can also be directed at humans, either individually or as a collective. The *Apocalypse of Abraham*, concerned that the nations currently mock and rule over God's people, describes an existing subterranean region that will enable a reversal of this situation at the eschaton (*Apoc. Abr.* 31.1-3).

The existing cosmos may also contain a storehouse for the instruments of change. The *Testament of Levi* describes such a place on the first and second sky, where fire, snow and ice are already prepared and held ready for the day of judgement, alongside powerful beings waiting to play their part (*T. Levi* 3.1-3. See also *1 En.* 66.1-2). Other storehouses hold the means of positive repair (*1 En.* 11.1).

---

[109] The *Ascension of Isaiah* is usually considered a composite work. Knibb holds that the Martyrdom of Isaiah (*Asc. Isa.* 1–5) reached close to its current form by the end of the first century CE, while the Vision of Isaiah dates from the second century CE, the two being combined at a later time. Knibb, 'The Martyrdom', 149–50. See also Yarbro Collins, 'The Seven Heavens', 74. Enrico Norelli holds that the Vision of Isaiah dates to around 100 CE with the Martyrdom written a few years later as an expansion of the prior work. Enrico Norelli, 'L' Ascension d'Esaïe est-elle vraiment un écrit unitaire?: une discussion avec Richard Bauckham', *Annali di Storia dell'Esegesi*, 32 (2015): 12–13. An alternative view is represented by Jan Dochhorn, who regards the *Ascension of Isaiah* as 'a unified composition, the result of a single act of authorship.' Jan Dochhorn, '"World" (ዓለም) in the Ascension of Isaiah', *Ephemerides theologicae Lovanienses*, 94 (2018): 241. Richard Bauckham has also argued for this position and dates the complete work to the decade 70–80 CE. Richard Bauckham, *The Fate of the Dead: Studies on Jewish and Christian Apocalypses*, Supplements to Novum Testamentum, vol. 93 (Boston: Brill, 1998), 368–80. While questions of composition remain unresolved, Jonathan Knight holds that the *Ascension of Isaiah* should be read as a whole. Knight, *The Ascension of Isaiah*, 10.

Whether places to which discordant powers can be removed or storehouses for the instruments of change, these already existing cosmic regions provide assurance that the cosmos will be repaired. In certain respects the cosmos is currently disordered, but humans who live in accord with the true cosmic order can know that their current experience of hardship, oppression and humiliation will be remedied in a restored cosmos, giving way to honour and abundance.

3.6 Conclusion: Existing assumptions

Every reader will bring assumptions to the text. Engaging with a sky-journey narrative, a modern Western reader will assume that the earth is a planet, the sky is a gaseous region surrounding the earth and the cosmos has no centre, and no true up and down. If the sky-journey narrative is a modern science-fiction novel, the modern reader will share the assumptions and experience of the implied reader. If the sky-journey narrative is an ancient apocalypse, these assumptions will distance this reader's experience from that of the implied hearer. It is highly implausible that the implied hearer of an ancient apocalypse shares those starting assumptions.

To move closer to the experience of Revelation's implied hearer, we have considered a range of cosmological conceptions that may plausibly be part of the implied hearer's starting assumptions, or already available in its mental library. The common conceptions and assumptions described in this chapter include:

- the earth as the 'ground floor' of the cosmos, often with 'basement levels' below, and coextensive with the cosmos on the horizontal axis.
- a material sky-structure reaching across the cosmos, often with openings to allow the meteorological functioning of the cosmos and/or the vertical movement of beings.
- layered sky-spaces between sky-structures, or at the underside of a sky-structure, as distinct from each other as they are from the earth-space.
- a cosmos-of-ordinary-human-experience, extending at least from the upper surface of the earth to the lower surface of the primary sky-structure.
- a distinct God-space at the highest cosmic level, beyond the cosmos-of-ordinary-human-experience, and often not accessible to humans at all, even after death or in an extra-ordinary experience. The nature of this space is likely to make it exclusive of conflict and rebellion.
- the lower skies, or firmament-space, defined by conflict (powerful inhabitants in conflict with God and/or each other).
- each cosmic space inhabited by beings appropriate to that space, including the visible sky which is filled with the bright powerful beings called stars (distinguished from other powerful beings, such as angels).
- the cosmos as it currently exists holds the means for fixing what is wrong in the cosmos (notably, the means of incapacitating rebellious/deviant powerful beings).

The following chapters will show how these common cosmological conceptions and assumptions all play a role in Revelation's cosmic-journey narrative.

4

The sky-journey, the sky-structure and the God-space

In the following chapters we consider select passages from Revelation which show how the sky-journey narrative operates in a four-tiered cosmic story-space. The four spaces are revealed and developed by the movements of the character John, the things that he sees and hears and the often identical but sometimes distinct movements of the audiovisual focalizer, which is the experiential perspective of the hearer. This chapter will show how the initial stage of the sky-journey moves the seer from the earth-space and upwards through an opening in the sky-structure, establishing the God-space at its upper surface. It will show how the there-and-back-again journey of the seer sometimes differs from the shifting location of the focalizer, and through these perspectives the nature of the sky-structure and the space above it are revealed. Chapter 5 will show how one narrative event (Rev. 9.1-11) involves three cosmic layers (under-earth, earth and sky-heaven) and is narrated from the perspective of the fourth and ultimate cosmic layer (the hyper-heaven). Chapter 6 will show how the audiovisual perspective locates conflict in the sky-heaven while the hyper-heaven is maintained as a consistently harmonious space, even in Rev. 12.1-18. In the subsequent chapters we consider the relationship between the present form of the cosmos and the changed cosmos at the end of Revelation's narrative. Chapter 7 will show what the foregoing discussion means for the nature and import of the cosmic changes in Rev. 20.1-15 and 21.1–22.5. Finally, Chapter 8 will show the rhetorical import of placing the hearer in a cosmos that has these four cosmic spaces and is also destined to change.

4.1 The earth-space

As in all sky-journeys, Revelation begins its narrative in the earth-space. The narrator is identified with the character John, using first-person pronouns and verbs (Rev. 1.9). Events are narrated from John's perspective, making the character and narrator also coincident with the focalizer. The hearer is invited into the seer's experience, which begins on earth.[1] Specifically, the narrator-character locates himself on the island

---

[1] This is noted because in some later parts of Revelation the focalizer is not coincident with the character John, and so the hearer is invited into an experience that is not identical with that of the seer.

called Patmos, that is, on land on the plane of the earth, although a small piece of land within the terrestrial sea.[2] Recalling the epistolary introduction (Rev. 1.4), the spatial scope is quickly expanded across the Aegean Sea to encompass the earthly region in which the addressees live (Rev. 1.11). Revelation's earth-space will be expanded further to include Jerusalem (Rev. 11.8) and Rome (Rev. 17.8). While it is not implausible that the implied hearer may be familiar with the concept of a spherical earth, it is far more familiar with the concept of a broad earth stretching from east to west, north to south. The expansion of the earth-space from Patmos to Asia Minor, and Jerusalem to Rome, certainly does not challenge this broad-earth concept. The ultimate expansion of the earth-space to the extremities of the earth at the four compass points (Rev. 7.1) connects with this primary assumption and reinforces it, as does the sight of the whole earth from extremity to extremity in one moment from a high vantage point (as in *1 En.* 83.11; Mt. 4.8; Lk. 4.5). The implied author allows, and in some ways encourages, the implied hearer to see the events unfolding on a broad earth.

It is unclear whether τὰς τέσσαρας γωνίας τῆς γῆς indicates to the implied hearer a square shape for the earth. We saw in Chapter 3 that the texts sometimes taken to indicate a four-cornered earth (*1 En.* 1–36; Job 37.3; 38.13; Isa. 11.12; 24.16) are ambiguous. Similarly, the τέσσαρες γωνία of Rev. 7.1 may suggest four actual corners that make the earth a square, or just the extremities of the earth in all four directions.

The narrator-character operates within this horizontal space as he turns to see the voice behind him (Rev. 1.12). There is no upwards or downwards movement, nor indication of upwards or downwards gaze; focalizer and object are together on the terrestrial plane. The extra-ordinary sight, then, is not due to an extra-ordinary location but an extra-ordinary mode of seeing; John has become 'in the spirit' (Rev. 1.10).[3] This is the encounter with an extra-ordinary being that occurs before the ascent into the skies (*2 En.* 1.1–2.2; *3 Bar.* 1.3-7; *Apoc. Abr.* 10.1–11.6; *Asc. Isa.* 6.6-9).

From 1.18–3.22 the narrator remains coincident with the character John but the character Jesus Christ speaks directly, so the narratorial function is temporarily transferred to this character.[4] His dictation of seven letters conjures up various images (including trees, doors, pillars and temples) but these are not seen by the character John as part of his visionary experience; he only hears the words. These images appear

---

[2] In the *Apocalypse of Abraham* an island is considered to be a part of the sea (*Apoc. Abr.* 21.4). Revelation does not appear to present this perspective, but even if we understand John to be in/on the sea he is still on the terrestrial plane.

[3] Note that 'spirit' here is a general term, and it is not necessary to capitalize it. Aune, *Revelation 1-5*, 83.

Labahn reads this differently, commenting, 'Das „Sein im Geist" beinhaltet eine örtliche Veränderung, die der textimmanente Erzähler mitsamt seinen Lesern / Leserinnen subjektiv berichtend erfasst.' Labahn, '"Apokalyptische" Geographie', 114. He holds that in Chapter 1 John relocates to heaven spiritually, while in Chapter 4 John relocates to heaven physically. This is possible, in which case there is an implied but unnarrated change in location from earth to hyper-heaven, but I suggest that this is better understood as the extra-ordinary encounter and visions that can occur in apocalyptic texts prior to (or sometimes independently of) the journey into the skies.

[4] Bal, *Narratology*, 8. I consider this framing to be more precise than Barr's, who describes Jesus Christ as the narrator of this section. Barr, *Tales*, 62–3.

only to the hearer, and they come and go. There are no narrative directions to locate them or display them in a specific part of the cosmos.

4.2 The journey through the sky-structure

The sky-journey proper begins in Rev. 4.1. Until this point there has been no indication of a change in location for the character John – he is still on Patmos on the plane of the earth. The first-person verb of seeing indicates that the visual focalizer is still coincident with the character John and so the hearer's experience of events begins from this location. The first-person verb of seeing is an indirect invitation for the implied hearer to share the experience and see as John sees. This is here made explicit as the narrator immediately follows with the same verb in imperative form – a direct invitation to the implied hearer to see.[5]

From this position, the sight indicated ἐν τῷ οὐρανῷ turns the gaze upward. We saw in Chapter 3 that οὐρανός and related words always indicated something upwards relative to the earth and Revelation allows the implied hearer to maintain this obvious assumption.[6] There was also the assumption that the sky (or at least the first sky-layer) could be seen from earth. Revelation's narrative has opened up a space stretching across the plane of the earth and now as the hearer's gaze is turned upward it expands that space from the surface of the earth up to that οὐρανός that can be seen from earth.[7]

The indicated sight in the οὐρανός is a 'door'. Koester writes, 'The open door signals that revelation is about to be given.'[8] Similarly, Aune surveys the ancient motif of an opening door as part of the epiphanic experience, and it is true that this motif is at play in Rev. 4.1.[9] Further to this, the door has meaning in terms of a tour through the cosmos.

In Chapter 3 we saw that in ancient conceptions it was almost universally understood that high above the earth is a material sky-structure, like a great cosmic ceiling. Various materials were proposed, including ice, bronze or something akin to animal skins, with a structure that accorded with its material composition. The apocalypses and the Hebrew scriptures described openings in the sky-structure, variously termed 'windows', 'doors' and 'gates', to allow beings to move between higher and lower cosmic layers and to allow the astronomical and meteorological functioning of the cosmos.

---

[5] Ureña writes that the call to attention contained in ἰδού requires the implicit or explicit presence of the addressees. 'It is as if John were saying: "I saw, but look with me, there before you is a door/throne/etc."' Ureña, *Narrative and Drama*, 19, 71, 77–9.

[6] If further confirmation is needed, we find it in the voice instructing the character John (and therefore the seeing-hearer) to 'come up here'. So too Charles, *Revelation*, vol. 1, 107.

[7] It would be unwise to draw firm conclusions from the singular οὐρανός. Revelation does not make a clear linguistic distinction between singular sky and plural skies as some ancient texts do. It uses οὐρανός almost exclusively in the singular, with the only exception being in Rev. 12.12 where the vocative heaven is plural. The other vocative heaven is singular in 18.20, and these are the only two instances in the New Testament of heaven being used vocatively. I am wary of Wright's claim that Rev. 12.12 'clearly' suggests multiple heavens. Wright, *Early History*, 132.

[8] Koester, *Revelation*, 367.

[9] Aune, *Revelation 1–5*, 281.

In some sky-journeys they allowed the seer to move upwards through the sky-layers (*3 Bar.* 2.2; 3.1; 4.2; 11.1-6; *T. Levi* 2.6; 5.1). I have argued that the implied hearer is already familiar with all of these concepts and Revelation's brief reference to a door in the sky is enough for the implied hearer to understand what is meant.[10] It is not necessary that the 'door' be narrowly literal; it is only necessary that it have meaning not only in terms of a general epiphanic experience but also specifically in terms of an experience involving movement through the cosmos.

Revelation 4.1-2 is, then, a narrative of the seer's movement from the earth, upward through the sky-structure. The upward movement is not narrated but is the direct implication of the narrative through 'narrative filling-in'.[11] When the hearer of Rev. 4.1-2 hears of a door open in the sky followed by a voice calling 'come up here', and then hears the description of a new scene from the perspective of the seer, the narrative inference is that the seer has moved upwards through that open door to reach this new location.[12] What is now described was not previously visible to the seer but can now be viewed because the seer has moved into a new position that enables him to view it.

4.3 The nature of the sky-structure

4.3.1 Material composition

Lourdes García Ureña has noted in Revelation the 'wide range of adjectives that refer to the materials that things are made of', namely χρυσοῦς, βύσσινος, ὑάλινος, σμαράγδινος, ἀργυροῦς, λίθινος, ξύλινος, χαλκοῦς, ἐλεφάντινος, θύϊνος, μύλινος, τρίχινος, σιδηροῦς and κεραμικός.[13] The use of these adjectives helps the hearer to 'visualize what John sees in a way that is realistic in a tactile sense, as the materials described are familiar ones and form part of their daily reality (wood, stone, iron), or are appreciated for their quality (gold, linen, emerald)'.[14] Revelation suggests familiar materials for the material composition of the sky-structure but by implication rather than explicit description.

In the second section of *2 Enoch* (*2 En.* 23–38) the sky-structures are composed of a crystalline substance, while *3 Baruch* allows that it may be clay or iron or copper/brass/bronze (Greek), or stone or glass or copper (Slavonic). But in most cosmic tours this question is not directly addressed. Revelation assumes a material sky-structure, but is ambivalent as to the material composition: Rev. 6.14 recalls the known concept of the sky-structure as something akin to cloth or animal skins stretched out across

---

[10] Malina is essentially correct to speak of 'a celestial vault or firmament' with 'an opening of sorts that allowed access to the other side'. Bruce J. Malina, *On the Genre and Message of Revelation: Star Visions and Sky Journeys* (Peabody: Hendrickson Publishers, 1995), 19.

[11] Chatman, *Story*, 31.

[12] In effect, this is the inference that Ureña has drawn when she writes, 'He sees a door opening to heaven and hears a voice commanding him to climb through it'. Ureña, *Narrative and Drama*, 22.

[13] Ureña, *Narrative and Drama*, 45.

[14] Ureña, *Narrative and Drama*, 46.

the cosmos, while Rev. 4.6 and 15.2 have resonances with the known concept of a crystalline structure.

Revelation 6.14 uses the familiar imagery of something that vanishes before the eyes (a scroll rolling up so that the page can no longer be seen) to add to its depiction of the sky-structure vanishing and leaving earth-beings exposed to the hyper-heaven. The imagery is traditional, indicating the moment of divine wrath (Isa. 34.4; *Sib. Or.* 3.82; 8.233, 413. See also Heb. 1.12; *Gos. Thom.* 111.1). But it also recalls the concept of a sky-structure composed of something akin to cloth or animal skins stretched out like a great cosmic tent (Job 9.8; Ps 104.2; Isa 40.22; 42.5; 44.24; 45.12; 51.13; Jer. 10.12; 51.15; Zech. 12.1. See also Mk 1.10. *Apoc. Abr.* implies that a sky is like a curtain).[15] The image of the sky rolling up like a scroll is itself drawn from the text which most persistently (Isa. 40.22; 42.5; 44.24; 45.12; 51.13) and explicitly (Isa. 40.22) describes the sky as like a tent. As scrolls and tents were composed of similar material the images work together. Against this background, Rev. 6.14 can suggest the material composition of the sky-structure.

By contrast, the imagery in Rev. 4.6 and 15.2 implies a sky-structure composed of a crystalline substance. From above the sky-structure, the 'something like a glass sea, like crystal' is described as part of the scene in front of the Throne. There is no indication that it functions as a heavenly lake in the sense that cranes may wade in it or souls wash in it; any watery implication of 'sea' is overpowered by the crystalline description.[16] This recalls the concept of a crystalline floor beneath the Throne of God (Exod. 24.10; Ezek. 1.22-26. See also *1 En.* 14.10, 17).

While 'in front of the Throne' implies a relatively small area, 'sea' implies a much larger area, allowing for the perception that this crystalline sea is the floor not only of the area immediately under the Throne but rather is the floor on which they all stand, that is, the sky-structure.[17] If the implied hearer is already familiar with the concept of a sky-structure composed of ice, crystal or glass (as implied in Exod. 24.10;

---

[15] Orlov, *Heavenly Priesthood*, 160, 175. MacRae, 'Some Elements of Jewish Apocalyptic and Mystical Tradition: And Their Relation to Gnostic Literature' (Cambridge, MA: Andover-Harvard Theological Library, 1981) 68. In the *Enuma Elish* the construction of the sky from the corpse of Tiamat is described as erecting a tent. See Greenwood, *Scripture*, 57.

[16] *3 Bar.* 10.1-9. While it is true that the sea is frequently a threatening image in the texts known to the implied reader, this clear crystalline sea does not retain any sense of threat. Contra Caird, *Commentary*, 62, 65, echoed by Harrington, *Revelation*, 78. See also Sweet, *Revelation*, 113. While not actually wet, it has more in common with the peaceful heavenly lake than the threatening cosmic sea.

[17] 'Although he describes the glass sea as lying in front of the throne, he probably meant that God's throne, surrounded as it is by the twenty-four thrones of the elders, the four living creatures and a rainbow, had the glassy sea extending from beneath it in all directions.' Richard B. Vinson, 'The Sea of Glass, the Lake of Fire, and the Topography of Heaven in Revelation', *Perspectives In Religious Studies*, 45/2 (2018): 132. Knight concludes, 'It is difficult to resist the conclusion that the primary reference in Rev. 4.6 is to the sky which features in much apocalyptic literature as the entity that divides the heaven(s) from the earth … apocalyptic literature promises to disclose what stands above the sky – what is ordinarily inaccessible to the human understanding'. Knight, *Revelation*, 60-1. Moo writes, 'This picture assumes that the sea of glass before the throne in Rev 4:6 is meant to be seen as a vast, glassy expanse forming at once the floor of heaven and—by extension—the ceiling above the earth.' Moo, 'The Sea', 152.

In Rev. 15.2 the victorious are seen standing on this crystalline lake, again suggesting that it is a kind of floor. For 'on' rather than 'beside' see Moo, 'The Sea', 153, n. 14.

Ezek. 1.22-26; described in *2 En.* 27; suggested as an option in Pseudo-Plutarch, *Placita Philosophorum* 2.11.2; *3 Bar.* 3.7 Slavonic), this would be enough to suggest such a composition for Revelation's sky-structure.[18] Obviously, the suggestion of a crystalline material conflicts with the suggestion of a material akin to animal skins. But while Revelation appears ambivalent as to the nature of the material it can hardly be doubted that it assumes a physical sky-structure.

It appears that at one point the implied author is conveying a message that works best if the narrative assumes a crystalline substance, while at another point the implied author is conveying a message that works best if the narrative assumes a material akin to animal skins. Yet the materiality of the sky-structure is always assumed, as are the spaces above and below the material sky-structure. In the following chapters we will see that structures and spaces remain important in Revelation's narrative, and the substance or matter of the cosmos less so. This will help us understand the nature of the new earth and sky in Rev. 21.1–22.5.[19]

4.3.2 Opacity

As suggested above, in moving upward through the sky-structure the seer has moved into a new position that enables him to view a new scene. Revelation suggests the reason why this scene cannot be viewed from earth: the sky-structure is opaque. That is, one cannot look upwards through the sky-structure to see what is above, though beings above the sky-structure can look downwards through it to see what is in the air or on the earth (Rev. 6.12; 7.1, 2; 8.13; 9.1). In that sense it functions more like one-way glass. Beings on earth are able to look upward into the space above the sky-structure only when the sky-structure is removed (Rev. 6.14-16).

The opacity of the sky-structure plays a role when the character John hears voices from the οὐρανός. Where the focalizer is coincident with the character John the way in which these voices are heard depends on John's location in the cosmos. When the cosmic journey currently has John above the sky-structure the voice is heard coming from a specific location in the vicinity of the Throne. The first-person ἤκουσα is used this way in Rev. 5.11; 6.1, 3, 5, 6, 7; 9.13; 16.1, 7, where it indicates a voice coming from a specific location within the hyper-heaven: from the angels and the four chimeric animals that surround the Throne, from the heavenly altar and from the heavenly temple.

However, when the audiovisual focalizer (coincident with the character John) is positioned on earth a voice may boom down from οὐρανός, but the precise source of the voice is not known. This first occurs in Rev. 4.1. The voice that says 'come up here' is identified with a previously heard voice, but the specific location from which it comes is not identified. Then from 4.2 to 9.21, where John is located above the sky-structure, his experience of hearing (ἤκουσα) includes identifying the specific

---

[18] Malina and Pilch write, 'Before (and behind and around) the throne is a sea of glass like crystal, which is the vault of the sky.' Malina and Pilch, *Social-Science*, 75. Similarly, Massyngberde Ford writes, 'Here the sea may be a crystal firmament.' Ford, *Revelation*, 74.

[19] See Chapter 7.

location from which the voice comes (Rev. 5.11, 13; 6.1, 3, 5, 7; 9.13).[20] But in Rev. 10.1-15.1 and 17.3-20.10, where John is located on earth, the voice is heard only ἐκ τοῦ οὐρανοῦ or ἐν τῷ οὐρανῷ (Rev. 10.4, 8; 12.10; 14.2, 13; 18.4), with no indication that he knows the specific location from which it comes.[21] The same is true in the one instance where the focalizer is briefly coincident with another character, when the two witnesses, located on earth, hear the voice ἐκ τοῦ οὐρανοῦ (Rev. 11.12).[22]

While John is on earth the narrator may still describe a sound coming from a specific location within the hyper-heaven but only where the focalizer is not coincident with the character John. Thus, while John is on earth in Rev. 11.16-18 the narrator describes singing within the hyper-heaven coming specifically from the twenty-four elders but does so without using first-person verbs of perception (or verbs with John as subject). While Ureña writes that John's 'repeated use of the formula καὶ εἶδον ... makes the focalization of his narrative exclusively his own',[23] I argue that this does not apply where εἶδον and other first-person verbs are not used and the narrator is describing something that John is not in a position to perceive. That is, the narrator conveys more audiovisual information to the hearer than is available to the character John. In these instances the focalizer is not coincident with John, nor with any other character. The hearer's experience, by definition identical with that of the audiovisual focalizer, diverges slightly from that of John; the hearer's virtual visionary journey has briefly returned it to the hyper-heaven while John has remained on earth. Here the 'oscillation in spatial context' noted by Ureña is not oscillation in John's position but in the position of the focalizer/hearer.[24] Similarly, it is not John who enables the hearer 'to perceive the surrounding atmosphere acoustically'[25] but the audiovisual focalizer.[26]

Not only does this aural phenomenon give additional confirmation of John's current location in his cosmic journey, it also reinforces the opacity of the sky-structure. Where the audiovisual focalizer is positioned on earth it cannot see through the sky-structure to identify the specific location that is the source of the heavenly voice, and so the source of the voice is identified no more specifically than οὐρανός. Whatever the material composition of the sky-structure, it prevents the upward gaze from peering

---

[20] In Chapter 6 I will show that the cosmic journey has John back on earth from Rev. 10.1.
[21] As described above, Rev. 1.9-20 is a vision that occurs on earth, and the gaze is horizontal; the sky-structure does not stand between the focalizer and object, and so the source of the voice can be identified. Note also Acts 2.2.
[22] As John is also on earth, the consistency remains even if we accept the reading ἤκουσα in 𝔓47.
[23] Ureña, *Narrative and Drama*, 125.
[24] Ureña, *Narrative and Drama*, 37.
[25] Ureña, *Narrative and Drama*, 73.
[26] The one instance where John is apparently on earth and hears a voice specifically from the Throne is in Rev. 21.3, where the Throne is also apparently on earth (read Rev. 21.1-4 together with 21.22 and 22.1-2). Without a sky-structure between himself and the Throne, he can hear/see the specific source of the voice. There is also an instance (Rev. 1.10) where John is on earth and hears a voice coming from a being on the same plane, but he is at first unable to discern the specific source of the voice. This is because the voice is coming from behind him, outside his field of vision, a situation which is rectified by turning around. But when the voice is coming from behind the sky-structure, there is no way for John to see the source of the voice.

into the space above. This is significant for understanding the narrative movements in Revelation 12 and the natures of the two sky-spaces.[27]

4.3.3 Single layer

As noted in Chapter 3 ancient sources almost universally held to the concept of a material sky-structure reaching across the cosmos, but in many cases the skies were composed of multiple layers. The Hebrew scriptures imply a single sky-layer, as do some of the apocalypses (*1 En.*; *2 Bar.*; *4 Ezra*), arguably some of the early Christian writings (Mark; Luke-Acts) and the Homeric literature. Others have three (some recensions of *T. Levi*; possibly 2 Cor.), seven (*Asc. Isa.*; *Apoc. Abr.*; some recensions of *T. Levi*; some recensions of *2 En.*; possibly *3 Bar.*; Plato, *Timaeus*), or ten (some recensions of *2 En.*). However, this numbering of the sky-layers is not always precise because in some cases there is an additional layer not counted in the seven; there is, so to speak, an eighth that belongs to the seven. Thus the second section of *2 Enoch* describes seven crystalline sky-layers with the throne of God sitting atop the seventh, but even this God-space has a ceiling above it. This ceiling is the ultimate upper limit of the cosmos, dividing the cosmos from nothingness. Unlike the seven crystalline sky-layers this ultimate border is composed of solidified light (*2 En.* 25.4). In a similar way, the seven planetary sky-spheres of Greek cosmological theorizing were actually surrounded by an eighth to which the regular stars were affixed.[28]

While Revelation assumes a sky-structure there is no indication in the narrative that it assumes more than one. As John passes upward through the opening in the sky-structure the immediate description of the God-space from his perspective implies that he only had to pass through the one. The implied hearer is already familiar with the concept of a single sky-structure and the simple implication of the narrative is sufficient communication. As the narrative progresses no additional layers are required to explain the movements through the cosmos. It should also be noted that the sky-journeys with multiple sky-layers label them with ordinal numbers (*T. Levi*; *2 En.*; *3 Bar.*; *Asc. Isa.*; *Apoc. Abr.*) and such might be expected here if John's journey took him through multiple layers.

In the ancient sources the number of sky-spaces does not always match the number of layered sky-structures. We saw in Chapter 3 that a sky-structure can divide the cosmos, creating a space above and a space below. The *Ascension of Isaiah*, for example, assumes seven sky-layers but describes ten distinct sky-spaces; one sky-space atop each of the seven sky-layers and an additional sky-space at the underside of the first, sixth and seventh sky-layer. Similarly, Revelation's clear indication of a single sky-structure is not an indication of a single sky-space. Indeed, Chapter 5 will show that Revelation's narrative operates in a certain manner in the sky-space above the sky-structure and in a different manner in the sky-space at the underside of the sky-structure.

---

[27] See Chapter 6.
[28] Wright, *Cosmology*, 50.

4.4 The God-space

4.4.1 Seeing the layout

Having set the location, Revelation begins to develop its God-space, initially through description of its appearance, layout and general operation (Rev. 4.2-11), followed by narration of events that modify the way the hearer views the scene (Rev. 5.1-14; 6.9-11; 7.9–8.5; 11.19; 15.2-8).[29] In Rev. 4.2 the first-person verb (ἐγενόμην) marks the focalizer as coincident with the character John, and the unfolding scene is viewed from above the sky-structure with a horizontal gaze. There is no indication of a shift in viewing position and this continuing visual perspective is affirmed again by the first-person verbs of seeing in Rev. 5.1, 2, 6, and 11. The Throne is thus seen not from below but front-on.

The hearer looks on as the scene is constructed piece by piece, beginning with the Throne and continuing with the scene surrounding the Throne.[30] It is at once striking, detailed and unclear. There is a being sitting on the Throne, seen only as a gleam of reddish light like the appearance of jasper and sardius.[31] Ureña notes that the colour red enhances the radiance of the rider in Rev. 19.11-16,[32] and this is also the case here. There is no further description of this being except that the participle 'sitting' is masculine in form. This contrasts with the detailed description of the head, hair, eyes, clothing, hands and feet of the Christ-figure in Revelation 1. The hearer assumes that he is human-like but glorious, much like the Christ-figure.[33] The narrator does not describe his head or eyes, or even the number of heads and eyes he has, nor does he specify whether this being has any non-human body parts – but in the absence of description the default image for a being sitting on a Throne is substantially human-like. More clearly, the absence of description is an indication that this being is God, reflecting the reluctance of many Judeans to make images of God, including verbal images.[34]

The ἶρις around the Throne recalls the hearer's image of brightness around the throne of God with the appearance of a multicoloured rainbow, known from Ezek. 1.27-28. An ἶρις can also be a single-coloured halo and so the image immediately

---

[29] Contra Ureña, it is not accurate to list this 'heaven' as an indefinite space, equivalent to the desert (Rev. 17.3) and the high mountain (Rev. 21.10). Ureña, *Narrative and Drama*, 37. It is not a known place in the same sense as Patmos or Ephesos, but unlike the desert and the mountain, it is given a specific location within the relatively coherent imagined cosmography, and once located it is described.

[30] As Bowman notes, 'The *throne* of God is henceforth the principal prop on the stage' (emphasis in the original). John Wick Bowman, *The Drama of the Book of Revelation* (Philadelphia: Westminster Press, 1955), 43.

[31] For ἴασπις and σάρδιον see *A Greek-English Lexicon of the New Testament and Other Early Christian Literature* (3rd Edition) (BDAG) and *Greek-English Lexicon of the Septuagint* (LEH). Neither has a clear match with modern classification of gems, but both appear reddish in colour.

[32] Ureña, *Narrative and Drama*, 80.

[33] Contra Sweet, *Revelation*, 117, the narrative does suggest a vague human shape to the reader, but it does so only implicitly.

[34] See *Apocalypse of Abraham* 17–18.

becomes as the narrator describes it – green like the gleam of an emerald.[35] This contrasts with the reddish gleam of the seated being. While the ἶρις could be seen as a horizontal circle around the Throne, part of the concentric circles that soon become apparent,[36] it is more likely that the implied hearer sees this as a glow all around the Throne.[37]

With the horizontal gaze continuing, a circle of thrones surrounding the Throne is now seen within the expanding frame.[38] The viewing position is just outside of this circle, looking inwards.[39] Still from this position, the camera zooms in to the Throne[40] and lightning bolts are seen coming from it, moving outwards towards the outer circle, and seven burning torches are seen in front of the Throne.[41]

With the gaze still focused in on the area close to the Throne, four more beings are now part of the scene. They do not move into the frame; they have always been there but now are seen by the hearer. The four beings are chimeric animals, full of eyes in front and behind. They are positioned very close to the Throne as they encircle it; this is the only visual that makes sense of the strange phrasing ἐν μέσῳ τοῦ θρόνου καὶ κύκλῳ τοῦ θρόνου.

Malina and Pilch present a different view, writing, 'With our seer, we are atop and on the other side of the vault of the sky, looking down from the perspective of the Throne.'[42] Thus they describe the four chimeric animals as constellations on the underside of the sky-structure.[43] However, the angle of gaze is not downwards but

---

[35] See Charles, *Revelation*, vol. 1, 115, and Malina and Pilch, *Social-Science*, 73. Contra Aune and BDAG, the colour description modifies the hearer's anticipation of a multicoloured ἶρις. Aune, *Revelation 1–5*, 286. William Arndt, Frederick W. Danker and Walter Bauer, *A Greek-English Lexicon of the New Testament and Other Early Christian Literature*, 3rd edn (Chicago: University of Chicago Press, 2000), 480.

[36] So Aune, *Revelation 1–5*, 286.

[37] Malina and Pilch describe it as 'an arch (like a rainbow) of emerald green light', comparable to the arch around a deity in a Graeco-Roman shrine. Malina and Pilch, *Social-Science*, 73.
   The glow of jasper, sardius/carnelian and emerald has an interesting parallel in Plato's description of the glorious ether-space, which lies atop the air-space of ordinary human living and contains far superior examples of jasper, carnelian and emerald (Plato, *Phaedo* 110d).

[38] The thrones are arranged in a large circle around the Throne. See Charles, *Revelation*, vol. 1, 115–16, and Aune, *Revelation 1–5*, 286. I am not persuaded by Bowman's description of a semicircle around the Throne 'after the mode of the Jewish Sanhedrin'. Bowman, *Drama*, 43.

[39] So also Ryan, *Hearing*, 66. Whitaker describes the scene from the middle, with the seer (and the hearers) looking out at the encircling twenty-four thrones. Whitaker, *Ekphrasis*, 110–11. Both positions are possible. I am inclined to understand that John (and the hearer) is just outside this circle. In Revelation the character John is invited up through the sky into the region surrounding the Throne; he is never invited to the very foot of the Throne, but he does interact closely with one of the twenty-four elders (Rev. 7.13-14). Further, in this visual description, it seems natural that the focalizer is in a position to see all twenty-four of the thrones described.

[40] The narrator's control over what is seen and *how* it is seen is analogous to the camera in cinema, 'with its shifts from long to medium to close-up shots'. Ureña, *Narrative and Drama*, 70, 125.

[41] The narrator informs the reader that these are the seven spirits of God. This strains the identification of the narrator with the character John, because it is not explained how the character John knows this information. Even while narrator and character are coincident, they are not absolutely identical. As Genette notes, 'The narrator almost always "knows" more than the hero, even if he himself is the hero.' Genette, *Narrative*, 194.

[42] Malina and Pilch, *Social-Science*, 75.

[43] See also Malina and Pilch, *Social-Science*, 77–86.

forwards. The viewing position is indeed above the sky-structure, brought there in Rev. 4.2, but the gaze has been directed horizontally, creating the scene around the Throne including the horizontal circle of twenty-four thrones. The focus moves closer in to the Throne to show the four animals but there is no indication in the narration that the angle of gaze has changed. These animals are seen on the same plane as the Throne, standing right next to the Throne as they encircle it.[44]

These are chimeric beings of the upper cosmos, not earthly animals, but the visual comparison with certain familiar animals enables the hearer to see them. Still, the narrator has only aided the hearer's imagination up to a certain point, as the third animal has a human face, but remains vague and undefined in other respects. They are 'filled with eyes in front and behind' and have six wings which are 'filled with eyes, around and inside'. A significant challenge is how to picture an animal 'filled with eyes'. As Charles noted, 'there is some difficulty in attaching to the conception of a creature with a face like a man and yet full of eyes in front'.[45] Responding to these difficulties, Mounce writes, 'Here as elsewhere we are dealing with visions that were meant to stir the imagination, not yield to the drawing board.'[46] Yet some have attempted to render these visions on the drawing board. Albrecht Dürer drew spots on the animals, similar to the 'eyes' on a peacock's tail.[47] This works well in a simple line drawing but doesn't resolve the question of how it would look up close and in colour, as the implied reader sees them in this virtual visionary experience. It appears that most commentators have either passed over this question, or suggested that the eyes are stars and imaged as such. Carrington writes, 'The Eyes, so suggestive of the peacock, unquestionably recall Stars.'[48] Similarly, J. Massyngberde Ford writes, 'They are probably not only for the purpose of sight, but for sparkling, as in Ezek. 1.18.'[49] For different reasons, Malina and Pilch understand eyes to be stars, and therefore a creature 'filled with eyes' as a constellation.[50] While I am not convinced by their reason for seeing it this way, and do not understand these creatures as constellations,[51] there may be something to seeing

---

[44] While the descriptive narration recalls for the implied reader the Ezek. 1.4-28 image of four creatures beneath a firmament with a throne above, it also recalls the Isa. 6.2 image of the six-winged seraphim above (Hebrew מִמַּעַל לוֹ) or around (Septuagint κύκλῳ αὐτοῦ) the throne, and the cinematic perspective in Revelation 4 directs that the four animals be added to the scene *around* the Throne (see also *1 En.* 71.7. The Ezek. 1 and Isa. 6 images are also combined in *Apoc. Abr.* 18.3-6). This is reaffirmed in 19.4 when the four animals prostrate themselves to the one sitting on the Throne, an image that works if the animals are on the same plane as Throne (see also 5.8). The prostration of the four animals in 5.8 and 19.4 also works against the suggestion of Hall, adopted by Ryan, that they are part of the Throne itself. Robert G. Hall, 'Living Creatures in the Midst of the Throne: Another Look at Revelation 4.6', *New Testament Studies*, 36/4 (1990): 609–13. Ryan, *Hearing*, 63.
[45] Charles, *Revelation*, vol. 1, 124.
[46] Robert H. Mounce, *The Book of Revelation, The New International Commentary on the New Testament* (Grand Rapids: Eerdmans, 1977), 125.
[47] Natasha O'Hear and Anthony O'Hear, *Picturing the Apocalypse: The Book of Revelation in the Arts over Two Millennia* (Oxford: Oxford University Press, 2015), 54.
[48] Philip Carrington, *The Meaning of the Revelation* (London: Society for Promoting Christian Knowledge, 1931), 115. Capitalization original.
[49] Ford, *Revelation*, 75.
[50] Malina and Pilch, *Social-Science*, 75.
[51] In Chapter 5 I show that stars are seen in the sky high above the earth, but not above the sky-structure in the region of the Throne.

these 'eyes' as points of light, or points of flame. Whitaker interprets the seven burning lamps, which are the seven spirits, in line with Zech. 4.10 'where the temple lamps or menorah are interpreted by the angel as "the eyes of the Lord, which roam the whole earth".'[52] If burning lamps can be eyes, and eyes can be a flame of fire (1.14), so it may be that the hearer sees these 'eyes' as points of flame. Note that while human eyes are spoken of in terms of weakness and suffering (Rev. 1.7; 3.18; 7.17; 21.4), the eyes of beings above are spoken of in terms of knowledge, power and glory – often described specifically as points of flame (Rev. 1.14; 2.18; 5.6; 19.12).

Revelation 5.1 begins the narration of events that modify how the hearer views the scene. Just as the four chimeric animals became part of the scene, revealed as having always been there, so in Rev. 5.6 the Lamb becomes part of the scene without movement into it, and yet the revelation of his presence is part of the developing narrative of searching for someone worthy. Also like the four chimeric animals, the description of his position is somewhat confusing (ἐν μέσῳ τοῦ θρόνου καὶ τῶν τεσσάρων ζῴων καὶ ἐν μέσῳ τῶν πρεσβυτέρων), but it appears to indicate a position near the Throne, from which the Lamb then moves to stand immediately at the Throne.[53] In response to this event, an encircling group of myriads of angels is now revealed surrounding the scene and this group now participates in the action.

It is in response to the opening of the fifth seal that the next addition is made to the scene. As with the four chimeric animals and the Lamb, the altar is now seen within the frame as something that has always been there. There is no description of its position within this space, so existing understanding of the space suggests its position. The Throne is the centre with the chimeric animals immediately at its four sides, while the concentric circles of thrones and angels are spaced further back. This leaves the area in front of the Throne, between the chimeric animals and the thrones, as the implied position of the altar.

It is the souls of the martyrs that potentially stretch the coherence of the scene. John is still in position atop the sky-structure, with the developing scene narrated from his perspective as the horizontal gaze is directed inward to the Throne and altar. An altar is understood to be a solid block, so the souls beneath the altar are down beside its base. The number of souls is not given but within Revelation's narrative sweep a number in the thousands would seem to be implied. It is the difficulty in picturing this number in the relatively small area that potentially threatens the coherence of the scene.

Despite the noted difficulties, the scene has been created in a way that is relatively clear. The Throne is the centre, with the four chimeric animals at its four sides. In the area in front of the Throne is the altar, and surrounding all this is a circle of twenty-four thrones, and surrounding this an encircling group of myriads of angels. It is when the narration begins to speak of a temple that the greatest ambiguity is introduced.

The heavenly temple comes into play several times (Rev. 7.15; 11.19; 14.15, 17; 15.5, 8; 16.1, 17) but its position within the scene is never described. This is also true of the altar, but the layout of the scene implied a simple position for the altar, whereas the nature and position of the temple is far more challenging and ambiguous. Most

---

[52] Whitaker, *Ekphrasis*, 115.
[53] Beale, *Revelation*, 350. Aune, *Revelation 1-5*, 352.

significant is the question of whether the temple encompasses much of the scene that has already been described or is a separate feature now added to the scene. In other words, does the temple enclose the Throne area or sit apart from the Throne? The challenge of locating the Throne in relation to the temple was noted already by Charles, who concludes that some parts of Revelation presuppose the Throne is within a temple and other parts presuppose that it is not.[54]

Revelation's God-space is suggestive of both a royal courtroom and a holy sanctuary. Not only do the elders on the encircling thrones prostrate themselves in obeisance to the Throne (Rev. 4.10), but also liturgical actions are performed on an altar (Rev. 8.3-5).[55] The entire scene can be understood in terms of a holy sanctuary with the area immediately surrounding the Throne equivalent to the Holy of Holies and the further concentric circles suggesting the outer areas of the temple or tabernacle, with decreasing levels of holiness.[56] Understanding the Throne area as the temple allows much of the narrative to make sense: those who are in front of the Throne worship God day and night in his temple (Rev. 7.15); the angel that comes from the temple is a messenger from God (Rev. 14.15);[57] the temple is filled with smoke from the glory of God (Rev. 15.8); and a loud voice comes from the temple, specifically from the Throne (Rev. 16.1).

There are also suggestions that within the hyper-heaven the temple is a bounded space (Rev. 14.15, 17; 15.5–16.1) that can be closed off (Rev. 11.19; 15.5-8), suggesting that it be seen as a building with walls. Such an image creates difficulties for the scene. The temple could be stretched to encompass the twenty-four thrones as required by the narrative (Rev. 4.9-10), but if it is a bounded space within the hyper-heaven then it surely cannot encompass the outer myriads of angels.[58] Yet temple walls that shut out the encircling angels from the central action would conflict with the description of these angels participating in this action (Rev. 5.11-12). Temple walls around the central area would also create difficulties for John's view of the scene. Unlike the seer of the Book of Watchers, who peers through an open door into the throne room (*1 En.* 14.14-25), John views the whole scene completely without impediment, from the Throne to the outer angels.

The heavenly temple could alternatively be seen as a building separate from the Throne. If Rev. 15.5-8 describes sequential events then the narrative movements suggest that the Throne is not within the temple, as the seven angels first exit the temple

---

[54] Charles, *Revelation*, vol. 1, 111–12. See also Vinson, 'Sea of Glass', 131. Some commentators have said that this is not a 'physical' temple at all, but a way of referring to being in the presence of God. Swete, *Apocalypse*, 102. Beale, *Revelation*, 441. There is truth in the view that the temple means being in the presence of God, but there remains the question of how the image works within the scene.

[55] Murphy, *Fallen*, 178. Not only is incense burnt on this altar, but the souls beneath the altar are the equivalent of the blood of sacrificial victims at the base of an altar. Charles is correct to note that the altar is suggestive of both the altar of burnt offerings and the altar of incense. Charles, *Revelation*, vol. 1, 172. Also Koester, *Revelation*, 398.

[56] Ryan, *Hearing*, 63.

[57] 'Some find it inappropriate that an angel commands Christ in this way, but that is to misconstrue the angel's role. The angel carries the message from the temple, where God resides.' Murphy, *Fallen*, 327.

[58] This is not because a heavenly throne room could never accommodate that number of beings (*1 En.* 14.22), but because of the way that Revelation creates the space and moves beings through it.

and then receive bowls from the chimeric animal who is next to the Throne. A separate position for the temple would also fit with John's unimpeded view from the central area to the outer angels and the participation of the outer angels in the central action. Yet a separate position would not fit well with the other aspects of the narrative nor accord with the sense that the whole central scene functions as both a royal courtroom and a holy sanctuary.

The lack of spatial clarity in the temple language presents no problem for its symbolic and emotive effects at key points in the narrative.[59] It is only a challenge for the visualization of a scene. And even with the reduction in visual clarity introduced by the temple language, the scene is clear enough for the hearer to understand it in spatial terms and to see how the Throne defines the space.

4.4.2 Nature of the space

Defined by the Throne

Bowman describes the Throne as the principal prop in the stage, which is true, but it is so much more.[60] It is the Throne that confronts the viewer from the moment the voice says 'come up here', followed by the impressionistic description of the one seated on the Throne. Each new element becomes part of the space through relationship with the Throne. The four chimeric animals are introduced first through their spatial relationship with the Throne; they are right at its base, on each side (Rev. 4.6). Likewise, the twenty-four thrones are introduced through their spatial relationship to the Throne – set back a little, they too encircle it (Rev. 4.3). So too the myriads angels. First described as surrounding the Throne, their position is immediately clarified as one step back again from the four chimeric animals and the twenty-four thrones (Rev. 5.11).

The relationship does not remain spatial only, as the narrative shows a responsive relationship between the Throne and the four chimeric animals (Rev. 4.8), and once the Lamb has come to the Throne, also between Lamb and the animals. It shows also a responsive relationship between the Throne and the next of the concentric circles; as the inner ring responds to the Throne in worship, the intermediate ring also responds to the Throne, the beings from the twenty-four thrones casting their crowns before the Throne and prostrating themselves before the one who is seated on it.

As with the inner ring, once the Lamb has come to the Throne the beings on the twenty-four thrones fall also before the Lamb and sing their response (Rev. 5.8-10). This pattern of response extends to the outer ring, as the outer ring is introduced to the scene responding in song to the Lamb's arrival at the Throne (Rev. 5.11-13).

The responsive relationship includes the aspect of obedience and full recognition of the authority of the one sitting on the Throne. Significant actions begin with the Throne and are put into full effect through the obedience of the beings/objects in the hyper-heaven. The first such action is the opening of the first four seals. This begins with the passing of the seven-sealed scroll from the one who sits on the Throne to the

---

[59] Barr, *Tales*, 116.
[60] Bowman, *Drama*, 43.

Lamb who stands right at the Throne, from the Lamb's opening of a seal to the response of a chimeric animal and from the chimeric animal's command to the horse's final action (Rev. 5.6–6.8). Thus the action begins with the Throne and moves outward, first to the Lamb who is at the Throne, then to the chimeric animals, then to the horses. At the opening of the seventh seal the action that has moved from the Throne to the Lamb now moves from the Lamb to the seven key angels who stand close by, and from the blowing of their trumpets to the completed action. With the sixth trumpet the action moves a step further, from the angel to the altar, whose response enables the completion of the action (Rev. 9.13).

With regard to the seven bowls, the temple language reduces the clarity of the image, but if the Throne is within the temple then a similar pattern applies: first bowls are passed from the four chimeric animals around the Throne out to the seven angels, then a command comes from the Throne/temple to the seven angels, leading to the response from the seven angels that completes the action (Rev. 15.5–16.21).[61] In every case all beings/objects act in full accord with the Throne.

Not only are the objects and beings of this space defined in relation to the Throne, even the floor of the space is defined by the Throne. The crystalline sea, while suggestive of a crystalline sky-structure, is introduced not in its own right but in relation to the Throne (Rev. 4.6), recalling the crystalline platform of God's moving throne in Ezek. 1.22. As in Ezekiel, where the crystalline platform of the throne is simultaneously the crystalline firmament, the crystalline sea that is defined in relation to the Throne becomes the floor of Revelation's upper cosmic space (Rev. 15.2).[62]

The way in which Revelation's Throne defines the space is even more striking when placed alongside similar scenes in *1 Enoch* and the *Apocalypse of Abraham*. As in Revelation, the seer of the *Apocalypse of Abraham* is taken from earth to the highest space without intervening stops and sights. But his first sight is not the throne. The space is defined first by its floor (the air as a kind of surface) and then by features and beings (*Apoc. Abr.* 15.4-7). The space defined, the throne of God then *enters into* this space (*Apoc. Abr.* 17–18). When the seer of *1 Enoch* is taken up onto the sky, at first he is not in the ultimate God-space. He moves horizontally into a palace complex whose

---

[61] These seven angels were not previously described within the scene, unless they are identified with the seven torches of Rev. 4.5.

[62] Some commentators argue that the glassy sea represents the presence of evil or chaos. Caird describes the heavenly sea of glass as 'the reservoir of evil out of which arises the monster (xii. I)'. Caird, *Commentary*, 65, 161, 259. Beale writes, 'It is possible that the "sea" symbolizes the realm of evil (4:6; 13:1; 15:2), within which Satanic forces operate and which imprisons all unbelievers.' Beale, *Revelation*, 1034. However, a sea in the sky need not represent evil. *2 Enoch* 3–6 describes the space above the first sky-structure, including a vast sea and various meteorological and astronomical phenomena. These are described in neutral or positive terms, and it is only in the space above the second sky-structure that evil/chaos/rebellion is seen in the cosmos. See also *T. Levi* 2.7. *3 Baruch* has a body of water on its fourth sky, presented positively as a place in which beings gather, wade and worship God, although it is called a lake rather than a sea (*3 Bar.* 10.1-5). Regarding the terrestrial sea, Revelation's narrative sometimes gives this sea a positive connotation (Rev. 5.13; 10.6; 14.7) and sometimes a negative connotation (Rev. 13.1; 21.1). It does not indicate a negative sense for its heavenly sea (Rev. 4.6; 15.2). In Rev. 15.2 its connotations are closer to the heavenly lake of *3 Bar.* 10.1-5.

Moo argues that the sea of glass mixed with fire connotes not rebellion against God, but rather the means of God's righteous, destructive judgement. Moo, 'The Sea', 154.

floor, walls and roof are described in awesome terms before peering through a door into the ultimate room. This room is described, and then God's throne is located within it (*1 En.* 14.8-18).[63] The palace complex is an awesome place appropriate to house God's throne but it is not defined by the throne.

Further to the contrast with these other apocalypses, there is also a notable difference between the way Revelation treats the Throne and its location and the way that Revelation locates all other objects and beings within spaces. As Ureña notes, Revelation's καὶ εἶδον descriptions begin by defining the stage before locating objects, beings and events on that stage.[64] Thus Rev. 13.1 does not read καὶ εἶδον θηρίον ἀναβαῖνον ἐκ τῆς θαλάσσης, but instead καὶ εἶδον ἐκ τῆς θαλάσσης θηρίον ἀναβαῖνον. The stage-first pattern holds true for the καὶ εἶδον descriptions in Rev. 1.12; 5.6; 14.14; and 19.11. Similarly, Rev. 12.1, 3 note the appearance of a σημεῖον ἐν τῷ οὐρανῷ before describing the being and its actions. By contrast, Rev. 4.2 calls to the hearer καὶ ἰδοὺ θρόνος before locating this ἐν τῷ οὐρανῷ – the Throne is prior to the Throne-space.

Despite the unclear temple language, Revelation's Throne is not located within a bounded space. The viewer can see the entire scene unimpeded, from the central area to the outer angels. There is no ceiling to define the space in which the Throne is located, nor horizontal edges.[65] The only spatial edge is the floor, which is defined in relation to the Throne and separates the Throne-space from the cosmos-of-ordinary-human-experience. There is little to define the Throne-space beside the Throne itself. The hearer is left with the sense that the Throne creates the space and without the Throne there would be no hyper-heaven. This has particular significance when cosmic spaces shift.[66]

What I discuss under the name 'hyper-heaven' is discussed in other terms by a number of scholars. There is, for example, substantial overlap between my 'hyper-heaven' and Gwyther's 'heaven' even though he understands this heaven in non-spatial terms. The overlap is in the nature of this heaven as 'the world where God lives and reigns'.[67] But Revelation 12 leads scholars to think that this heaven is also the scene of conflict. The dragon pulling down stars, opposing armies of angels battling in the οὐρανός and Satan standing in front of the Throne are commonly held to introduce elements of evil/rebellion into the 'heaven' that is the 'dwelling place of God' or the place 'where God is enthroned'.[68] Contrary to this common belief, in Chapter 6 I will show

---

[63] Enoch's movement is sometimes understood as vertical, through three heavenly tiers that are also three areas in a vertical heavenly temple. Christopher R. A. Morray-Jones, 'Paradise Revisited (2 Cor 12:1-12): The Jewish Mystical Background of Paul's Apostolate. Part 1: The Jewish Sources', *HTR* 86/2 (1993): 203. Christopher R. A. Morray-Jones, 'The Temple Within', in *Paradise Now. Essays of Early Jewish and Christian Mysticism*, ed. April. D. De Conick, SBL Symposium Series 11 (Leiden: Brill, 2006), 46. I am more persuaded by Esler's analysis of this space in terms of a walled palace complex and find simple horizontal movement sufficient. Esler, *God's Court*, 114, 38, 51.

[64] Ureña, *Narrative and Drama*, 72–3.

[65] The throne-space of *1 Enoch* has walls and a ceiling (*1 En.* 14.15-17). The throne-space in the second section of *2 Enoch* has a ceiling (*2 En.* 25.4).

[66] See Sec. 7.1 and Sec. 7.2.

[67] Howard-Brook and Gwyther, *Unveiling*, 121–2. Similarly, Jordaan describes heaven as 'a qualitative reference to a situation where all and everyone live in God's presence, in ceaseless praise, worship and obedience to him as Lord'. Jordaan, 'Cosmology', 3, 5.

[68] Jordaan, 'Cosmology', 3; Wink, *Naming*, 119.

that Revelation 12 maintains the consistent picture of a hyper-heaven characterized by full recognition of the authority of the one who sits on the Throne. The apocalypses considered in Chapter 3 all had a God-space free of rebellion, and also free of beings undergoing punishment for their former rebellion, and we will see that this is also the case in Revelation.

Limited accessibility to humans

We also saw in Chapter 3 that while the cosmic tours always revealed a God-space free of rebellion, there was variation in whether the God-space is accessible to humans. At one end of the scale the *Ascension of Isaiah* shows a God-space accessible to many living humans in extra-ordinary experiences and to all the righteous dead.[69] At the other end of the scale, *3 Baruch* (Greek) has a God-space that is not accessible to living humans even in extra-ordinary experiences, nor to the righteous dead, who have a blessed dwelling place in a mid-range sky-level. Others fall somewhere in the middle. *1 Enoch* has a God-space accessible to a living human in an extra-ordinary experience, but the current and future dwelling place of righteous humans is in/on the earth.[70] The same is true of the *Apocalypse of Abraham*.[71] Similarly, *2 Enoch* has a God-space accessible to at least one living human in an extra-ordinary experience, but the places for the dead, both righteous and unrighteous, are in mid-range sky-levels.

Revelation's God-space also falls somewhere in the middle of this spectrum. While it is a holy place in full harmony with the Throne, above the cosmos-of-ordinary-human-experience, its nature does not prevent John's extra-ordinary experience of a journey into this space. It is temporarily accessible to some, but not all, of the righteous dead. While Rev. 1.18 mentions ὁ θάνατος καί ὁ ᾅδης, with the implication that it is speaking of a dwelling place for dead people, it is in Rev. 6.9 that a place for the dead is first shown to the hearer. There the altar becomes part of the scene in front of the Throne, introduced as something that has been there all along, with an implied position in the area in front of the Throne and within the circle of thrones. While the image of the souls at its base is lacking in clarity, and the nature of their existence is likewise vague, the image does have resonances with the blood of sacrificial victims under the altar, with the concept of life-blood and with the blood/souls that cry out for vengeance.

---

[69] The *Ascension of Isaiah* implies that a number of Christians were having similar experiences to its seer. Knight, *The Ascension of Isaiah*, 9–10. Hall, 'The Ascension of Isaiah: Community Situation, Date, and Place in Early Christianity', *Journal of Biblical Literature*, 109/2 (1990): 294.

[70] *1 En.* 22; 51.

[71] *Apoc. Abr.* 21.6 depicts the garden of Eden on the plane of the earth, in ways implying that it is the place of blessed rest for the righteous dead. Box wrote, 'Note that Paradise is here located on the earth, though the transcendental Paradise is meant.' G. H. Box, *The Apocalypse of Abraham, Translations of Early Documents. Series I, Palestinian Jewish Texts (Pre-Rabbinic)* (London: Society for Promoting Christian Knowledge, 1918), 67. But the *Apocalypse of Abraham* makes no clear reference to a 'transcendental' paradise and it is equally possible that its place of blessed rest is at the eastern extremity of the earth, across the encircling river.

Their position at the base of the altar makes them equivalent to the blood of animal sacrifices, which is dashed against the sides of the altar[72] or poured at its base.[73] As these are people who have been executed for their faithful witness the image gives meaning to their deaths. But is also suggests a place of rest and care for those who have died in this way.

The equivalence between blood and the life/soul of a person recalls the idea from the Hebrew scriptures that the blood is the life. This is the basis for the prohibition against eating blood or meat that has not been properly drained of its blood (Gen. 9.4-5; Lev. 17.10-16; Deut. 12.23. See also Acts 15.20, 29), and can be used to explain the role of blood in sacrifice (Lev. 17.11). When an animal is killed in the field, its life-blood should go into the ground (Lev. 17.13).

The concept is at play in the story of Cain and Abel. Killed like an animal in the field, Abel's life-blood goes into the ground. The life-blood being all that is left of Abel's life, it is the life-blood that calls out from the ground for vengeance (Gen. 4.10-11). The Book of Watchers draws on this story when depicting its equivalent of Sheol in a mountain at the edge of the earth, with the souls of the righteous crying up to heaven for just vengeance (*1 En.* 22.5-12). While the souls of the righteous have their own section within the mountain, and a slightly better existence than the souls of sinners, they are still far less than their living selves; they are more like life-blood crying out from the ground than full beings experiencing a real afterlife.

All this is recalled in Rev. 6.9, which goes a step further than the Book of Watchers, since the special place for these souls is not a section within the mountain/Sheol/Hades but in front of the Throne in the hyper-heaven.[74] It is a place of rest and honour but they remain far less than their living selves. While their existence involves a degree of conscious rest and comfort, and even participation in the action through their cries for justice, they are not fully alive actors in the way that John is, nor even as the other beings around the Throne appear to be.[75] They are under the Throne while they wait for something to change.

It is not accurate to describe these souls as 'resurrected' or 'alive'.[76] They are described only as 'souls' and their only action is to cry out for justice as they impatiently wait for vindication, reflecting 'the cry of innocent blood for vengeance'.[77] Nor is their receipt of white robes an act of resurrection or receipt of heavenly bodies.[78] While glorious (sometimes white) robes as the heavenly body and/or resurrection body is a familiar image (*Asc. Isa.* 9.9; 4 Ezra 2.39-45; 1 Cor. 15.53; 2 Cor. 5.1-4), the hearer is most immediately familiar with white robes as a symbol of purity or victory (Rev. 3.4, 18; 4.4; 6.2). These souls are not seen to 'come alive' until Rev. 20.4 where the scene is on earth.

---

[72] Exod. 24.6; 29.12, 16, 20; Lev. 1.5, 11, 15; 3.2, 8, 13; 5.9; 7.2; 8.19, 24; 9.12, 18; 17.6; Num. 18.17; 2 Kgs 16.13, 15; 2 Chron. 29.22.
[73] Lev. 4.7, 18, 25, 30, 34; 5.9; 8.15; 9.9; Deut. 12.27.
[74] See also *1 En.* 47.1-2
[75] Ureña acknowledges that John is more than narrator and becomes an actor in the narrative. Ureña, *Narrative and Drama*, 28, 55.
[76] Contra Paul Barnett, *Apocalyse Now and Then: Reading Revelation Today* (Sydney: Aquila Press, 1989), 82.
[77] Sweet, *Revelation*, 141.
[78] Contra Charles, *Revelation*, vol. 1, 176.

Thus Revelation's God-space is accessible only to some among the righteous dead and only in this special sense, not as a blessed home for life beyond death but as a place of waiting. The rest of the righteous dead, together with the unrighteous dead, have gone into the ground and so are in Hades, or have drowned and sunk into the sea (Rev. 20.13).[79] In Chapter 7 we will see that the cosmic changes of Revelation 20–22 involve a change to this aspect of the God-space.

4.5 Conclusion: Structures and spaces

This chapter has shown Revelation's narrative functioning as a cosmic tour, taking the seer into the skies and showing him the four corners of the earth. Following a common pattern in cosmic tours, the extra-ordinary experience begins on earth as an encounter with an extra-ordinary being and continues as an ascent into an extra-ordinary location. Revelation's cosmic tour narrative maintains the most basic assumptions about the cosmos (a broad earth, a material sky-structure) but makes choices regarding the number of sky-structures and the way in which the spaces are developed.

There is a single sky-structure with a sky-space above and a sky-space below. This chapter showed the nature of the structure and the space above, leaving the sky-space at the underside of the sky-structure for subsequent chapters. The narrative assumes the materiality of the sky-structure but different parts of the narrative assume a different material composition. The substance of which the cosmos is composed appears less significant than its structures and spaces.

While cosmic tours commonly locate a God-space at the highest cosmic level, they typically define an awesome space and locate God and God's throne within it. By contrast, Revelation's narrative showed the Throne defining the space, leaving the hearer with the sense that the Throne creates the Throne-space. Regarding its accessibility to humans, Revelation's God-space fell somewhere in the middle of the existing spectrum, being accessible to at least one human in an extra-ordinary experience and to some, but not all, of the righteous dead. We will see a change in this characteristic of the God-space when it merges with the earth-space.[80]

As this chapter focussed on the earth and the space above the sky-structure, the following chapters will show how the narrative uses the space at the underside of the sky-structure and the space below the earth. Story-space will be seen to incorporate the four spaces of hyper-heaven, sky-heaven, earth and under-earth, each with distinct characteristics and beings appropriate to the space. Chapters 5 and 6 will show how the nature of the spaces and their beings interacts with the functioning of the narrative that employs them as story-space and actor.

---

[79] Kiddle writes, 'He must wait the final judgement in the cheerless underworld of the dead, full of unknown terrors. Only the Christian, perhaps only the martyr, could expect to be delivered from the miseries of Death and Hades.' Martin Kiddle, *The Revelation of St. John*, *The Moffat New Testament Commentary* (London: Hodder and Stoughton, 1940), 118. Kiddle is essentially correct, although it may not be true that Hades is full of 'terrors' and 'miseries'.
[80] See Sec. 7.2.

5

Four cosmic layers in operation

This chapter will show how all four cosmic layers (hyper-heaven, sky-heaven, earth and under-earth) play a role in Revelation's narrative. The focus is Rev. 9.1-11, which is sometimes noted for its use of 'all three' cosmic tiers but here we will see that the narrative operates in all four.[1] The central actor in this narrative is a star, though commentators have often assumed that it is not really a star but an angel. This assumption is based on the modern cosmological understanding that stars are not living beings. Because a star is not a living being, a star that behaves as a living being must be a metaphor for something else.[2] Revelation's implied author and implied hearer do not share this assumption.

In this chapter I demonstrate how the narrative operates across the cosmic tiers, with the star behaving as a star. This is not an assertion of 'literalism' but a recognition of how the narrative is functioning within itself. The narrative certainly has a more-than-literal meaning, but translating 'star' into 'angel' does not move us towards the more-than-literal meaning of this narrative.[3] Treating the star as a star, we begin by considering the normal position of stars within Revelation's cosmos before noting the role that this 'fallen' star plays in Rev. 9.1-11. Finally, we return to Rev. 5.6-14 to see the four cosmic levels at play in the narrative and the division between the highest level and the lower three.

5.1 The position of stars

Knowing the sights common to many sky-journeys, it is notable that Revelation's seer does not see sun, moon, stars, clouds or winds in his initial movement from earth

---

[1] Ryan, *Hearing*, 2. Jon K. Newton, *A Pentecostal Commentary on Revelation. Pentecostal Old Testament and New Testament Commentaries* (Eugene: Wipf and Stock, 2021), 183.
[2] 'The star is conceived as a personal being here, *i.e.* as an angel.' Charles, *Revelation*, vol. 1, 238. 'The "star" is a supernatural being, i.e., an angel.' Aune, *Revelation 6–16*, 625.
[3] This point can be expressed by analogy. Aesop's story of the tortoise and the hare certainly has meaning beyond itself, specifically in the area of human behaviour and character traits. But within the story the hare is not a human being, and nor is the tortoise. Within the story the hare is faster than the tortoise because hares have the characteristic 'fast' and tortoises have the characteristic 'slow'. The story maintains this characteristic of the tortoise even as it finds a way for the tortoise to win the race. The more-than-literal meaning of the story does not require that the hare represent an athletic human and the tortoise represent an unathletic human.

to the highest cosmic layer. Some or all of these are seen in their normal positions and normal movements as part of the (first) upward journey in *2 Enoch* and *3 Baruch* and are seen in their normal positions and movements soon after the (first) upward journey in *1 Enoch* and the *Apocalypse of Abraham*. By contrast, in Revelation they are not seen as part of the (first) upward journey and are introduced only in narration of abnormal movements and changes (Rev. 6.12-14), so some consideration must be given to the assumed normal position of stars.[4]

5.1.1 Position of stars in ancient sources

We noted in Chapter 2 that the sky-structure in Genesis is a barrier that holds back the upper cosmic waters. Set into this sky-structure, or moving through the space beneath it, are sun, moon, stars and birds (Gen. 1.14, 20). These beings are similarly located in *1 Enoch* (*1 En.* 33.1-4; 75.3) which also has a single sky-structure. There is one place in *1 Enoch* that could imply that the stars are affixed to a turning sky (*1 En.* 18.4) but numerous and detailed descriptions of the stars as self-moving entities travelling across the underside of the unmoving sky-structure. In Greek cosmological theorizing stars are affixed to the underside of a turning sky-structure. In Anaximander's model this is a single hemispherical sky-structure, while in later models it is the outermost of eight concentric spheres.[5]

Some apocalypses with multiple sky-layers present sun, moon and stars not with reference to the sky above them but with reference to the sky below them. The seer of the *Apocalypse of Abraham* looks down from the seventh sky to see the stars atop the fifth sky (*Apoc. Abr.* 19.9). *3 Baruch* does not speak of stars, but sun and moon are seen after its seer emerges onto the third sky-layer (*3 Bar.* 6–9). The seer of *2 Enoch* sees the rulers of the stars in his (first) upward journey as he emerges onto the first of seven/ten sky-layers, then as he emerges onto the fourth sky-layer he sees the sun, accompanied by stars in its movement across the cosmos (*2 En.* 3.3–4.2; 11.1-3). However, the second section of *2 Enoch* places stars at the underside of the first of seven sky-spheres (*2 En.* 30.4 J recension).

There is no instance of stars in the God-space. *1 Enoch* has its stars at the underside of the sky-structure and its God-space above it; the first section of *2 Enoch* has its stars on the first/fourth sky and its God-space on the seventh/tenth; Aristotle had stars set into the underside of the ultimate (eighth) sky-sphere, understanding that beyond this boundary was divinity (*De Caelo* 278b12-15); the second section of *2 Enoch* (J recension) has its God-space atop the seventh crystalline sky-sphere and *below* the ultimate (eighth) sky-sphere of solidified light, but its stars are at the underside of its first sky-sphere. The normal positions for stars are thus: (1) at the underside of the single/first sky-structure, (2) at the underside of the uppermost sky-structure or

---

[4] While there is subsequent mention of the place where the sun rises in the east in the normal course of the day (Rev. 7.2) and the ordinary experience of a harsh summer sun (Rev. 7.16), these do not show where the daytime sun is positioned in the cosmos.
[5] Wright, *Cosmology*, 42, 50.

(3) above a mid-level sky-structure. They are never in the God-space. This is the range of cosmological conceptions with which the implied hearer is plausibly familiar and from which its initial assumptions are drawn.

5.1.2 Stars in Revelation 1–3

The occurrences of ἀστήρ prior to the beginning of the sky-journey give no clues as to their normal position. As noted in Chapter 3 Rev. 1.9-20 operates within horizontal space on the island of Patmos. While in an ordinary place the seer enters into an extraordinary mode of seeing in which he encounters the extra-ordinary being before his ascent into the sky.[6] There is no upwards or downwards movement, nor indication of upwards or downwards gaze, so the visionary scene is created on the plane of the earth. Revelation assumes that its hearer understands this as a vision and goes on to explain the allegorical meaning of key elements in the vision: these 'stars' represent angels (Rev. 1.20).[7]

The occurrences of ἀστήρ in the seven letters likewise give no clues as to the normal position of stars. From Rev. 1.18–3.22 the narratorial function is temporarily transferred to another character (whom the hearer understands to be Jesus Christ) who dictates the seven letters with their various images. The character John does not see these trees, doors, pillars, temples and stars with his eyes; there is no camera eye that locates them within a frame. While the images of stars may appear fleetingly to the hearer, they lack narrative directions to locate them spatially and certainly give no indication of the normal position of stars within Revelation's cosmos. It is only the cosmic tour that can begin to locate stars.

5.1.3 No stars above the sky-structure

It is notable that as Revelation's seer emerges into the space above the sky-structure, and views the scene with a horizontal gaze, he does not observe astronomical or meteorological phenomena: no sun, moon or stars, no storerooms of hail, no clouds collecting rainwater from heavenly lakes. What is described are features of a royal courtroom and a holy sanctuary. The initial description of the scene (Rev. 4.2-11) does not include every significant feature and subsequent narration modifies the way the hearer views the scene (Rev. 5.1-14; 6.9-11; 7.9–8.5; 11.19; 15.2-8), notably adding the altar and surrounding myriads of worshipping angels. But despite the increasingly detailed construction of the scene, astronomical and meteorological entities are never added to it and there is no suggestion that their presence would be appropriate in this space, so the starting assumptions of the implied hearer are confirmed.

It has been argued by some that the eyes of the chimeric animals are actually stars, which would locate stars above the sky-structure. Carrington wrote that they

---

[6] Note *2 En.* 1.1–2.2; *3 Bar.* 1.3-7; *Apoc. Abr.* 10.1–11.6; *Asc. Isa.* 6.6-9.
[7] Koester, *Revelation*, 252–3.

'unquestionably recall Stars'[8] but Malina and Pilch go a step further, arguing that a heavenly creature 'filled with eyes' is literally a constellation.[9] I argued in Chapter 4 that the eyes of beings above are spoken of in terms of knowledge, power and glory, and often visualized as points of light or flame (Rev. 1.14; 2.18; 5.6; 19.12), but they are not called ἀστέρες. While Revelation refers to ἀστέρες they are never linked with ὀφθαλμοί or described as a component part of a being, not even of the heavenly woman of Revelation 12. This woman has a crown composed of stars, not a body composed of stars; likewise a body clothed with the sun, not composed of the sun. While points of light may be part of the visualization of the chimeric animals, the hearer does not understand them to be composed of ἀστέρες. The space above the sky-structure does not contain stars.

5.1.4 Assumed position of sun, moon and stars in Rev. 6.12-14

Revelation's story-space has expanded horizontally from the island of Patmos to the cities of Asia Minor and upwards from the surface of the earth to the underside of the sky-structure, where the door is seen, and has further incorporated a space above the sky-structure. The hearer is prepared for sun, moon and stars at the underside of a sky-structure (whether set into it or moving across it). It is also prepared for stars above a sky-structure, but only a mid-level sky-structure within multiply-layered skies – not above the single (or ultimate) sky-structure, and not in the God-space. Revelation has affirmed a single sky-structure and a God-space above it that is not inclusive of astronomical or meteorological phenomena. Within the story-space in which Revelation's narrative is operating, the only place that is appropriate to stars is the underside of the sky-structure.

In Rev. 6.12, the focalizer is coincident with the character John (καὶ εἶδον), still above the sky-structure with no indication of a change in location. But within the passage (Rev. 6.12-17) there is reference to γῆ, ὄρος and νῆσος, and various categories of earth-dwelling humans, all of which draw the gaze downward. Either the viewing position remains atop the sky-structure, with the gaze directed below it, or the increasing distance from καὶ εἶδον allows John to temporarily be forgotten and the focalizer to drift downward.[10] The focalizer's gaze is now showing ἥλιος, σελήνη and ἀστέρες, together with ὄρος and νῆσος, in the space extending from the surface of the earth to the underside of the sky-structure; the ἀστέρες are seen falling from the underside of the sky-structure to the surface of the earth. The assumed normal position of sun, moon and stars is at the underside of the sky-structure.

---

[8] Carrington, *Meaning*, 115. Capitalization original.
[9] Malina and Pilch, *Social-Science*, 75.
[10] Ureña suggests that John may perhaps have 'left heaven to witness first-hand what is taking place on earth' in Rev. 6.12-17. Ureña, *Narrative and Drama*, 37. I suggest that the truth in this is better expressed by the idea of the focalizer drifting to earth, while John's cosmic journey still has him in the hyper-heaven.

5.2 Four cosmic layers in the narrative (Rev. 9.1-11)

5.2.1 Narrator, focalizer, character

The character John has been above the sky-structure in the vicinity of the Throne from Rev. 4.2. There has been no indication of travel to another part of the cosmos, whether explicitly (as in Rev. 17.3; 21.10), by clear narrative inference (as in Rev. 4.2) or discerned through the audiovisual perspective (as in Rev. 10.1; 15.2). Through most of Revelation 4–6, the first-person verbs of perception made the focalizer coincident with the character John and maintained John's position above the sky-structure.[11] This remains true throughout Revelation 7–8 (note especially Rev. 7.9 and 8.2), and at 9.1 this is still John's position. The first-person καὶ εἶδον again indicates the visual perspective of the character John, making him coincident with focalizer and narrator. The viewing position is thus from above the sky-structure, gazing downward through it to see the star on earth. As noted in Chapter 4 the sky-structure is opaque when looking upward from below but clear when looking down from above.

While the earth-space initially extended from the Aegean Sea into Asia Minor, by this point in the narrative the story-space has expanded horizontally to encompass the entire earth, as in Rev. 7.1 the focalizer gazes from its hyper-elevated position in the cosmos down to the extremities of the earth at all four compass points. The star could be anywhere on this earth.[12]

5.2.2 What is the star, and where has it come from?

The narrator describes the sky-being as having fallen to earth. It is generally thought that because it is an actor in the narrative it is not truly a star,[13] and it is often thought

---

[11] In Rev. 6.12-17, the focalizer may temporarily drift downwards, away from John's location.

[12] The angel is at the place where the abyss opens up onto the earth. Revelation does not specify where that is. Sean Michael Ryan concludes that his Hearer-Construct One understands the opening of the abyss to be at the very edge of the earth, in fact at the far edge of the encircling Ὠκεανός, specifically at the north-west. Ryan, *Hearing*, 85–90. This is a plausible reading for his HC1, whose textual knowledge includes the biblical prophets, Psalms, Exodus and the Book of Watchers as the only extra-biblical apocalypse. However, the Book of Watchers has a very distinctive focus on placing cosmically significant locations at the horizontal extremities of earth and sky, while apocalyptic literature more generally has a stronger vertical focus. The Book of Dream Visions (*1 En.* 83–90) has abysses in the middle of the earth (*1 En.* 88.1; 90.24-26). Revelation's implied hearer is less strongly dominated by the particularities of *1 Enoch* 17 than is Ryan's HC1.

[13] Gebhardt, *Doctrine*, 36. Swete, *Apocalypse*, 112. Charles, *Revelation*, vol. 1, 238. Caird, *Commentary*, 118. Ford, *Revelation*, 143. Mounce, *Revelation*, 150. M. Eugene Boring, *Revelation, Interpretation* (Louisville: John Knox Press, 1989), 136. Geoffrey C. Bingham, *The Revelation of St John the Divine* (Blackwood: New Creation, 1993), 89. Murphy, *Fallen*, 242. Tim LaHaye, *Revelation Unveiled* (Grand Rapids: Zondervan, 1999), 168. Beale, *Revelation*, 491–3. Aune, *Revelation 6–16*, 625. Ben Witherington, *Revelation. New Cambridge Bible Commentary* (Cambridge: Cambridge University Press, 2003), 150. Brian K. Blount, *Revelation: A Commentary* (Louisville: Westminster John Knox Press, 2009), 173. Joseph L. Mangina, *Revelation, Brazos Theological Commentary on the Bible* (Grand Rapids: Brazos Press, 2010), 122. Ian A. Fair, *Conquering with Christ: A Commentary on the Book of Revelation* (Abilene: Abilene Christian University Press, 2011), 221. Gordon D. Fee, *Revelation: A New Commentary* (Eugene: Cascade, 2011), 125. Koester, *Revelation*, 455.

that because it is 'fallen' it is evil or in rebellion against God.[14] Neither of these conclusions is justified.

While a 'star' can be an allegorical stand-in for an angel in apocalyptic literature (*1 En.* 85–90), and indeed in Revelation (Rev. 1.9-20), apocalypses also allow that a star is fully capable of being an actor in its own right. That stars are living beings is also known in Greek culture. Even Aristotle, in arguing that the stars are not self-moving, feels the need to explain how this is possible *given that stars are living beings* (Aristotle, *De Caelo* 292a15-b19).[15] We saw in Chapter 3 that different cosmic spaces are inhabited by beings appropriate to that space and stars are beings appropriate to certain sky-spaces. Thus the Book of Watchers has an awesome space above its sky-structure inhabited by cherubim and watchers/angels, while the space just below the sky-structure is inhabited by stars who generally move across it in ordered ranks (*1 En.* 33.1-4) but are fully capable of conscious disobedience (*1 En.* 18.13-15; 21.3-6. See also Jude 14).

A star that is an actor in a narrative is not automatically an allegory for an angel. This can be clearly seen in the Book of Watchers, which distinguishes between sinful stars and sinful angels, both in the nature of their sin and the punishment each group receives. Stars sin when their horizontal journey deviates from the set itinerary (*1 En.* 18.13-15; 21.3-6. See also *1 En.* 80.4-6), while angels/watchers sin when they leave the sky-space that is their appropriate dwelling and descend to earth to live in the manner of an earth-being (*1 En.* 6.1-8; 12.4; 15.1-7). There is a place of imprisonment/punishment in which deviant stars are currently held and a separate place of imprisonment/punishment that will be used for rebellious angels/watchers in the eschaton (*1 En.* 18.11–19.1; *1 En.* 21.1-10).[16] Stars and angels are distinct beings and not automatically an allegory one for the other.

The narration of the punishment of deviant stars certainly has significance beyond astronomical speculation. In the Book of Watchers (*1 En.* 1–36) stars serve as an example to be emulated because they do not deviate from their path (οὐ παραβαίνουσιν τὴν ἰδίαν τάξιν) but move across the sky according to their role in the cosmic order (*1 En.* 2.1).[17] Yet ancient people who observed the night sky noted a small number of 'wandering' stars. The stars who deviate from their correct path then serve as a negative example (*1 En.* 18.12-16; *1 En.* 21.1-6).[18] The broader significance is effected specifically because the narrative is about stars.

---

[14] Caird, *Commentary*, 118. Ford, *Revelation*, 143. Harrington, *Revelation*, 109. Barr, *Tales*, 162. Beale, *Revelation*, 492. Blount, *Revelation*, 173. Fee, *Revelation*, 125. Waal, *Socio-Rhetorical*, 145. Peter S. Williamson, *Revelation. Catholic Commentary on Sacred Scripture* (Grand Rapids: Baker Academic, 2015), 167. Newton, *Pentecostal Commentary*, 183.

[15] See also Plato, *Laws* 898d–899b; *Timaeus* 39e–40b.

[16] *1 En.* 18.11–19.1 and *1 En.* 21.7–10 appear to give slightly different pictures. In the first, the one place currently holds the deviant stars and in the eschaton will also be used for the rebellious angels/watchers. In the second, these are two separate places and the place for angels/watchers is currently empty. Alternatively, Dillman argued that *1 En.* 18.11–19.1 could also be read as indicating two separate places, if 19.1 is taken as the explanation for 18.11 rather than the explanation for 18.12. August Dillmann, *Das Buch Henoch übersetzt und erklärt* (Leipzig: Vogel, 1853), 118. Either way, stars and angels/watchers are treated differently.

[17] Hahne, *Corruption*, 38.

[18] Hahne, *Corruption*, 166.

Similar themes are found in other parts of *1 Enoch*. The Astronomical Book (*1 En.* 72–82) is so named because it describes the orderly movements of sun, moon and stars in line with the cosmic cycles of days, months, seasons and years. Yet it also predicts a time when 'many of the chiefs of the stars shall make errors in respect to the orders given to them; they shall change their courses and functions and not appear during the seasons which have been prescribed for them'.[19] Several parts of *1 Enoch* are concerned with the obedience or disobedience of actual stars.

It is perplexing that the Animal Apocalypse (*1 En.* 85–90) is so often cited to show that stars are an allegory for angels.[20] It is of course true that the Animal Apocalypse depicts all animals and stars as an allegorical stand-in for something else – stars represent angels, sheep represent Israelites and other animals represent different categories of humans.[21] But the Animal Apocalypse does not show that the stars in *1 En.* 18.13-15; 21.3-6 are really angels any more than it shows that the sheep in *1 En.* 82.19 are really Israelites. Nor is the Animal Apocalypse cited as evidence that the πρόβατα of Rev. 18.13 are really Israelites.

Stars *can* represent angels and when they do there are indicators of this. Functioning as an actor in the narrative is not in itself an indicator that a star represents an angel. In fact, where Revelation presents a vision in which stars do represent angels (Rev. 1.9-20) the stars are not actors. Here the seer is in an ordinary place but viewing an extra-ordinary scene because he is seeing in an extra-ordinary manner. This is not a straightforward viewing of a place on Patmos. Elements in the scene are a visual representation of something else and explained so by the figure who acts in the role of interpreting angel. This device is employed a second time in Revelation 17, which is likewise not a straightforward viewing of a place in the desert but a visionary scene with elements that are interpreted as representing something else. Their interpretation in the visionary scenes is not an indication that they will carry the same meaning throughout Revelation. Horns may always connote power, but they do not always represent kings (Rev. 5.6; 17.12) and nor is Rev. 1.20 an indication that stars will always represent angels wherever they occur in Revelation (6.13; 8.10-11; 12; 9.1; 12.1, 4). Rev. 9.1-11 does not share the features of Rev. 1.9-20 that indicate that the star represents an angel. The implied hearer already knows that stars are powerful sky-beings and with this cosmological assumption feels no need to interpret the star as something else.

---

[19] *1 En.* 80.5-6. Translation Isaac, '1 (Ethiopic Apocalypse of) Enoch'.

[20] Charles, *Revelation*, vol. 1, 238. Charles H. Talbert, *The Apocalypse: A Reading of the Revelation of John* (Louisville: Westminster John Knox Press, 1994), 42. Beale, *Revelation*, 492. Aune, *Revelation 6–16*, 525. Blount, *Revelation*, 173.

[21] The Animal Apocalypse is a detailed allegory in which *every* described being stands for something else, and only in this context do stars stand in for angels/watchers. Lydia Gore-Jones, 'Animals, Humans, Angels and God: Animal Symbolism in the Historiography of the 'Animal Apocalypse' of 1 Enoch', *Journal for the Study of the Pseudepigrapha*, 24 (2015): 270–1. The 'star' of *1 En.* 86.1 is clearly the angel/Watcher named Asael, and the cattle are clearly humans. Annette Yoshiko Reed, *Fallen Angels and the History of Judaism and Christianity: The Reception of Enochic Literature* (Cambridge: Cambridge University Press, 2005), 74–5. Daniel C. Olson, *A New Reading of the Animal Apocalypse of 1 Enoch: All Nations Shall be Blessed*, Studia in Veteris Testamenti Pseudepigrapha, vol. 24 (Boston: Brill, 2013), 153.

While most commentators state that the star is really an angel or some other being, scholarship is more divided on whether it is 'fallen' in a moral sense or in rebellion against God.[22] Those who have argued that it is not in rebellion include Charles, Aune and Koester.[23] While Beale writes that the language of a 'falling star' is 'uniquely reserved for evil angels in the OT, Jewish writings, and the NT',[24] in fact in the Septuagint (LXX) πίπτω and ἀστήρ are never used together[25] and outside of Revelation they are used together in the New Testament only in Mt. 24.29 and Mk 13.25, neither of which conveys the sense of 'evil angels'.[26] This is also true of the two prior occurrences in Revelation (Rev. 6.13; 8.10).

None of the references to falling stars in the *Sibylline Oracles* suggest that the falling stars are in rebellion (*Sib. Or.* 2.202; 8.190; 8.341; 14.269); there is only the mockery of Memphis which imagined it was as high as the stars but has now fallen from its elevated status (*Sib. Or.* 5.72. See also *Pss. Sol.* 1.5). The only text that comes close to speaking of falling stars as evil is the *Testament of Solomon*. This asserts that stars are in fact firmly set in the firmament and do not fall, and the meteorological phenomenon that appears to be a falling star is in fact a falling demon (*T. Sol.* 20.14-17). But this unusual theory is not at play in Revelation, which does not describe the actor as having the visual appearance of a falling star (as though it may actually be a demon), instead the narrator shares its reliable knowledge that the visualized actor *is* a fallen star.

The normal place for stars is high above the earth, usually at the underside of a sky-structure, but the sight of a star falling to earth is also part of ordinary human experience and is not considered an indication that the star is evil or in rebellion

---

[22] Ian Fair comments, 'Considerable discussion has also been given to the phrase *a star that had fallen from the sky to the earth* … The discussion centers not on whether this star represents an angel, but on whether this angel is a good angel or a "demonic" angel' (emphasis in the original). Fair, *Conquering*, 221. Koester comments, 'The star that fell in 8:10 was a heavenly body, but the star in 9:1 is an angel … The disputed question is whether this star is a demonic being.' Koester, *Revelation*, 455.

[23] Charles, *Revelation*, vol. 1, 238. G. E. Ladd, *A Commentary on the Revelation of John* (Grand Rapids: Eerdmans, 1972), 129. Mounce, *Revelation*, 192. L. Morris, *The Revelation of St. John*, Tyndale New Testament Commentaries (Grand Rapids: Eerdmans, 1987), 127. Aune, *Revelation 6–16*, 525. Koester, *Revelation*, 455–6.

[24] Beale, *Revelation*, 492.

[25] Only Isa. 14.12 comes close to using πίπτω and ἀστήρ in conjunction. Here the words are ἐκπίπτω and ἑωσφόρος, translating the Hebrew הֵילֵל. It is possible but by no means certain that the ἑωσφόρος/הֵילֵל should be understood as a star. John D. W. Watts, *Isaiah 1–33. Word Biblical Commentary* (Nashville: Thomas Nelson, 2005), 264.

[26] Beale's citation of Lk. 10.18 is likewise misleading. Beale, *Revelation*, 492. The word used is not ἀστήρ but ἀστραπή. That Jesus sees Satan fall from οὐρανός in a way that visually resembles lightning falling to earth is not the same as saying that falling stars are evil or in rebellion against God.

Duvall agrees that the star of 9.1 is not evil or in rebellion against God, but also cites Jude 13 as possible support for the opposing view. J. Scott Duvall, *Revelation, Teach the Text*, ed. John H. Walton Mark L. Strauss (Grand Rapids: Baker 2014), 131. Note, however, that the stars in Jude 13 are ἀστέρες πλανῆται – *wandering stars* not *falling stars*. Appropriately, the Greek term ἀστήρ πλανήτης is the origin of the English word 'planet'.

Charles was essentially correct when he wrote, 'The participle πεπτωκότα does not convey when connected with ἀστέρα the idea of a fallen or lost angel … Its use here is due to the fact that ἀστήρ is used … It is different, however, when the subject of πίπτειν is not a star, but an angel.' Charles, *Revelation*, vol. 1, 238–9.

against God. It is not falling to earth that indicates a star is in rebellion against God but deviating in its horizontal movements across the cosmos (*1 En.* 18.13-15; 21.3-6; 80.4-6; Jude 14).[27]

While Revelation uses καταβαίνω to describe the downward movement of angels, the star's (completed) downward movement is described with πίπτω. The different verb is appropriate to a sky-being with different characteristics. Unsurprisingly for beings associated with the messenger function, ἄγγελοι are capable of vertical movement between cosmic layers, both downward and upward, unless prevented in some way (by divine decree or imprisonment, *1 En.* 14.5; by the exclusive nature of the gated upper space, *3 Bar.* 11-17). Stars are a different kind of sky-being, native to different sky-spaces, and not capable of controlled movement between higher and lower cosmic layers. There remains the possibility that they may fall or be pushed out of their high position and so downward movement of stars is appropriately described with πίπτω or σύρω (Rev. 6.13; 8.10; 9.1; 12.4).[28] Being incapable of controlled vertical movement, a star that has come to be on earth does not return to the skies. As the narrative of Rev. 9.1-11 calls its central actor an ἀστήρ, so it depicts the actor's movements in ways that are consistent with an ἀστήρ. Thus its downward movement from sky to earth is depicted with πίπτω rather than καταβαίνω. As a sky-being that has come to be on earth, its status as 'fallen' does not indicate that it is evil or in rebellion against God; it merely indicates that within the narrative of Rev. 9.1-11 it is behaving as a star.[29]

The fact that it is 'entrusted with the key' to a major cosmic region makes it highly unlikely that this being is in rebellion against God.[30] In the Revelation narrative rebellious beings are 'given' the power/means/permission to perform certain damaging actions (notably in Rev. 13) but control over the cosmos belongs to God and to select beings in absolute obedience to God (Rev. 7.1-3; 11.4-6; 20.1).[31]

The narrator-character's knowledge that this star had fallen ἐκ τοῦ οὐρανοῦ and εἰς τὴν γῆν possibly comes from the character's knowledge that a star's proper place is at the underside of the sky-structure, so a star upon the earth must have fallen to that position.[32] Alternatively, we may understand this as another example of the narrator

---

[27] *1 En.* 43.1-44.1 speaks of the righteous movements of stars, and in this context notes that a star can become lightning and never again dwell in the ranks of the stars. Nickelsburg and VanderKam, *1 Enoch 2*, 146. In this text a star falling to earth is part of the normal course of events and does not constitute rebellion against God or the godly cosmic order.
[28] Or in the case of something that closely resembles a falling star, with βάλλω (Rev. 8.8).
[29] In Rev. 20.1 an angel is seen καταβαίνοντα ἐκ τοῦ οὐρανοῦ holding the key to the abyss. This image and action has significant similarities with the star of Rev. 9.1-11, leading Charles to the reasonable conclusion that they are the same being. Charles, *Revelation*, vol. 1, 239. It should be noted, however, that in Rev. 9.1-11 the actor behaves as a star within the narrative, while in Rev. 20.1-3 the actor behaves as an angel, καταβαίνοντα ἐκ τοῦ οὐρανοῦ. Thus any identification between the two can only occur beyond the frames of each narrative.
[30] Aune, *Revelation 6-16*, 238.
[31] This is possibly also suggested in Rev. 9.14-16, if the four angels have the power to dry up the Euphrates to allow armies to cross, and in 16.4-6, if the angel of the waters has authority over the waters.
[32] 'The nuance of the perfect tense πεπτωκότα ('had fallen') is that John did not see the star fall but saw it after it had fallen and identifies it as such.' Beale, *Revelation*, 491.

knowing more than the character, even as they are coincident.[33] In either case, as a star that has fallen to earth, it has come from the underside of the sky-structure.

Excursus: What purpose the angel interpretation?

I have argued that within the frame of the narrative the star is truly a star; yet the narrative of Rev. 9.1-11 also has a more-than-literal significance in which this identity is not important. The parallel between the trumpets narrative and the bowls narrative is instructive in this regard. These narratives follow the same pattern. The first four strikes are against the four components of the cosmos-of-ordinary-human-experience: earth, sea, river, sky (Rev. 8.7-12; 16.2-9). That is to say, they are indirectly against humans. The fifth strike is directly against humans, specifically those who participate in the the kingdom of the beast (Rev. 9.1-11; 16.10-11). The sixth strike is against that kingdom itself, as actions are taken to facilitate the attack from the kings and armies beyond the Euphrates (Rev. 9.13-19; 16.12).[34]

The significance for the first real hearers is how the narrative of destructive judgement positions them in their social, political and economic context.[35] Pagan empire, and those who fully participate in it, are marked as under judgement from the greater cosmological and eschatological perspective. Those who fully participate in pagan empire do so in spite of the greater cosmological and eschatological reality which they should understand to be good reason for changing their worship and allegiance.

The trumpets narrative achieves this significance with Rev. 9.1-11 depicting a being from the sky opening the abyss, yet the parallel narrative achieves the same significance with no sky-being and no abyss. Beyond the frame of the narrative the sky-being is unimportant. At this level of signification it makes no difference whether the being exists at all, much less whether it is a star or an angel.

There is, perhaps, an intermediate level of signification, beyond the narrative frame of Rev. 9.1-11 but still within the narrative frame of Rev. 1.4–20.10. At this level it might be argued that the implied author intends the implied hearer to identify the sky-being of Rev. 9.1 with the sky-being of Rev. 20.1, connecting God's act of unleashing harm with

---

[33] This is more probable than Charles's solution that 'the Seer saw the angel just alighting'. Charles, *Revelation*, vol. 1, 238. Similarly, Lilje writes, 'A great meteor falls on the earth; as the meteor flashes past the seer he thinks he sees a great key.' Hans Lilje, *The Last Book of the Bible*, trans. Olive Wyon (Philadelphia: Fortress Press, 1957), 146. This is visually engaging and captures the drama but is not an accurate description of John's experience.

The chapter concludes with the narrator relating that rest of humankind did not repent at these judgements of partial destruction (Rev. 9.20). This is related not specifically as a description of what the character John saw but as factual information that the narrator passes to the narratee.

[34] Kings who are, perhaps, outside the οἰκουμένη. In a vain attempt to counter the kings from outside the οἰκουμένη the dragon, beast and false prophet gather all the kings from within the οἰκουμένη (Rev. 16.14). This recalls Isaiah's oracle against Babylon: 'Listen, an uproar of kingdoms, of nations gathering together! The LORD of hosts is mustering an army for battle. They come from a distant land, from the end of the heavens, the LORD and the weapons of his indignation, to destroy the whole earth' (Isa. 13.4-5 NRSV).

Within the οἰκουμένη there are fifty or sixty ἔθνη. Wan, *Contest*, 141.

[35] DeSilva, *Seeing*, 69–72.

God's act of restraining harm.[36] Identifying these two beings is not straightforward, as the actor of Rev. 9.1-11 is called ἀστήρ and behaves as an ἀστήρ within the narrative while the actor or Rev. 20.1-3 is called ἄγγελος and behaves as an ἄγγελος within the narrative. But if we identify these two beings then it may help to understand the star as an angel or the angel as a star.

This identification is possible at this intermediate level of signification, but for the narrative of Rev. 9.1-11 we gain nothing by saying that the star is really an angel. Within the frame of the narrative the star acts as a star and we only confuse the narrative by translating 'star' into 'angel'. Beyond the frame of the narrative, the significance of Rev. 9.1-11 for its first real hearers does not depend on the precise identity of this being or even the existence of this being. Translating 'star' into 'angel' clarifies neither the function nor the significance of the narrative.

5.2.3 Locating the abyss through narrative and visual perspective

While the star has come from the underside of the sky-structure, the viewing position is from its upper surface. The angel blowing the trumpet is seen relatively close to the focalizer with a horizontal gaze. The angle of gaze, however, is drawn downward by γῆ, φρέαρ and ἄβυσσος.

As noted in Chapter 3 an abyss is assumed to be downward from earth. Even in the Book of Watchers, which places the opening of the abyss at the western extremity of the earth (*1 En.* 17.8), the abyss still stretches downward from the plane of the earth. In some cosmic schemata any traditionally subterranean regions are relocated to the skies, and in one case this includes a region of imprisonment/punishment for powerful beings who threatened the cosmic order (*2 En.* 7.1-5; 18.3), but these texts do not have a place called 'abyss' located in the skies. The Greek texts cited by Malina and Pilch to support an abyss in the sky in fact speak of Hades or a θάλασσα, not an ἄβυσσος.[37]

A φρέαρ is likewise associated with the earth, commonly referring to an artificial well or well-shaft which has been dug into the ground and sometimes referring to a pit.[38] A φρέαρ τῆς ἀβύσσου is suggestive of the στόμα τῆς ἀβύσσου of *1 Enoch* 17.8, which is located at the western extremity of the cosmos on the plane of the earth. And while ἄβυσσος is not ᾅδης, it is also suggestive of the openings in the earth that lead to the subterranean Hades, known in Greek cultural stories and located on the landscape.[39]

In keeping with the nature of the earth and the sky-structure, the hearer gazes downward through the sky-structure to see the entrance of the abyss but does not see through the earth into the abyss itself.[40] The opacity of the earth conforms to

---

[36] Witherington, *Revelation*, 150. See also Mounce, *Revelation*, 150. Charles, *Revelation*, vol. 1, 239.
[37] Malina and Pilch, *Social-Science*, 133–5.
[38] BDAG. For a well that has been dug in the ground, see LXX Gen. 21.30; Num. 21.18. For a pit, see LXX Ps. 54.24; 1 Macc. 7.19.
[39] Strabo, *Geographica* 5.4.5; 14.1.11; Virgil, *Aeneid* 6.274. Dyer, 'The Four Horsemen', 138–40.
[40] Contra Barr, *Tales*, 115. Koester writes, 'John writes as a visionary, who sees heaven, earth, and the underworld from a cosmic vantage point.' Koester, *Revelation*, 457. This is true, although to be more

ordinary human experience in which a person on the earth cannot see downwards through it. In Chapter 4 we saw that when the audiovisual focalizer is located on earth it can gaze upward to see the sky-structure but cannot look through it to see the beings and objects in the hyper-heaven, though it may hear loud voices coming down from the hyper-heaven. A similar situation applies to the earth. The audiovisual focalizer can gaze downward to see the surface of the earth but cannot look through it to see the beings in the lower regions, though it may hear voices coming up from these regions. Thus the audiovisual focalizer, located in the hyper-heaven, *sees and hears* the angels around the Throne in Rev. 5.11-12 but only *hears* the response from the creatures under the earth in Rev. 5.13. The hearer's visual experience of the abyss is in keeping with its assumed position beneath the earth. For the same reason the entrance to the abyss cannot be in the sky of a southern hemisphere as argued by Malina and Pilch,[41] because the focalizer, here coincident with John high above Patmos, Ephesos and Smyrna, would be unable to gaze downward through the earth to observe actors and locations in the sky of a southern hemisphere.

In addition to the visual perspective, the logic of the narrative movements also locates the entrance of the abyss on the earth rather than somewhere in the sky. A star comes down from sky to earth and then opens the pit; the narrative inference is that there is a causal connection between these two actions, that is, moving from sky to earth put it in the correct position to open the pit. This locates the pit on the earth. Ordinarily, if the φρέαρ τῆς ἀβύσσου were opened by a star that would indicate a position in the sky, but this φρέαρ τῆς ἀβύσσου is opened specifically by a star that has moved from the sky to earth.

The narrative of Rev. 9.1-11 is operating on all four cosmic levels. The focalizer, coincident with the character John, is in the highest cosmic level above the sky-structure and views the initial action with a horizontal gaze: the angel blows the trumpet. This action initiates subsequent events, which draw the focalizer's gaze downward to lower cosmic levels. The focalizer's gaze shows a star on the earth, and the narrator shares the knowledge that it came to this position by falling from the underside of the sky-structure. The star is then seen opening a shaft that leads downward to a cosmic level beneath the earth, and beings from this place emerge up onto the plane of the earth. Revelation's narrative is not operating in three cosmic levels but in four, which I label hyper-heaven, sky-heaven, earth and under-earth.

Rev. 9.1-11 directly utilizes all four cosmic levels. In Chapter 6 we will see how Revelation 12 utilizes hyper-heaven, sky-heaven and earth. There I will show that distinguishing the two sky-spaces in which the narrative is operating gives a better understanding of the story that Revelation is telling.

---

precise, he sees *the entrance of* the underworld and the things that emerge from it. He sees smoke pouring from the shaft of the abyss but does not gaze into the abyss to see the fire that is creating this smoke.

[41] Malina and Pilch, *Social-Science*, 129–30, 33–5.

5.2.4 Nature of the abyss

In Chapter 3 we considered two broad concepts of an under-earth region: the appropriate dwelling-place for whatever remains of the human person following death and the region associated with a powerful threat to the cosmic order. The latter is called תְּהוֹם in the Hebrew scriptures and translated ἄβυσσος in the LXX. In these texts there is a sense that this watery place is itself is a potential threat to the cosmic order, though the threat may also come from its water-dwelling monsters. In Greek stories this concept is found under the name τάρταρος, where it is not associated with water and the potential threat comes from the beings that are imprisoned in it. An early Christian writing mentions the concept under the name ἄβυσσος (Lk. 8.31), yet there the concept appears closer to the τάρταρος of Greek stories, serving as a place of imprisonment for non-water-dwelling beings. Another early Christian writing mentions the concept under the name τάρταρος (2 Pet. 2.4). In its Greek form the Book of Watchers refers to this concept using both ἄβυσσος and τάρταρος but predominantly ἄβυσσος (*1 En.* 9.4; 17.7; 20.2; 21.7).

Most texts assume that there is only one place rightly called 'abyss' – the deepest Part of the cosmos.[42] But the Book of Dream Visions (*1 En.* 83–90) speaks of (a) a great, deep, watery abyss (*1 En.* 83.4, 7), (b) a narrow, deep, empty, dark abyss (*1 En.* 88.1) and (c) a fiery abyss, paired with a second fiery abyss (*1 En.* 90.24-27).[43] The first can be understood as the archaic concept of the primordial sea. The second is an extremely deep enclosure – a dark holding place for a powerful being as it awaits judgement (*1 En.* 90.21). The third is a deep place of fiery punishment/destruction following the judgement.[44]

For Revelation's implied hearer ἄβυσσος has a limited range of connotations. It always connotes threat but does so in two distinct ways: firstly, as a potential source of cosmic destruction, and secondly, as a prison for beings that could threaten the cosmic order, that is, as a place that *prevents* cosmic destruction. It tends to connote water but does not demand it.

Consider how Revelation's narrative uses and modifies the connotations of ἄβυσσος in the context of the trumpet strikes. The first trumpet initiates a strike against the earth, the second initiates a strike against the sea, the third against springs/rivers and the fourth against the (luminaries of the) sky. These four strikes against these four key parts of the cosmos-of-ordinary-human-experience function like the plagues of Egypt, partly punishing and partly calling to repentance those who still refuse to repent.[45] They are God's action against an ungodly human world expressed by partial destruction

---

[42] Some texts use ἄβυσσος in plural form but it is unlikely that this is a true plural. See *4 Ezra* 8.23; *Jub.* 2.2, 16; *Hist. Rech.* 4.9; *Pss. Sol.* 17.19; *1 Clem.* 20.5; 28.3; 59.3; Justin, *Dialogue with Trypho* 61, 129; Theophilus, *To Autolycus* 1.4, 7. Most likely this usage is only plural in the way that מַיִם and שָׁמַיִם are plural in the Hebrew scriptures and does not suggest separate watery deeps.

[43] See also *1 En.* 54.1-6; 'a deep valley burning with fire … and cast them into the abyss of complete condemnation'.

[44] See also *1 En.* 21.7, which has a cleft extending into 'the abyss, full of pillars of fire'.

[45] The four trumpets have struck the four components of the cosmos-of-human-experience: land, sea, rivers and sky. While the Genesis 1 cosmogony describes the cosmos in terms of three components, there is some precedent for considering river a significant entity alongside sea. Some Hebrew scriptures make a point of placing sea and river in parallel (Lev. 11.9; Ps. 24.1-2; 66.6; 89.26; Isa.

of the world around them, of which they are part.⁴⁶ This is confirmed by the eagle John sees after the fourth trumpet, flying below him at the midpoint between sky and earth, announcing three more woes to those dwelling further below on the earth.⁴⁷ The opening of the pit of the abyss occurs at this point in the narrative as a further strike by God upon those still refusing to repent but now directly upon them rather than upon their world. Therefore, whatever the creatures of the abyss 'really are' they are enacting God's own strike on the human world in a fairly direct way. They have a king over them, presumably leading them into war, who is the angel of the abyss named Destroyer. This king is not identified with any other character in Revelation.⁴⁸ For the implied hearer, who hears the narrative echoes of the plagues on Egypt, the name Destroyer suggests identity with הַמַּשְׁחִית of Exodus 12.23, and just as the Hebrews were exempted by the sign over the door so now the servants of God are exempted by the sign on their foreheads.⁴⁹

Although they are frightening and sickening in appearance and action, the creatures of the abyss play a similar role to the four winds held by four angels at the corners of the earth (Rev. 7.1-3) and also to the four angels bound at the Euphrates (Rev. 9.13-15).⁵⁰ The four winds remain in place until the right time for them to damage earth and sea, when God's faithful have received a mark of protection from God's action against the earth. The abyss of Rev. 9.1-11 then is functioning as a cosmic location of stored destruction/judgement.⁵¹

11.15; 50.2; Nah. 1.4; Hab. 3.8), as does the Ugaritic Baal Cycle ('The message of Yam, Your Lord, Of Your master Judge River' KTU 1.2 I 3-34). Greek mythology tells of Pontos, the primordial sea (or god of the primordial sea), and Okeanos, the primordial river (or god of the primordial river). This primordial river encircles the extremities of the earth and is also the source of the freshwater springs and rivers throughout the inhabited earth.

⁴⁶ Barr notes, 'Unlike the previous series, all of the trumpets are signals of doom and destruction … In one sense these trumpets are simply an amplification of the sixth seal, revelations of divine judgement on the earth.' Barr, *Tales*, 155.

⁴⁷ For μεσουράνημα see Sec. 5.4.

⁴⁸ It is not identified with satan, devil, dragon, serpent, beast, false prophet, prostitute, Babylon or unclean spirits. Charles writes, 'We have no means of identifying the angel of the abyss beyond the statement here.' Charles, *Revelation*, vol. 1, 245. Contra Beale, the implied hearer does not identify this king with the star of 9.1. Beale, *Revelation*, 492. Instead they see the star standing outside the abyss, opening it and standing aside as horrific creatures pour forth. It later understands that within the abyss was a being, their king, who leads them out of the abyss and across the earth. Koester notes, 'It seems unlikely that the angel with the key in 9:1 is the same as … the Destroyer in 9:11 since the first angel opens the abyss from outside, whereas the second angel is king of the locusts that are inside the abyss.' Koester, *Revelation*, 456.

⁴⁹ Rev. 9.11 reads ὄνομα αὐτῷ Ἑβραϊστὶ Ἀβαδδών, καὶ ἐν τῇ Ἑλληνικῇ ὄνομα ἔχει Ἀπολλύων. The Greek name means 'the destroyer' (BDAG). The alternate name, transliterated from the Hebrew אֲבַדּוֹן, means 'destruction' (BDB) and is often associated with death and the grave. In Exod. 12.23 the word is מַשְׁחִית, which also literally means 'destruction' or 'ruin' (BDAG), and yet is consistently translated into English as 'the destroyer' (or 'the Angel of Death', probably under the influence of 1 Chron. 21.15). It is translated 'the destruction' only in Young's Literal Translation. As in Exodus 12 so in Revelation 9 the narrative leaves ambiguity over whether this is a 'good' angel or a 'bad' angel, but its function is to serve God's purpose. See also Ps. 78.49 (77.49 LXX).

Bowman is incorrect to say, 'Both God's people and the pagan world undergo this *torment*, but with quite differing feelings and attitudes and hence with opposing results on character.' Bowman, *Drama*, 65.

⁵⁰ Apocalyptic literature does know of powerful beings who serve God but cannot fully control their violent tendencies. *Apoc. Abr.* 18.10.

⁵¹ See Sec. 3.5.

While ἄβυσσος tends to connote water it does not demand water and the descriptive elements of Rev. 9.1-11 instead connote something hot and airy. Besides the term ἄβυσσος itself there is no connection with the sea or with water of any kind.[52] The abyss is not directly described as fiery but the smoke rising from it like smoke from a furnace could imply that the abyss itself is like a furnace, connoting the concept of a cosmically deep fiery cavern.[53] But it is not depicted as a place of *fiery torment* or *punishment* or *destruction*.[54]

With the echoes of other apocalyptic literature, the abyss may be understood as a locked chamber beneath the earth, very large but limited in size and unconnected with any other cosmic location except through the shaft to the earth above. In Rev. 9.1-11 the abyss is not functioning as a hell-hole of rebellion against God but as a storehouse of divine judgement – a cosmic assurance of destructive judgement against unrighteous earth-dwellers. At least in this limited sense, Rev. 9.1-11 does with the abyss what Ps. 104.26 does with Leviathan; the threat to the cosmic order becomes part of the cosmic order, a creature under God.[55]

Later in the narrative, however, the abyss functions somewhat differently. The powerful being that emerges from the abyss in Rev. 11.7 is a θηρίον. When used of an extra-ordinary creature, this term always describes a being in rebellion against God – not only in LXX Daniel but throughout Revelation (Dan. 7.1–8.4; Rev. 11.7; 13.1-18; 14.9-11; 15.2; 16.2, 10, 13; 17.3-18; 19.19-20; 20.4, 10). Further, the abyssal Beast of Rev. 11.7 makes war. While the abyssal beings of Rev. 9 are described as looking and sounding like horses going to war, they are not described as *making war*. In Revelation, making war is always an act of rebellion against God, conducted against those who are obedient to God, either on earth or in the sky (Rev. 11.7; 12.7; 13.7; 16.14; 19.19; 20.8). The Beast of Rev. 11.7 is depicted killing righteous humans, which is an expansion on the comment that it makes war.

The Beast that comes up from the abyss is not functioning as an expression of God's destructive judgement. Its violence is not directed against the unsealed but against God's servants and ultimately against the world as God would wish it to be. Further, the Beast coming up from the sea in Rev. 13.1 recalls the earlier narration of the Beast coming up from the abyss, creating an association between the abyss and the sea.[56] This, in turn, recalls the concept of the watery abyss that threatens the cosmic order.[57]

While the inside of the abyss is never described, Revelation's narrative assumes (a) an abyss as a huge, deep, subterranean cavity, the cosmic storehouse of (powerful

---

[52] 'So far as the ἄβυσσος is conceived as a surging, imprisoned flood, it has no connection with our text.' Charles, *Revelation*, vol. 1, 240.
[53] In *Apoc. Abr.* 15.1 the smoke like that of a furnace implies a *fire* like that of a furnace. For a fiery cavern, see *Apoc. Abr.* 31.3.
[54] Contra Beale, the narrative does not describe the abyss as a place where demons are tormented. Beale, *Revelation*, 493.
[55] There is also a parallel with the Greek story in which Zeus recruits the Hekatoncheires and Kyklopes, releasing them from Tartaros to help him defeat the Titans and establish the civilized cosmic order. Robin Hard, *The Routledge Handbook of Greek Mythology* (London: Routledge, 2004), 68–9.
[56] Although this θηρίον is grammatically anarthrous the hearer naturally associates this image with the earlier image of a warlike beast rising from the abyss.
[57] But contra Bousset, it does not identify the sea as the abyss. Bousset, *Offenbarung*, 358.

beings that are) a means of punishment for unrighteous humans and (b) an abyss as a watery, chaotic region at the deepest level of the cosmos, characterized by martial rebellion against the good order and true peace of the cosmos as a whole. Though contradictory, these cosmic features are somehow the one abyss. The narrative description is insufficient to create a second abyss (with different characteristics), and thus the hearer's understanding of the abyss must be expanded. It is full of beings with the potential to emerge onto the earth and cause great harm, not only in the sense that it is a storeroom for the means of God's destructive judgement but now also in the sense that it is the native dwelling of a powerful enemy of God's people. It is a bounded, lockable space controlled by God (Rev. 9.1-2; 20.1-3), yet also a deep, chaotic region from which may emerge a powerful threat to the godly order of the cosmos. It is the abyss that most challenges the coherence of Revelation's imagined cosmography.

5.2.5 The abyss and Hades

Some scholarship maintains a distinction between Hades and the abyss, while other scholarship treats Revelation's ᾅδης and ἄβυσσος as essentially synonymous.[58] As noted previously, Sean Michael Ryan defines a hearer-construct (Hearer-Construct One) that in many ways is similar to the implied hearer of Revelation. His Hearer-Construct One is familiar with texts including Isaiah, Jeremiah, Ezekiel, Daniel and notably Psalms, and on that basis Ryan argues that this hearer makes a close connection between Hades and the abyss, even to the point where there is no distinction between the two.[59] Contrary to Ryan, a hearer familiar with these texts would not fail to distinguish between Hades and the abyss. There may be a loose poetic association between them implied by Ps. 18.4-5 (17.5-6 LXX), in which the cords of death/Sheol are parallel to the *torrents* of destruction, and by Ps. 88.3-7 (87.4-8 LXX) in which the Psalmist laments that the state of his life is so bad that he is close to the grave/Sheol, concluding 'you overwhelm me with all your *waves*'. But these loose poetic associations are not enough to lose the distinction between Sheol/Hades and the watery deep/abyss, even for Ryan's hearer-construct. While there is occasional use of ἄβυσσος for the subterranean realm of the dead (Ps. 70.21 LXX; Romans 10.7), the distinction between ἄβυσσος and ᾅδης is usually maintained. The distinction is part of the starting assumptions of Revelation's implied hearer and helps it recognize the distinction that Revelation maintains between the narrative functions of Hades and the narrative functions of the abyss. Revelation's abyss has conflicting characteristics but it never serves as the dwelling place of humans, whether living or deceased, righteous or unrighteous. For its part, Hades never serves as the dwelling place of powerful beings, either as their natural home or a place to which they have been confined. Hades and the abyss remain distinct.

---

[58] The two are treated as synonymous in Ryan, *Hearing*, 86–8. Mangina, *Revelation*, 122. Malina and Pilch, *Social-Science*, 129–30. J. J. Elar, *The Apocalypse the Antichrist and the End* (London: Burns and Oates, 1906), 74.

[59] Ryan, *Hearing*, 86–8.

While Revelation depicts a being called 'Hades' moving through a higher cosmic level, as a cosmic region Hades remains under the earth. Unlike the hyper-heaven, sky-heaven, earth and abyss, Revelation's Hades is not shown in spatial relationship with other cosmic locations through visual narrative. Rev. 1.18 refers to Hades within the direct speech of Jesus Christ; it is not shown through the audiovisual perspective of the focalizer or located through narrative movements. Rev. 20.13 briefly describes an action of Hades in a context in which there is no longer any earth or skies for spatial relationships to exist. And while the 'Hades' of Rev. 6.8 is seen and narrated, this Hades is not the cosmic region but a being or personification. We recognize this because:

1. Hades is grouped with beings that represent concepts or actions (conquest, war, hardship, killing, death), not with beings that function as part of the cosmic structure (as Leviathan arguably does in *Apoc. Abr.* 21.4).
2. Hades is moving. Hades, as the place in which dead people dwell, does not move in any other text, and its movement here is an additional reason why the implied hearer understands that this is something other than a cosmic region. One text has something called Hades which is simultaneously a being and the place where dead people dwell, but even there it does not move (*3 Bar.* 5 Greek).

With the dwelling-place of the dead not positioned in the cosmic structure through the visual narrative, the hearer's assumption of a subterranean Hades is allowed to persist. Hades is located under the earth in all cosmic pictures with which the hearer may be familiar, except those few that dispense with an underworld entirely and place *all* traditionally under-earth locations in the skies.[60] Revelation, however, has not dispensed with the underworld as it retains the subterranean abyss and thus the hearer's assumption of the subterranean Hades.

In comparison with the other great cosmic regions, Revelation shows relatively little interest in Hades. Death is a reality in the cosmos and so Hades is assumed to exist also. The assumptions concerning Sheol/Hades that come to the hearer from the Hebrew scriptures and their Greek-language equivalents are neither challenged nor revised by Revelation. While some other apocalypses give Sheol/Hades a positive slant for the righteous, or a negative slant for the unrighteous, Revelation's Hades is simply the neutral place of the ordinary human dead (righteous and unrighteous) assumed by those whose cosmic picture is shaped by the Hebrew scriptures and the common ideas they share with most apocalypses, early Christian writings and Greek cultural stories.[61] Revelation's under-earth level must then be understood as a set of two: Hades and the abyss.

---

[60] See Sec. 3.3.2.
[61] There is some insight in Boll's comment that the base of the heavenly alter is equivalent to the chambers of souls in *4 Ezra* 7, but it is misleading to say that Revelation therefore has Hades in heaven. Boll, *Aus der Offenbarung Johannis*, 35. At the base of the alter is the life-blood (souls) of the sacrificial victims, that is, those who were executed for their faithful witness (see Sec. 4.4.2). When Revelation uses the term ᾅδης it speaks of the current dwelling of the righteous dead more generally, along with the unrighteous dead (Rev. 20.13).

5.3 The Throne and the sub-Throne cosmos (Rev. 5.6-14)

In previous sections I have distinguished the four cosmic levels: hyper-heaven, sky-heaven, earth and the under-earth regions. With the four levels distinguished in this way we can now return to Rev. 5.6-14 to see how they play a role in the narrative. The character John has been above the sky-structure from Rev. 4.2 and first-person verbs of perception have maintained the coincidence of character and focalizer. The hearer shares John's visual perception (καὶ εἶδον) of the Lamb moving to the Throne and taking the scroll, where the elders and chimeric animals respond by falling down in worship.[62] The aural part of their response is narrated without verbs of perception but there is no indication to the hearer of a change in the audiovisual perspective. It is explicitly through John's perception (εἶδον καὶ ἤκουσα) that the subsequent liturgical response from the surrounding myriads is seen and heard.

A discernable shift in perception comes when the liturgy is joined by πᾶν κτίσμα ὃ ἐν τῷ οὐρανῷ καὶ ἐπὶ τῆς γῆς καὶ ὑποκάτω τῆς γῆς καὶ ἐπὶ τῆς θαλάσσης (Rev. 5.13). Uniquely in John's first sky-journey (Rev. 4.2-9.21) the focalizer perceives this through hearing (ἤκουσα) but not through sight.[63] In part the shift in perception is required by the participation of the beings under the earth, who cannot be seen from above due to the opacity of the earth. But it is also a natural shift if the focalizer's gaze is directed horizontally and does not show sights in lower cosmic levels.

The liturgical contribution of this latter grouping is experienced differently from the liturgical contributions of the beings that have been positioned around the Throne, whether near (Rev. 5.8-10) or further back (Rev. 5.11-12). Combined with the nature of the liturgical back-and-forth, this gives the impression that just as every being above the sky-structure has voiced its praise, now every creature below the sky-structure responds. This means that in Rev. 5.13 the creatures ἐν τῷ οὐρανῷ are not in the Throne-space but at the underside of the sky-structure.[64] Rev. 5.13 does not ennumerate the species that participate in the liturgy, but τὰ ἐν αὐτοῖς πάντα indicates that they are the creatures that normally dwell in these spaces. Guided by the rest of Revelation, and by familiar literature including Genesis 1, the creatures on earth include horses and sheep and other animals, creatures in the sea include fish and other marine animals and creatures in the οὐρανός include sun, moon, stars and probably

---

[62] Bryan observes that in apocalyptic literature chimeric creatures represent the destruction of created boundaries and a threat to cosmic order, but this does not hold true for creatures native to the divine realm. Bryan, *Cosmos*, 211.

[63] The combined audiovisual perception is sometimes conveyed by the phrase εἶδον καὶ ἤκουσα (Rev. 5.11; 8.13). In Rev. 6.1-8 it is conveyed through the hearing of voices from specific positions within the Throne-space and by the parallel narration suggesting that John saw the opening of each seal (Rev. 6.1, 3, 5, 7).

[64] Which creatures of the cosmos are included in v. 14 is considered by Charles. He lists four options: (a) the birds of the air, and all creatures of earth, under-earth and sea; (b) the sun, moon and stars of the sky, plus all creatures of earth, under-earth and sea; (c) all creatures of the greater cosmos excluding the four animals and twenty-four elders; and (d) all creatures of the greater cosmos. Charles, *Revelation*, vol. 1, 150. A visual-narrative reading with a cosmological focus shows that it is both (a) and (b), including the sun, moon, and stars that dwell at the underside of the sky-structure, together with the large birds that fly at the midpoint between the sky-structure and the earth, plus all creatures of earth, under-earth and sea.

also the large birds that fly through the air at the midpoint between the earth and the sky-structure (Rev. 8.13; 19.17; Gen. 1.14-25. See also Philo, *De gigantibus* 6-8).[65] It is very difficult to know which under-earth creatures are recruited into the liturgy but it is rhetorically effective that all sub-Throne regions are heard responding to the Throne-space.[66] In creating a division between the Throne-space and the sub-Throne regions, Rev. 5.6-14 anticipates what we will find in the conflict and contest narratives of Revelation 12.[67] There we will see the same event narrated across hyper-heaven, sky-heaven and earth, but in such a way that the event is characterized differently in the hyper-heaven than it is in the lower spaces.

5.4 Mid-heaven

In describing the cosmic regions, I have so far given only cursory attention to the μεσουράνημα (Rev. 8.13; 14.6; 19.17). This 'mid-heaven' is most commonly understood as the midpoint between east and west – the cosmic apex or central section of the sky.[68] There is good reason for this, based on the use of μεσουράνημα or similar words in other texts: the *Sybilline Oracles* speaks of the μέσος οὐρανός as the part of the sky where certain constellations are found (*Sib. Or.* 5.208);[69] Strabo's *Geographica* uses μεσουράνησις for the high point of the moon's orbit over the earth and the verb μεσουρανέω to describe the movement of the sun as it reaches its highest point between rising and setting (Strabo, *Geographica* 1.3.11; 2.5.1); and *Moralia* uses μεσουρανοῦν and ἀντιμεσουρανοῦν respectively for the position of the sun at midday and midnight. Similarly, Josh. 10.13 LXX reports καὶ ἔστη ὁ ἥλιος κατὰ μέσον τοῦ οὐρανοῦ.[70]

This use of very similar terms would be good reason to understand the μεσουράνημα as the cosmic apex were it not for the distinctly different use of this mid-heaven in Revelation's narrative. The mid-heaven is never designated as the location of sun, moon or stars, which would indicate a position at the underside of the sky-structure. Nor is it the location of objects or structures, which could suggest a position atop the sky-structure or on the earth. Rather, it is the location of beings that are in the act of flying (πέτομαι), specifically an angel (Rev. 14.6), an extra-ordinary bird (Rev. 8.13) and ordinary birds (Rev. 19.17). It is not the abode of beings that have no need of wings (sun, moon, stars or the wingless dragon). A distinct characteristic of mid-heaven, then, is its presentation as a region in which beings fly but do not stand. Beings are seen

---

[65] The beings in the Throne-space ascribe seven terms of glory and power to the Lamb, while the creatures ἐν τῷ οὐρανῷ καὶ ἐπὶ τῆς γῆς καὶ ὑποκάτω τῆς γῆς καὶ ἐπὶ τῆς θαλάσσης ascribe four terms of glory and power both to the Lamb and to the one seated on the Throne. Scholars often hold that the number four symbolizes the creation, which would support the perception that these regions are all below the sky-structure. Beale, *Revelation*, 59. See also Ford, *Revelation*, 95.
[66] DeSilva, *Seeing*, 262.
[67] See also *2 Bar.* 59.3: 'the heavens which are under the throne of the Mighty One'.
[68] Gebhardt, *Doctrine*, 43. Swete, *Apocalypse*, 111. Charles, *Revelation*, vol. 1, 237. Ford, *Revelation*, 139-40. Aune, *Revelation 6-16*, 523. Koester, *Revelation*, 451. Malina and Pilch, *Social-Science*, 86.
[69] See also Hesiod, *Works and Days* 609: Εὖτ' ἂν δ' Ὠρίων καὶ Σείριος ἐς μέσον ἔλθῃ οὐρανόν.
[70] Malina and Pilch describe the mid-heaven as the midway point between east and west along the line of the ecliptic. Malina and Pilch, *Social-Science*, 39, 94, 128, 204.

standing on the hyper-heaven (Rev. 5.6; 7.9, 11; 8.2, 3; 15.2) and on the earth (Rev. 7.1; 10.5, 8; 11.11; 12.18) and even in the sky-heaven (12.4; 19.17) but never in mid-heaven. The narrative assumes that the mid-heaven has no surface on which an object may rest or a being may stand.

The narrative treats mid-heaven as the region of air at the midpoint between earth and sky-heaven. In all three instances the beings in the mid-heaven have a function closely connected with humans on earth: in Rev. 8.13 and 14.6 they shout a message down to those dwelling on earth, while in Rev. 19.17 the birds of mid-heaven are invited down to the earth to eat the corpses of military casualties. In the Hebrew scriptures and the Septuagint the most frequently noted carrion birds are eagles/vultures – large birds that in ordinary human experience are seen flying at a great height above the earth, though notably lower than the sun and moon. There are fewer mentions of crows/ravens, but the Epistle of Jeremiah speaks of them ἀνὰ μέσον τοῦ οὐρανοῦ καὶ τῆς γῆς (Ep. Jer. 54).[71] Rev. 19.17 is calling to the birds that fly at the midpoint between earth and sky, inviting them to go down to earth.[72]

Beings at the midpoint between sky and earth are appropriate broadcasters of a message that comes from sky to earth. In this sense there is truth in Hansen's description of mid-heaven as one of the 'middle spaces that serve as the site of transversals across the boundaries'.[73] While flying horizontally across the mid-heaven, the beings at this level facilitate the vertical movement of messages from the skies above to the earth below.[74] Rather than a cosmic tier in its own right, the μεσουράνημα is a kind of half-level at the midpoint between οὐρανός and γῆ.

5.5 Conclusion: The fourfold cosmos

This chapter has shown how the narrative of Rev. 9.1-11 operates across the four cosmic levels. The upper sky-space, the lower sky-space, the earth-space and the under-earth-space were each utilized as part of the story-space. Ancient conceptions held that each cosmic space has its own native inhabitants with distinct characteristics appropriate to the space.[75] In Rev. 9.1-11 a being from the lower sky-space was employed as the central actor in the narrative in ways consistent with its nature as a being from that space.

---

[71] See also *1 En.* 90.2: 'I saw with my own eyes all the birds of heaven – eagles, vultures, kites, and ravens – coming; the eagles were the ones who were leading all the birds; and they began to eat those sheep, to dig out their eyes, and to eat their flesh.' Translation Isaac, '1 (Ethiopic Apocalypse of) Enoch'. The Animal Apocalypse uses these 'birds of heaven' to allegorically represent the destructive activity of the Macedonian armies. Nickelsburg, *1 Enoch 1*, 395.

[72] Thus we are not left to wonder, with Boll, why only the birds from the middle section of the sky are called down to earth. Boll, *Aus der Offenbarung Johannis*, 38. Rather, *all carrion birds* are called down to earth, and carrion birds are understood to fly at the midpoint between earth and sky.

[73] Hansen, *Silence*, 38.

[74] Ascent and descent through the cosmic layers does not involve πέτομαι or πτέρυγες, but remaining in mid-heaven or moving across mid-heaven does involve πέτομαι and/or πτέρυγες.

[75] 'It is necessarily true that the universe [κόσμος] must be filled with living things in all its parts, since every one of its primary and elementary portions contains its appropriate animals and such as are consistent with its nature: the earth containing terrestrial animals, the sea and the rivers containing aquatic animals … and the heaven [οὐρανός] containing the stars.' Philo, *De gigantibus* 6–8. Translation Yonge, *Philo*. See also 1 Cor. 15.39-41.

We also saw that the lowest cosmic space is a set of two: Hades and the abyss. As the cosmic journey does not include any stops in the underworld, and the opacity of the earth prevents the gaze from seeing into the underworld from above, the focalizer's gaze showed only the entrance to the abyss where it opens up onto the earth. Thus the under-earth space is less clearly defined than other spaces, but the respective roles of Hades and the abyss showed the distinction between them. While there is no overlap between the roles of Hades and the abyss, in certain respects the assumed nature of the abyss in some parts of the narrative differs from its assumed nature in other parts of the narrative. In Chapter 7 we will see that Koester is correct to distinguish Hades, the abyss and the lake of fire as three distinct regions.[76]

Finally, as we returned to Rev. 5.6-14 we saw that this spatial perspective aids our understanding of the universal liturgy. We observed a distinction between the hyper-heaven and all other cosmic tiers, as the responsive liturgy begins in the Throne-space and is joined by all beings in the sub-Throne cosmos. This includes the beings in the sky-heaven, who are grouped with the beings of earth and sea in their response to the beings of the hyper-heaven.

While the meaning and nature of Revelation's heaven has often captured scholarly attention, with contributions from Hermann Gebhardt, G. B. Caird, Walter Wink, Anthony Gwyther, Gert Jordaan and others, the scholarly discussion has always assumed a single heaven.[77] The four-tiered cosmic structure changes that conversation. As the narrative operates in the four-tiered structure it defines two spaces that are both called οὐρανός, one of which is home to the beings called stars, neither of which can be dismissed as 'just the sky'. In the following chapters we will see how Revelation differently characterizes the sky-heaven and hyper-heaven and what this four-tiered structure means for cosmic eschatology, rhetorical cosmology and the meaning of 'heaven'.

The Book of Watchers has an upper sky-space that is the native home of awesome beings called cherubim and watchers/angels and a lower sky-space that is the native home of stars, who move across the cosmos in ordered ranks (1 En. 33.1-4) but are also capable of individual acts of rebellion (1 En. 18.13-15; 21.3-6. See also 1 En. 80.4-6; Jude 14). For stars as living beings in their appropriate cosmic space see also Plato, Laws, 898d–899b; Timaeus 39e–40b; Aristotle, De Caelo 292a15-b19.

[76] Koester, Revelation, 456. See Sec. 7.3.
[77] Gebhardt, Doctrine, 50–1. Caird, Commentary, 62. Wink, Naming, 119. Gwyther, 'New Jerusalem Versus Babylon', 48–50. Jordaan, 'Cosmology', 3. See also Moo, 'The Sea', 152, n. 9.

6

The distinct natures of the two sky-spaces (Rev. 12)

This chapter will show how Revelation's narrative operates in two distinct sky-spaces, one above the sky-structure and one below, imbuing each space with distinct characteristics. The space at the underside of the sky-structure, which I have called sky-heaven, is seen as a site of conflict. But the space above the sky-structure, which I have called hyper-heaven, is established as a consistently harmonious space. This is Revelation's God-space, the space defined in relation to the Throne and characterized by full recognition of authority of the one who sits on the Throne.[1]

Existing scholarship holds that this picture of the God-space is not consistent. The dragon pulling down stars, opposing armies of angels battling in the οὐρανός, and Satan standing in front of the Throne are commonly held to introduce elements of evil/rebellion.[2] Even Gwyther, who defines heaven as the aspect of reality in which 'God lives and reigns' and 'the truth of God is believed and practised',[3] comments that 'heaven was a battleground in which competing claims were played out'.[4] Contrary to the prevailing scholarly view, this chapter argues that the narrative of Revelation 12 operates across the two sky-spaces in such a way that the harmony of the God-space is maintained, affirming the implied hearer's expectation of a God-space free of rebellion.

---

[1] Minear speaks of 'the throne-heaven'. Paul S. Minear, *I Saw a New Earth: An Introduction to the Visions of the Apocalypse* (Washington: Corpus Books, 1968), 273.

[2] Gebhardt defines heaven as 'the region of being beyond time and space' and here locates 'the travail of the woman, the birth and taking away of the child, Michael's struggle with and conquest over the dragon'. Gebhardt, *Doctrine*, 50–1. Resseguie describes heaven as 'the dwelling place of God', 'the place where God's throne is found', yet also as a place where 'good and evil coexist' and the location of military conflict between Michael and Satan. Resseguie, *Revelation Unsealed*, 85–6. Beale speaks of 'the spiritual, timeless dimension of God's heavenly council' and locates the woman and dragon in this same heaven. Beale, *Revelation*, 319, 625. Koester speaks of the dragon operating in the same heaven where the child is enthroned. Koester, *Revelation*, 562. Witherington distinguishes between 'sky' and 'heaven', locating the woman, dragon and angelic war in heaven. Witherington, *Revelation*, 167, 70. See also Swete, *Apocalypse*, 150. Caird, *Commentary*, 62. Mounce, *Revelation*, 235. Wink, *Naming*, 119. Barnett, *Apocalypse*, 89. Harrington, *Revelation*, 78. J. Nelson Kraybill, *Apocalypse and Allegiance: Worship, Politics, and Devotion in the Book of Revelation* (Grand Rapids: Brazos Press, 2010), 74. Jordaan, 'Cosmology', 3. John Christopher Thomas and Frank D. Macchia, *Revelation, The Two Horizons New Testament Commentary* (Grand Rapids: Eerdmans, 2016), 220. Newton, *Pentecostal Commentary*, 227.

[3] Gwyther, 'New Jerusalem Versus Babylon', 48.

[4] Gwyther, 'New Jerusalem Versus Babylon', 50.

6.1 Narrator, focalizer, character

6.1.1 There and back again

While the narrative of John's cosmic journey has him above the sky-sheet from Rev. 4.2 to 9.21, from 10.1 the visual and aural perspective of the focalizer, and its coincidence with the character John, demonstrate that at this stage of his journey he is on earth. The implied author is able to shift the seer to earth at this point without explanation because the implied hearer is prepared for a there-and-back-again cosmic journey.

The return to earth is a standard feature of the sky-journey narrative, often at the conclusion of a simple there-and-back-again journey (*Apoc. Abr.* 30.1; *3 Bar.* 16.2; *T. Levi* 5.7; *Asc. Isa.* 11.35), but Enochic literature features a multi-stage journey with more than one moment of departure. This feature of Enochic literature exists for two reasons. First, as expansions on Gen. 5.24, stories of Enoch's journey into the skies must conclude with Enoch in the skies, but for Enoch to share his heavenly knowledge he must return to earth. This conundrum is resolved by a double sky-journey: Enoch travels into the skies, learns heavenly knowledge, returns to earth to share this heavenly knowledge (*1 En.* 81.5; *2 En.* 38), then returns to the skies to take up permanent residence (*1 En.* 70; 81.6; *2 En.* 67; 68.1-3).[5] The second reason is the composite nature of *1 Enoch* which means that the first sky-journey is retold with an additional moment of departure (*1 En.* 14.8; 39.1). Shared knowledge of multi-stage cosmic journeys allows Revelation's implied author to shift the seer's position without explanation.

In cosmic journey narratives these shifts in position are usually narrated, but unnarrated shifts also occur. Nickelsburg and VanderKam note such a shift in *1 En.* 43.1. The Book of Watchers (*1 En.* 1–36) features a cosmic journey that serves as a prototype for a similar journey in the Book of Parables (*1 En.* 37–71), but where the earlier journey narrates movement from the throne room to a new location the Book of Parables simply describes the new location: 'Enoch, without any indication of movement, is simply "there".'[6]

Another unnarrated relocation occurs in Revelation 12, where it is not the seer who is relocated but the woman and/or dragon. This woman is in the sky in Rev. 12.1 and flees into the earthly wilderness in 12.6.[7] Her move to earth may happen somewhere between v. 1 and v. 6, as assumed by Barr, in which case it is implied and not narrated.[8]

---

[5] 'The passage as interpreted here recounts Enoch's final assumption after he has returned to earth from his first ascent (described in 39:3) and, necessarily, after he has transmitted the account of his heavenly and cosmic journeys and visions contained in the Parables (cf. 81:5–82:3).' Nickelsburg and VanderKam, *1 Enoch 2*, 317.

[6] Nickelsburg and VanderKam, *1 Enoch 2*, 143.

[7] It is the 'earthly' wilderness in terms of its vertical positioning within story-space. However, Minear points out that there is also a sense in which 'the earth' and 'the wilderness' are distinct realities. Minear, 'The Cosmology', 30.

[8] Barr, *Tales*, 213. Charles wrote, 'In [verse] 4 a descent to earth on the part of the woman and the Dragon is silently presupposed.' Charles, *Revelation*, vol. 1, 314. See also Ford, *Revelation*, 200. Aune, *Revelation 6–16*, 686.

Alternatively, v. 6 may be taken as a narration of her movement from the sky directly to the wilderness on earth. But this reading does not eliminate the unnarrated move because the second telling (Rev. 12.13-14) has her on earth prior to her horizontal flight into the wilderness. Thus there is an unnarrated relocation, at least in the second telling.

6.1.2 Earthly position in Revelation 10

Commentators recognize that Rev. 10.1 has John on earth[9] or viewing events as if he were on earth.[10] One commentator expressed the alternative opinion that John is still in the skies at the beginning of the chapter but moves to earth in Rev. 10.9 when 'the seer in his rapture quits his position at the door of heaven (iv. 1), and places himself before the great Angel whose feet rest on sea and land'.[11] Why is it so widely agreed that John shifts to earth in Revelation 10? Generally, commentators give little explanation of why they believe this. It appears that Revelation has conveyed the shift to these readers in subtle ways that they may not consciously recognize. I believe they are correct to see this shift in Revelation 10 (and in v. 1 rather than v. 9) for several reasons: the phrase καταβαίνοντα ἐκ τοῦ οὐρανοῦ, the implied visual perspective, the aural perspective, the narrative's easy fit to an earthly position, John's horizontal movement and the prophetic commissioning.

When John sees an enormous angel καταβαίνοντα ἐκ τοῦ οὐρανοῦ the phrase itself implies a viewing position on earth, gazing upwards to see the descending angel. Unlike the English words 'come' and 'go', the verb καταβαίνω does not indicate the position of the viewer relative to the movement. But καταβαίνοντα/καταβαίνουσαν ἐκ τοῦ οὐρανοῦ occurs only when John is on earth (Rev. 18.1; 20.1; 21.2, 10). Even when John's position is atop a high mountain (Rev. 21.10) he is still below the sky-structure, having to look upward as the city begins to descend from above. This use of καταβαίνοντα/καταβαίνουσαν ἐκ τοῦ οὐρανοῦ is appropriate as it is suggestive of the hearer's ordinary viewing position as a human being on earth, having to look upward to see something in the sky or coming down from the sky.

Further to this, the content of the scene creates an implied visual perspective from a position on earth. The vividness of 'his right foot on the sea and his left foot on the earth' brings the camera eye close to this position, which then allows the aesthetically fitting image of the huge being reaching a hand up to the sky. Gazing upward to see his hand reaching the sky impresses on the hearer a sense of his immense size and power. Viewing the scene from above would be far less effective. In itself, the visual perspective implied by the content only means that the focalizer is on earth and not necessarily the character John. But combined with εἶδον καταβαίνοντα ἐκ τοῦ οὐρανοῦ it strengthens the sense that John is on earth.

---

[9] Isbon T. Beckwith, *The Apocalypse of John: Studies in Introduction with a Critical and Exegetical Commentary* (New York: Macmillan, 1919), 573. Charles, *Revelation*, vol. 1, 258. Bingham, *Revelation*, 97. Murphy, *Fallen*, 250. Beale, *Revelation*, 522.
[10] Barr, *Tales*, 158. Koester, *Revelation*, 488.
[11] Swete, *Apocalypse*, 128.

The sense that John is on earth is confirmed by the aural perspective. As explained in Chapter 4, when the audiovisual focalizer is positioned atop the sky-structure it hears voices from specific beings/objects/locations within the God-space.[12] But when it is positioned on earth it cannot identify the precise source of the heavenly voice and so the voice is described generically as ἐκ τοῦ οὐρανοῦ. Thus in Revelation 10, where first-person verbs of hearing mark the audiovisual focalizer coincident with the character John (Rev. 10.4, 10), the perception of a voice ἐκ τοῦ οὐρανοῦ confirms John's position on earth.

This earthly location facilitates a simple understanding of the narrative. John sees the immense angel towering above him, with his hand reaching up to the sky but his feet on the plane of the earth. John then walks over to those feet and the angel hands down the scroll.[13] A position atop the sky-structure would be awkward, even comical: it would require John to walk to a position directly above the angel and reach down to take the scroll from the angel's upstretched hand. But the implied author is creating an awesome scene, not a comical one, and John's position on earth fits with the narrative.

John's horizontal movement towards the angel is another indication of his position on earth because when John is in the God-space, horizontal movement is not part of his cosmic tour experience. This characteristic is shared with the sky-journeys of several other apocalypses. The *Ascension of Isaiah* describes the vertical movement of its seer through seven sky-layers to the space atop the seventh. While in this space the seer observes 'the righteous and the angels' moving horizontally towards the one who is worthy of worship (*Asc. Isa.* 9.28, 33-34, 41) but the seer himself does not move. Indeed, the seer's interaction with worthy beings occurs when they move to his position (*Asc. Isa.* 9.39). Similarly, the seer of the *Apocalypse of Abraham* remains standing on the ultimate sky while the fiery throne-chariot moves towards him (*Apoc. Abr.* 17.1). 3 Baruch and 2 Enoch have horizontal movement only in mid-level skies, not in the God-space on the ultimate sky (*3. Bar.* 6.1; 8.1; *2 En.* 10.1). Only the Book of Watchers has horizontal movement on the same cosmic level as the God-space, but even here the seer comes only into the penultimate God-space, stopping at the doorway of the ultimate God-space and refraining from horizontal movement into it (*1 En.* 14.9-25).[14]

The characteristic common to most sky-journeys is observed also in Revelation. While in the God-space John sees the horizontal movement of a being approaching the Throne (Rev. 5.7; see also 8.3; 15.5-8) but does not do so himself, nor does he move horizontally when he speaks to the being sitting on one of the twenty-four thrones (Rev. 7.13). When horizontal movement is required for John to speak to an angel, it is the angel who comes to John (Rev. 17.1). The lack of horizontal movement in the God-space is suggestive of the special privilege of entering this awesome space and the

---

[12] See Sec. 4.3.2.

[13] This is how Albrecht Dürer drew the scene in 1498. O'Hear and O'Hear, *Picturing*, 45.

[14] Some scholarship argues that Enoch's movement into the penultimate God-space is actually vertical. Morray-Jones, 'Paradise', 203. Morray-Jones, 'The Temple Within', 46. However, I am persuaded by Esler's analysis of this space in terms of a walled palace complex, which lends itself to simple horizontal movement after the initial journey onto the sky-structure. Esler, *God's Court*, 114, 38, 51.

impropriety of moving freely within it. But the earthly location of Revelation 10 allows the seer to move horizontally to the feet of the great angel.

Finally, a location on earth is appropriate for a scene of prophetic commissioning (or re-commissioning). Revelation's first prophetic commission occurred on earth in Rev. 1.9-20.[15] Rev. 10.1-11 is another commissioning scene that follows a similar pattern to the first: while in an ordinary location John sees and hears an extra-ordinary being (Rev. 1.9-16; 10.1-7), receives the instruction to be the messenger of revealed knowledge (Rev. 1.11, 19; 10.11) and receives much of this knowledge from his earthly position (Rev. 2.1–3.22; 11.1–15.1) before he is taken into the hyper-heaven (Rev. 4.2; 15.2). Hebrew prophets were likewise on earth when they received their prophetic commissioning through eating the words of God (Jer. 1.9; 15.16; Ezek. 2.8–3.3). Apocalyptic seers also frequently encounter an extra-ordinary being on earth before they are taken on their journey into extra-ordinary places (*2 En.* 1.1–2.2; *3 Bar.* 1.3-7; *Apoc. Abr.* 10.1–11.6; *Asc. Isa.* 6.6-9).

6.1.3 Earthly position continues

John's earthly position remains unchanged from Rev. 10.1 to the visions of Revelation 12. The position of the visual focalizer is less stable. From Rev. 10.1–11.3 the first-person verbs of perception and speech directed to 'me' mark the audiovisual focalizer coincident with John on earth (Rev. 10.1, 4, 5, 8, 9, 11; 11.1). From Rev. 11.4 the focalizer remains on earth but is not explicitly coincident with any character until Rev. 11.12 where it is briefly coincident with the two witnesses on earth. But Rev. 11.16-18 narrates a scene around the Throne in the hyper-heaven. The focalizer is now in this space, allowing the implied hearer to see the twenty-four elders prostrating themselves and to hear the words of worship coming specifically from these beings. This audiovisual experience of the hyper-heaven is related without first-person verbs or pronouns: John has remained on earth while the focalizer has shifted to the hyper-heaven, giving the implied hearer an experience slightly different to that of the character John.[16]

In contrast with the focalizer, there are no indications of a change in position for the character John. There is no narration of movement, nor is a change in position required by the audiovisual perspective or other literary markers. On earth from Rev. 10.1, John is in the correct location to measure the temple in Rev. 11.1-3. His continuing position on earth is confirmed by the solitary first-person verb in Rev. 12.10. John hears a loud voice ἐν τῷ οὐρανῷ but does not perceive the precise source of the voice, thus indicating that he is on earth hearing the voice boom down from beyond the sky-structure. John's position on earth is a factor in how the sights of Revelation 12 are experienced and where they are located in the cosmic schema.

---

[15] See Sec. 4.1.
[16] John has not shifted to the hyper-heaven. Contra Charles, *Revelation*, vol. 1, 109, 314. Aune, *Revelation 6–16*, 638. For this reason it is not accurate so say 'the seer now sees the twenty-four decans'. Malina and Pilch, *Social-Science*, 149. Aune, *Revelation 6–16*, 635.

6.2 Narrative structure and narrative resonances

Revelation 12 is distinctive as it is composed of three embedded narratives. The first evokes a form of the combat myth (Rev. 12.1-6, 13-17). Embedded within this is the second narrative, evoking a second form of the combat myth (Rev. 12.7-9). And embedded within this is the third, evoking the image of the accuser in the heavenly court (Rev. 12.10-12).

The first combat myth involved the attack of a serpentine dragon on a pregnant woman and her offspring, as in the Egyptian myth of Seth-Typhon's attack on the goddess Isis and her child Horus, or the Greek myth of Python's pursuit of the goddess Leto and her unborn twins Apollo and Artemis.[17] The second combat myth involved war in the sky between opposing armies and the throwing down of the defeated combatant.[18]

However, while the narrative of Revelation 12 evokes the hearer's knowledge of the combat myth, primarily in its Greek form as discussed by Adela Yarbro Collins, there are two significant aspects of its images and narrative that do not appear in the Apollo-Python-Leto or Horus-Typhon-Isis forms. The first aspect that is missing in the Apollo-Python-Leto myth is the link between the dragon and the chaotic sea. In fact in this Greek myth Python seems to be associated with the land and is thwarted by the sea and the god of the sea.[19] In Rev. 12.13-18 the role of land and sea/river is reversed, instead affirming the hearer's assumptions deriving from the Hebrew scriptures and associated traditions, regarding the threat of primordial watery chaos.

The second aspect of Revelation 12 that is missing in these Greek and Egyptian myths is the seven heads of the dragon, which is an important feature of the Babylonian Tiamat and the Canaanite Litan. This is reflected in the Leviathan of the Hebrew scriptures, which in Psalm 74.14 is known to have multiple heads. However, as Barker notes, the Hebrew scripture does not say how many heads Leviathan had, so the seven heads of the dragon in Revelation 12 evoke the hearer's knowledge not only of the Hebrew scriptures but also of associated traditions.[20]

While the implied hearer knows of cosmic combat (order vs. chaos, land vs. sea) in connection with the dragon image, when hearing of a sky war between opposing armies of powerful beings (Rev. 12.7-9) it anticipates that the leader of the rebellious army will be pictured as a powerful humanoid, under a name such as Azazel, Mastema

---

[17] Yarbro Collins, *Combat Myth*, 83. Collins favours the latter as the source for Revelation 12. A similar pattern is found in other myths, including the attempt of Kronos to swallow each of his children at birth to prevent them from growing to surpass him in strength.

[18] Yarbro Collins, *Combat Myth*, 80. One version of this myth was used to mock the king of Babylon in Isaiah 14.12-20.

[19] 'Python, offspring of Terra, was a huge dragon ... When Python know that Latona [Leto] was pregnant by Jove [Zeus], he followed her to kill her. But by the order of Jove the wind Aquilo [Boreas] carried Latona away, and bore her to Neptune [Poseidon]. He protected her ... he took her to the island Ortygia, and covered the island with waves.' From *Hyginus*, cited in Aune, *Revelation 6–16*, 670.

[20] Margaret Barker, *The Revelation of Jesus Christ: Which God Gave to Him to Show to His Servants What Must Soon Take Place (Revelation I.I)* (Edinburgh: T&T Clark, 2000), 217.

or Beelzebul.[21] By embedding the second combat myth within the first, Revelation identifies the leader of the rebellious army with the dragon of cosmic chaos. As Collins notes, narrative constraints determine that the leader be pictured as a dragon rather than a humanoid being,[22] but this is still an unusual and striking image for the hearer. Another effect of embedding the second combat myth at this point is that the vanquisher of the dragon is Michael, rather than the man-child himself.[23]

The third story or cosmological concept known to the implied hearer, the accuser in the heavenly court, is embedded in the second combat story (Rev. 12.10-12). This heavenly court could make a judgement regarding the righteousness or unrighteousness of humans, so a function within this court was bringing accusations against human beings or testing their righteousness and faithfulness. This concept is known in the Hebrew scriptures under the epithet שטן, translated by διάβολος in the Septuagint (LXX). In the four contexts where שטן is used in relation to sky-beings (Num. 22; 1 Chron. 21; Job 2; Zech. 3), it has the specific connotation of a legal opponent or accuser.[24] Under the names σατανᾶς and διάβολος early Christians retained a similar concept: a particular being who accuses humans and tests their righteousness and faithfulness (Mt. 4.1-11; 16.23; 1 Cor. 5.5; 2 Cor. 12.7; 1 Tim. 1.20. See also Jude 9). Revelation has already evoked this concept in the messages to the seven churches (Rev. 2.9-10, 13; 3.9) so the hearer is prepared for its use in Rev. 12.10-12.

6.3 The embedded narratives in the cosmic structure

6.3.1 Star wars in the sky-heaven

The appearance of the great woman and dragon ἐν τῷ οὐρανῷ elicits scholarly debate as to whether they are in 'the sky' or in 'heaven'.[25] A visual-narrative reading shows

---

[21] In *1 Enoch* a powerful sky-being who leads a group of similar beings in rebellion against God is known by the name Azazel nine times (*1 En.* 8.1; 9.6; 10.4, 8; 13.1; 54.5; 55.4; 69.2 twice) and Satan once (*1 En.* 54.6). In *Jubilees* we find such a being named three times Mastema (*Jub.* 10.8; 19.28; 49.2), nine times Prince of Mastema (*Jub.* 11.5, 11; 17.16; 18.9, 12; 48.2, 9, 12, 15) and Satan once (*Jub.* 10.11). In the Hebrew scriptures and their Greek equivalent the epithet 'satan' (or 'devil') is never used as a label for such a being. In early Christian writings there are occasional references to a powerful leader of powerful beings who rebel against God and/or cause physical harm to human beings without God's consent. Such a being is called Beelzebul seven times (in four places: Mt. 10.25; 12.22-32; Mk 3.22; Lk. 11.14-23) and Satan six times (in five places: Mt. 12.26; Mk 3.13-27; Lk. 10.18; 11.18; 13.16).

[22] Yarbro Collins, *Combat Myth*, 109.

[23] Although in the interpretation (Rev. 12.10-12) the vanquisher is indeed the man-child.

[24] The noun שטן appears in five contexts in the Hebrew scriptures with human referents, three of which are military contexts, indicating an opponent in battle (1 Sam. 29; 1 Kgs 5; 11), and two are legal contexts, indicating a legal accuser (2 Sam. 19; Ps. 109). See also *Apoc. Zeph.* 6.16–7.9.

[25] Those who locate them in the 'sky' include Swete, *Apocalypse*, 144. Beckwith, *Apocalypse of John*, 616. Bingham, *Revelation*, 112. G. R. Beasley-Murray, *The Book of Revelation*, New Century Bible (London: Butler and Tanner, 1974), 197. Barr, *Tales*, 203. Leonard L. Thompson, *Revelation. Abingdon New Testament Commentaries* (Nashville Abingdon Press, 1998), 133. Mangina, *Revelation*, 147. Williamson, *Revelation*, 205. Those who locate them in 'heaven' include Gebhardt, *Doctrine*, 51. Barnett, *Apocalypse*, 102. Beale, *Revelation*, 625. Witherington, *Revelation*, 167. N. T. Wright, *Revelation for Everyone* (Louisville: Westminster John Knox Press, 2011), 108. Fair, *Conquering*, 251.

that these signs are seen from earth, looking upward at the underside of the sky-structure. Revelation 12.1-9 does not mark coincidence of focalizer and character with first-person verbs and pronouns, but reads naturally if the focalizer is assumed to be coincident with John. As there is no indication that the focalizer's perspective is different to John's, we may assume the coincidence of the functional focalizer-narrator with the nominal narrating character. There is then a smooth transition into Rev. 12.10-12 which explicitly marks the focalizer coincident with John (καὶ ἤκουσα).

Further, wherever ἰδού is used of a sight present in the narrative (as here in Rev. 12.3) the perspective is identical with John's. Sometimes ἰδού allows the hearer to anticipate an event coming later in the narrative (Rev. 1.7; 9.12; 11.14; 16.15; 22.7, 12), but when speaking of a present sight in the narrative the word ἰδού either is spoken by a character addressing John (Rev. 1.18; 5.5; 21.3, 5) or comes from the voice of the narrator, coincident with the focalizer and the character John (4.1, 2; 6.2, 5, 8; 7.9; 14.1, 14; 19.11). The latter is the case in Rev. 12.3. Thus, when the narrator directly invites the hearer to see the dragon, it is an invitation to share the perspective of the character John. The viewing position is on earth with John and the gaze is directed upward.[26] Given the opacity of the sky-structure the upward gaze can only reach as far as its underside.[27] The woman and dragon are thus located in the οὐρανός, that is the sky-space at the underside of the sky-structure.

This position for the woman and dragon is confirmed by the accompanying sky-beings. Sun, moon and twelve stars are the woman's accoutrement, while many other stars are attacked by the dragon.[28] As explained in Chapter 5 the underside of the sky-stucture is the normal position of sun, moon and stars in Revelation's cosmic schema.[29] Contrary to much Revelation scholarship, the stars of Revelation 12 are normal stars in their normal position in the cosmos. I also argued that most Revelation scholarship incorrectly assumes that the star of Rev. 9.1 is an angel, often a rebellious or morally 'fallen' angel.[30] The same is often true of the stars in Rev. 12.4.[31] Thus deSilva writes that the dragon 'is able to rally a third of the angels to his cause' and 'drew one-third of the spirit beings away from [God's] order'.[32] However, the dragon cannot be understood to seduce the stars into sin or lead them in rebellion.

Recognizing the dragon as a combat monster, the implied hearer sees this powerful assailant defeating large numbers of sky-beings (stars) and throwing them from the underside of the sky-structure down to the earth. The defeat and casting down of these

---

Thomas and Macchia, *Revelation*, 215, 19. Charles notes arguments for the two alternatives. Charles, *Revelation*, vol. 1, 314.

[26] Thus I dispute Koester's comment that 'whether he watches from heaven, earth, or some other location is not clear'. Koester, *Revelation*, 116.

[27] See Sec. 4.3.2.

[28] 'So wird der Himmel als Firmament, an dem die Himmelskörper nach traditionellem Verständnis befestigt sind.' Labahn, '"Apokalyptische" Geographie', 122.

[29] Contra Charles, who suggests that if the scene is 'in heaven' this fits with the presence of sun, moon, and stars. Charles, *Revelation*, vol. 1, 314. See Sec. 5.1.4.

[30] See Sec. 5.2.2.

[31] Charles, *Revelation*, vol. 1, 319. Bingham, *Revelation*, 112. Barr, *Tales*, 220. Aune, *Revelation 6–16*, 686. Beale, *Revelation*, 636–7. Osborne, *Revelation*, 461. Witherington, *Revelation*, 168. Newton, *Pentecostal Commentary*, 223.

[32] DeSilva, *Seeing*, 105, 13.

beings is a familiar pattern to the implied hearer. In Daniel 8.10 the goat monster's little horn exalts itself as high as the army of the skies (or in the LXX, ἕως τῶν ἀστέρων τοῦ οὐρανοῦ) and throws some of the stars to earth and tramples them. The dragon in the primary combat narrative (Rev. 12.1-6) is depicted as neither leader nor persuader but as combat monster. It is only in the embedded combat narrative (Rev. 12.7-9) that the dragon takes on the role of military leader. This embedded narrative evokes the second form of the combat myth, involving war in the sky between opposing armies and the throwing down of the defeated combatant.[33] In this form of the combat myth the military leader is normally depicted as humanoid but Revelation 12 embeds the military leader myth into the combat monster myth and so depicts him as a dragon. It is within this embedded narrative that the dragon becomes part of the composite evil called Dragon-Serpent-Devil-Satan, whose actions include accusation (satan) and seduction into sin (ancient serpent).[34] But in the primary combat narrative of Rev. 12.1-6 the dragon is the combat monster. Neither a military chief leading the stars in rebellion nor a persuader seducing the stars into sin, he is a combat monster knocking them out of the sky.[35]

Commenting on this destructive image, Aune notes, 'The destruction of one-third of the stars corresponds to the destruction of a third of various parts of the cosmos as the result of the plagues unleashed by the seven trumpets (8:7–9:19).'[36] This image fits well with stars, who have a set place in the cosmic schema and whose removal is therefore an act of cosmic destruction. Stars are sky-beings native to a particular sky-space and are not capable of controlled movement between higher and lower cosmic layers.[37] Being incapable of controlled vertical movement, a star that has come to be on earth does not return to the skies; throwing them down to earth is a true act of destruction. The destructive image makes far less sense if the sky-beings of Rev. 12.4 are angels. Angels have no set place in the cosmic structure so removing them from their current location is not an act of cosmic destruction.

Revelation 12.4 depicts ordinary star-beings in their normal position in the cosmos before they are thrown to earth. Visually, the falling of the stars appears similar to the 'falling stars' that are seen in ordinary experiences of the night sky. The woman and the

---

[33] Yarbro Collins, *Combat Myth*, 80.

[34] 'Satan' evokes the accuser of the Hebrew scriptures. In the four contexts where שׂטן is used in relation to sky-beings (Num. 22, 1 Chron. 21, Job 2, Zech. 3) it has the specific connotation of a legal opponent or accuser. Of the sky-being who comes to Balaam 'as a satan' in Numbers 22, Day writes, 'If we allow that the announcement of divine wrath is a paralegal expression, then Balaam in [chapter 22] verse 32 stands charged with undertaking a journey without divine consent.' Day, *Adversary*, 67. See also *Apoc. Zeph.* 6.16–7.9. 'Then I asked him, "Who is the great angel who stands thus, whom I saw?" He said, "This is the one who accuses men in the presence of the Lord." Translation O. S. Wintermute, 'Apocalypse of Zephaniah', in *The Old Testament Pseudepigrapha*, ed. James H. Charlesworth, vol. 1 (Garden City: Doubleday, 1983).

'Ancient Serpent' evokes the snake of Genesis 3.

[35] The image of stars militarily removed from the sky to a lower cosmic level also recalls the image in Isaiah 14. The hoped-for military defeat of a powerful human ruler is compared with the concept of a star that is cut down from the sky (Isa. 14.12). Note that in this image the star is not *led* or *seduced* down from the sky but forcefully removed by a powerful opponent.

[36] Aune, *Revelation 6–16*, 686.

[37] See Sec. 5.2.2.

dragon are associated with these stars, together with the sun and moon, and are seen together in the sky-space at the underside of the sky-structure.

A shift from sky-heaven to earth occurs at some point in the narrative. In Rev. 12.14 the woman is given the wings of the great eagle to aid her horizontal movement from one earthly location to another, but her movement from the sky-heaven to the first earthly location is not narrated. Where this issue is noted, scholarship usually understands the shift to occur in Rev. 12.4. Charles wrote, 'In [verse] 4 a descent to earth on the part of the woman and the Dragon is silently presupposed'.[38] This view is shared by Aune and is also expressed in Barr's narrative-critical commentary on Revelation.[39] It is thus thought that when the dragon stands in front of the woman, ready to devour her child, this occurs on earth.

I propose a different reading. If we grant full weight to the perfect tense of ἕστηκεν then the dragon does not take up position in front of the woman in v. 4 but has been there from the moment he appeared in the sky.[40] The whole sky-scene of Rev. 12.1-3 has the dragon already in place to devour the child: the woman is in the sky, she is labouring in the sky, she gives birth in the sky and then she flees from the sky to the earthly wilderness (Rev. 12.6). There is no unnarrated change in location in Rev. 12.1-6.

The unnarrated change in location occurs only when v. 6 is retold in vv. 13-14. The first telling had the woman and dragon in the sky, with the woman fleeing directly from this unsafe sky location to the safe earthly location. The second telling has the woman and dragon on earth, with the woman fleeing from this unsafe earthly location to the safe earthly location. In the second telling, the woman's unnarrated shift to earth occurs at a moment in the storyline prior to the dragon pursuing the woman across the earth.

With the birth occuring at the underside of the sky-structure, the snatching up of the child means movement from the sky-heaven to the hyper-heaven, that is, from a conflicted space to a safe space.[41] While Aune writes, 'The statement that the child will be caught up to heaven (v. 5) indicates that the confrontation between the dragon and the woman takes place on the earth', this is not accurate.[42] Revelation 12.5 does not state that the child was caught up to οὐρανός but rather to the Throne. The child's initial position at the underside of the sky-structure is sufficient prerequisite for his subsequent upward movement into the Throne-space.[43]

---

[38] Charles, *Revelation*, vol. 1, 314.
[39] Aune, *Revelation 6-16*, 686. Barr, *Tales*, 213. See also Fair, *Conquering*, 253. Thomas and Macchia, *Revelation*, 219.
[40] 'The dragon has taken his stand before the woman' (Worrell New Testament). 'And the dragon standeth before the woman' (American Standard Version). 'The Dragon was standing' (Weymouth New Testament). Malina and Pilch comment that the 'grammatical form points to a condition enduring into the present ... The word does not describe behaviour, as though the Dragon were elsewhere and then came and stood.' Malina and Pilch, *Social-Science*, 156. In Sec. 5.2.2 we gave full weight to the perfect tense of πεπτωκότα in Rev. 9.1, as do most commentators and translations.
[41] Malina and Pilch write, 'The first piece of action after the presentation of the characters is the birth of a son from one constellation, the Pregnant Woman, and his removal to the other side of the vault of the sky, with God.' Malina and Pilch, *Social-Science*, 157.
[42] Aune, *Revelation 6-16*, 686.
[43] 'Der Mythus des Apokalyptikers läßt das Kind entrückt werden am Himmel selbst, zu seinem Thron ... Die Mutter dagegen muß zur Erde hinabfliehen.' Boll, *Aus der Offenbarung Johannis*, 112.

The narrative of Rev. 12.1-6 uses cosmological concepts already known to the implied hearer. These concepts are the sky-structure that create distinct spaces above and below and conflicted lower sky-spaces combined with harmonious upper sky-spaces.[44] Already familiar with the basic concepts, the implied hearer readily understands the narrative moves and the safety achieved by lifting the child from conflicted space at the underside of the sky-structure to the God-space above.

6.3.2 Battle angels in the sky-heaven

The visual perspective that prevailed through the first combat narrative (Rev. 12.1-6) continues into the second (Rev. 12.7-9). The character John has not moved from this earthly position as there is no narration of movement, nor is a change in position required by the audiovisual perspective or other literary markers. The focalizer was on earth with John through vv. 1-6, and in vv. 7-9 there is nothing in the visualization of the scene to indicate that the focalizer's perspective is different to John's. The coincidence of the functional focalizer-narrator with the nominal narrating character continues into the second combat narrative (Rev. 12.7-9) and is explicitly affirmed in the accuser narrative (Rev. 12.10-12).

The actors in the second combat narrative are Michael with his angelic army and the dragon with his own angelic army. The dragon is the only continuing actor from the first combat narrative to the second. His continuing role is striking because the agonist of the second combat myth is typically a humanoid being rather than a monstrous being. The continuing role of the dragon makes the second combat narrative a continuation of the first.

The dragon has not changed position since it was first seen in front of the woman in Rev. 12.3-4. The woman has fled from him (Rev. 12.6) but the dragon has not been moved either through explicit narration or narrative inference. The description of events ἐν τῷ οὐρανῷ assumes the same οὐρανός in which the dragon was seen in the first combat narrative. The visual perspective also assumes this οὐρανός as the focalizer is still on earth gazing upward at the underside of the sky-structure.

The second combat narrative (Rev. 12.7-9) begins when Michael and his angelic army attack the dragon's position.[45] As expected in the second form of the combat myth the dragon is now a military leader commanding his own angelic army. But even here the dragon's own combat strength is important and it is found insufficient to withstand the military assault. The casting down of the dragon (Rev. 12.9) is a dramatic climax because until now the dragon has maintained its position in the sky-heaven.[46]

---

[44] See Sec. 3.4.2 and Sec. 3.4.3.
[45] 'It is Michael, commander of God's armies, who takes the initiative.' Boring, *Revelation*, 58–9. This is contrary to the readings in which the dragon assaults the gates of heaven or attempts to pursue the child into the safe space. Swete, *Apocalypse*, 150. Charles, *Revelation*, vol. 1, 320. Herschel H. Hobbs, *The Cosmic Drama* (Waco: Word Books, 1971), 122–3. Mounce, *Revelation*, 235. Barnett, *Apocalypse*, 104. Thomas and Macchia, *Revelation*, 220.
[46] Contrary to those readings that shift the dragon to earth prior to v. 5. Charles, *Revelation*, vol. 1, 314. Hobbs, *Cosmic Drama*, 122. Ford, *Revelation*, 200. Aune, *Revelation 6–16*, 686. Barr, *Tales*, 213. Fair, *Conquering*, 253. Thomas and Macchia, *Revelation*, 219.

The permanent effect of this action (οὐδὲ τόπος εὑρέθη αὐτῶν ἔτι ἐν τῷ οὐρανῷ) parallels the permanent effect of casting stars down to earth (Rev. 12.4. See also 6.13; 8.10; 9.1). Unlike more recent depictions of dragons, this dragon does not have wings or the power of flight or any other means of moving upward into the skies.[47] He is more like a star than an angel; his initial dwelling-place is the sky-heaven but once he finds himself on earth he has no means of returning to the sky-heaven.[48]

6.3.3 Legal battles in the hyper-heaven

The focalizer's coincidence with the character John becomes explicit in the transition from the second combat narrative to the accusation narrative (Rev. 12.10-12). Specifically, they share the aural perception of a voice ἐν τῷ οὐρανῷ. This accords with John's position on earth from Rev. 10.1. As explained in Chapter 4 the experience of a voice ἐν τῷ οὐρανῷ or ἐκ τοῦ οὐρανοῦ not only indicates the coincidence of character and focalizer, but it also indicates their position on earth.[49]

While the position of the focalizer in unchanged there is a significant shift in perception – from visual to aural. The narrative of Rev. 12.10-12 is not *seen* by the audiovisual focalizer but *heard*. This shift in perception indicates a change in the location of action from the underside of the sky-structure to the space above, such that the audiovisual focalizer is allowed the aural experience of a great voice booming down from above the sky-structure but not the visual experience of the scene that is hidden by the sky-structure. The change in the site of action is also indicated by the designation ἐνώπιον τοῦ θεοῦ, equivalent to ἐνώπιον τοῦ θρόνου.

Along with the new location are new actors. Like the combat narratives, the accusation narrative is a contest between opponents, but the identity of the opponents has changed. Michael has been replaced with ὁ ἀρνίον – or more accurately by οἱ ἀδελφοί ἡμῶν who enact victory by τὸ αἷμα τοῦ ἀρνίου and by the word of their testimony. Ὁ δράκων has been replaced with ὁ διάβολος.

Ὁ διάβολος has an accusatory function in Rev. 12.10-12. In the Hebrew scriptures the accusatory function is enacted by a שטן, which is transliterated into Greek as σατανᾶς or translated as διάβολος. As the LXX translation of שטן the epithet διάβολος

---

[47] Ancient depictions showed dragons as serpentine monsters and did not give them wings. See Koester, *Revelation*, 544–5. Aune, *Revelation 6–16*, 683. The implied hearer's primary image of dragons does not include wings. The implied author clarifies aspects of the image (such as the number of heads) but does not add wings.

[48] In Revelation only angels and the angelomorphic Christ-figure move freely between earth and the higher cosmic layers (for significant movement of angels see Rev. 7.2; 8.13; 10.1; 14.6-10, 17-19; 17.1-3; 18.1; 20.1; 21.10). Certainly no earth-dwelling creatures, including humans, are ordinarily capable of vertical movement through the cosmic layers. Birds are never seen as high as the sky-heaven, being limited to the midpoint between sky-heaven and earth (Rev. 8.13; 19.17). The creatures from the abyss in Revelation 9 emerge up onto the land but show no sign that they are capable of moving further upward to the sky-heaven. Even the four chimeric animals show no sign that they are capable of vertical movement, despite the fact that in Ezekiel (Ezek. 1.4-28) and the *Apocalypse of Abraham* (*Apoc. Abr.* 17.1–18.14) the equivalent beings are the means by which God's throne moves. In Revelation the Throne does not move but remains in place as the defining point of the greater cosmos. But see Chapter 7.

[49] See Sec. 4.3.2.

already carries connotations of accusation, and the identity of ὁ διάβολος is developed further by the additional epithet ὁ κατήγωρ, the accuser. The accusation narrative describes a contest (or the results of a contest) between the one accusing and the ones testifying. It is a legal contest that plays out ἐνώπιον τοῦ θεοῦ, that is, ἐνώπιον τοῦ θρόνου. The Throne-space is functioning as the heavenly courtroom (Job 1–2; Zech. 3). In this space the ones who testify achieve a legal victory over their adversary by maintaining their testimony even at the cost of their lives. For the accuser, this legal defeat results not merely in a rebuke (Zech. 3.2; Jude 9) but in permanent removal from the Throne-space.

6.4 Conclusion: A consistent hyper-heaven

The foregoing analysis has shown the narrative operating across the cosmic tiers, maintaining the distinct character of the ultimate tier. The first combat narrative (Rev. 12.1-6) showed a combat monster in the sky-heaven, partially destroying the cosmic order (pulling down stars from their rightful place) and threatening the woman's child. The second combat narrative (Rev. 12.7-9) showed the same being still in the sky-heaven but now as a military chief leading other powerful beings in a battle against angelic armies loyal to God. The accusation narrative (Rev. 12.10-12) spoke of a legal contest in the hyper-heaven between the accuser and the testifiers.

In this way the narrative imbues each space with distinct characteristics. The sky-heaven is seen as a site of conflict, rebellion and danger, while the hyper-heaven is maintained as a space defined by the Throne and in which all beings acknowledge the authority of the one sitting on the Throne. By his very actions the accuser acknowledges the authority of the Throne: to act as a functionary of the heavenly court is to affirm the authority of the heavenly court, and to bring accusations before the Throne is to acknowledge the authority of the Throne.

It is also true that in Rev. 12.9 and 20.2-3 the dragon and the accuser are identified as the same being, named as ὁ δράκων, ὁ ὄφις ὁ ἀρχαῖος, ὁ διάβολος καὶ ὁ σατανᾶς and ὁ πλανῶν. As the sky-dragon and the hyper-heavenly accuser are the same being one might be inclined to see rebellion in the hyper-heaven, but this would miss a key narrative distinction. The narrative speaks of ὁ δράκων in the sky-heaven doing draconian actions and ὁ διάβολος/κατήγωρ in the hyper-heaven doing the actions of an accuser. The distinct epithets and actions fit the distinct locations, and in this way the narrative maintains the distinct character of each space. In the sky-heaven the being is experienced as the dragon while in the hyper-heaven it is experienced as the accuser. While the conflict below the sky-structure involves rebellion against God's good order, the legal accusation above the sky-structure works within the heavenly court system and implicitly acknowledges the authority of the Throne.

The different actions in the different spaces maintain their distinct character even though they are, in some sense, the same event. We saw the military rebellion narrative play out in the sky-heaven with an equivalent action in the hyper-heaven – somehow the same event, even though the action in the hyper-heaven is neither military nor rebellious in character. The military defeat of the dragon is somehow the same event as the legal defeat of the accuser. The military victory of Michael in the sky-heaven is somehow the same event as the legal victory of the testifiers in the hyper-heaven.

In fact, the legal victory of the testifiers occurs not only in the hyper-heaven but also on earth: 'They have conquered him by the blood of the Lamb and by the word of their testimony, for they did not cling to life even in the face of death' (Rev. 12.11 NRSV). Maintaining their testimony in the face of the satan's accusations is an action that occurs on earth (Rev. 2.9-10, 13; 3.9), the victory achieved by holding their testimony 'even unto death' (Rev. 2.13; 12.11). The slaughtering (σφάζω) of Christians (Rev. 6.9) is the same type of ironic victory as the slaughtering (σφάζω) of Christ (Rev. 5.9).[50] The legal victory achieved, the Highest Possible Court no longer acknowledges the charges brought against Christians.[51] Thus even on earth the satan's accusations have lost their validity, although the cosmic opponent still has the power to put Christians to death (Rev. 12.17). In this way the same event occurs in three cosmic layers but looks very different in each space.

The differential characteristics of the event across the cosmic layers means that the common view of 'heaven' is not correct. Contrary to the predominant scholarly view, Revelation does not exhibit tension in its portrayal of heaven, between heaven as a site of conflict and heaven as the realm in which God truly reigns.[52] Rather, the implied hearer is shown a sky-heaven characterized by archetypal conflict between powerful sky-beings and a hyper-heaven defined by full recognition of the Throne.

In this way Revelation maintains and further develops the cosmic story-space it first began to reveal in Revelation 1. In Chapters 4 and 5 we saw how Revelation's narrative operates in a story-space coextensive with the cosmos on the horizontal and vertical axes. On the vertical axis this story-space extends through four cosmic tiers: hyper-heaven, sky-heaven, earth and under-earth. As the narrative operates across these four distinct spaces the specific characteristics of each are developed.

While scholarship generally assumes a single heavenly tier in Revelation, we saw that this is not completely accurate. Rather, the single sky-structure divides the space above it from the space immediately below it, thus creating the two sky-spaces that I have called hyper-heaven and sky-heaven. Above the sky-structure the Throne is the constitutional existent. The Throne defines the space while all beings, objects and structures within it are defined through their spatial and functional relationship with the Throne. As such, the space is characterized by full recognition of the authority of

---

[50] As Boring writes, '"Witness", "martyr" and "testimony" preserve their legal connotations and already have the overtones of "holding fast to one's Christian convictions when tried before the pagan courts", even to the point of death, thereby giving testimony to the truth of the Christian message. In this sense Jesus was the prototypical martyr (1:5; 3:14; 22:20).' Boring, *Revelation*, 145.

[51] The term 'Highest Possible Court' is from Day, *Adversary*, 126.

[52] Of the Throne-space Caird writes, 'In spite of the presence of God ... it contains symbols of the world's evil (iv. 6; xxi. 7; xii. 1).' Caird, *Commentary*, 62, echoed in Harrington, *Revelation*, 78. McDonough writes, 'While there are indications in 12:7-12 of primordial struggles in heaven ... for the most part heaven serves as the place, as in the Lord's Prayer, where God's will is done.' McDonough, 'Revelation', 182. Gert Jordaan describes heaven as 'a qualitative reference to a situation where all and everyone live in God's presence, in ceaseless praise, worship and obedience to him as Lord' but also identifies the οὐρανός of Rev. 12.1-9 (in which the dragon attacks the cosmic order and leads his army in battle against the hosts of heaven) as 'a metaphor for the dwelling place of God'. Jordaan, 'Cosmology', 3, 5.

the one sitting on the Throne. This was seen in the responsive relationship between the Throne and each concentric circle around the Throne, and in the significant actions that begin with the Throne and are put into full effect through the obedience of the beings/objects in this space. The apocalypses considered in Chapter 3 all had a God-space free of rebellion and this was found to be the case also in Revelation. The narrative of Revelation 12 operates across the earth and the two sky-spaces in such a way that the harmony of the God-space is maintained, affirming the implied hearer's expectation of a God-space free of rebellion.

7

Cosmic change (Rev. 20–22)

Steven Friesen writes that 'the imagery of Revelation often eludes systematization. But there is a relatively coherent imagined geography in the visionary's world'.[1] This study has thus far argued a similar view. The narrative of Rev. 1.4–20.10 operates in a cosmic story-space with four spatial levels (Figure 7.1). The highest level (hyper-heaven) was able to be visualized through the spatial and functional relationship between the Throne and all other existents, although the heavenly temple language eludes systematization. The next highest level (the sky-heaven) was seen as the dwelling place of sun, moon and stars. The earth is the location of Ephesos and Smyrna, Jerusalem and Rome. The earth-space is sometimes divided into earth and sea (the Mediterranean Sea) with Patmos as a small piece of land within this terrestrial sea.[2] The under-earth is the location of Hades and the abyss. These two cosmic regions are distinguished by their character and role in the narrative, although in some respects the abyss eludes systematization.[3]

From Rev. 21.11 onwards, the narrative makes changes to its story-space. This chapter examines the cosmic changes in Rev. 20.11-15 and 21.1–22.5 from a narratological perspective. I describe the narrative cause of the deletions in cosmic story-space and the later reappearance of cosmic spaces. As the lake of fire, a previously unseen region, makes its appearance in the narrative of cosmic change, I argue that it is paradoxically located outside the cosmos. Finally, I offer a narratological contribution to the question of whether Revelation expects the destruction of the real cosmos.

---

[1] Friesen, *Imperial Cults*, 152.
[2] The earth-space can perhaps be divided further into earth, sea and river, although there is no direct reference to an encircling ocean-river. River is one of the four components of the cosmos-of-ordinary-human-experience: sky, earth, sea, river (Rev. 8.7-12; 14.7, 16.2-9). Some Hebrew scriptures place sea and river in parallel (Lev. 11.9; Ps. 24.1-2; Isa. 50.2; Nah. 1.4; Hab. 3.8). Greek mythology distinguishes between the primordial sea and the primordial river. The primordial river encircles the earth and is the source of the freshwater springs and rivers throughout the earth. While river is one of Revelation's four cosmic components, it is not clear that river is distinguished as a part of space in the way that the sea is.
[3] See Sec. 5.2.4.

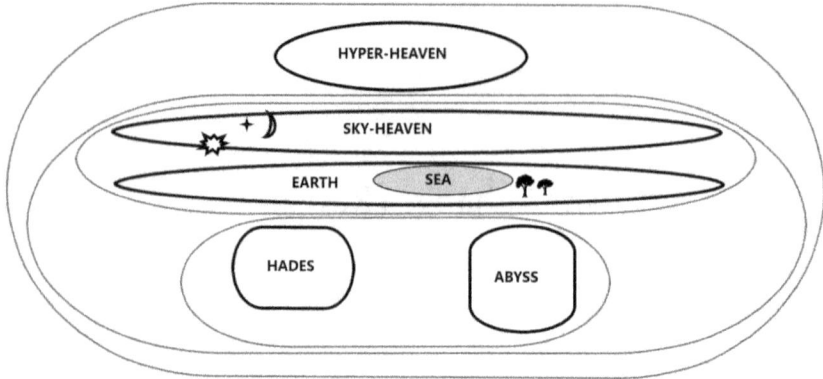

Figure 7.1 The cosmos of Revelation 1.4–20.10.

7.1 No cosmos but the Throne (Rev. 20.11-15)

7.1.1 Narrator, focalizer, character

In Rev. 17.3 John was taken into an earthly wilderness, and this location continues through to Rev. 20.11 as there has been no indication of travel to another part of the cosmos, whether explicitly (as in Rev. 17.3; 21.10), by clear narrative inference (as in Rev. 4.2) or discerned through the audiovisual perspective (as in Rev. 10.1; 15.2). Where the character John is coincident with the audiovisual focalizer his continuing location on earth is confirmed by aural perspective (Rev. 18.4; 19.1, 6). Specific voices in the hyper-heaven are narrated only where the lack of first-person verbs allows the focalizer's perspective to differ from John's (Rev. 19.4-5). The visual perspective also suggests the continuing position on earth. As noted above, καταβαίνοντα/καταβαίνουσαν ἐκ τοῦ οὐρανοῦ only occurs when John is on earth (Rev. 10.1; 18.1; 20.1; 21.2, 10) and is suggestive of the hearer's ordinary viewing position as a human being on earth, having to look upward to see something in the sky or coming down from the sky.[4]

John's cosmic journey has taken him from a remote earthly location to the hyper-heaven (Rev. 4.2), from hyper-heaven to a central earthly location (Rev. 10.1), from this earthly location back to the hyper-heaven (Rev. 15.2) and from hyper-heaven to another remote earthly location (Rev. 17.3). He has seen extra-ordinary things in an extra-ordinary location (Rev. 4–5; 15) but he has also seen extra-ordinary things in ordinary locations (Rev. 1; 10–14; 17–19). When John sees the souls of the martyrs come to life and sit on thrones (Rev. 20.4) this is another extra-ordinary sight in an ordinary location.[5] But when he gazes on the Throne something unprecedented is happening with story-space.

---

[4] See Sec. 6.1.2.
[5] Contra Malina and Pilch, the thrones are seen on earth. Malina and Pilch, *Social-Science*, 233. The cosmic journey currently has the seer on earth and there is no indication of upward gaze.

7.1.2 Deletions in story-space

Revelation's story-space initially stretched across the Aegean Sea but soon expanded horizontally to the extremities of the earth and vertically through all four cosmic levels. In this way story-space became co-extensive with the cosmos and differentiated into its four distinct spaces. It is therefore a striking change when Rev. 20.11-15 deletes some of these spaces, leaving the narrative to operate in bare and undifferentiated space.

This deletion is effected through the development of the scene. The focalizer's gaze now falls on a great white throne and the one seated on it. The throne's description 'differs from other references to thrones in Revelation in that this throne is both "great" and "white"'.[6] Its singularity, however, marks it as the hyper-heavenly Throne (Rev. 4.2) and the description is insufficient to create an additional singular throne. From a position on earth, the focalizer cannot gaze upon the Throne: this contradiction is immediately resolved by the flight of ἡ γῆ καὶ ὁ οὐρανός from the face of the one sitting on the Throne.

This cosmic change goes beyond Rev. 6.14 where the sky-structure is pulled aside, exposing earth-dwellers to the face of the one sitting on the Throne. Revelation 6.12-17 features partial cosmic destruction, with the sun and moon damaged, stars fallen from sky-heaven to earth, the sky-structure pulled back and mountains and islands shifted out of their usual position. The sun and moon remained in the lower sky-space and humans remained in the earth-space, despite the removal of the sky-structure that ordinarily separated the distinct spaces.

In Rev. 20.11-15 the flight of ἡ γῆ καὶ ὁ οὐρανός affects story-space such that former earth-dwellers have no differentiated space in which to stand – they find themselves in front of the Throne. Their experience is not merely a lack of objects to hide behind. Without the differentiated earth-space, lower sky-space and upper sky-space, former earth-dwellers are left with no space in which to be distant from the Throne. Undifferentiated space also means that the position of the visual focalizer is less meaningful and does not limit perception. Its gaze shows the Throne, with the former earth-dwellers in front of it.[7]

The ordinary location is on earth, which has significance for the debate on whether the 'millennial reign' is earthly or heavenly. See Beale, *Revelation*, 991–1002. Charles Homer Giblin, 'The Millennium (Rev 20.4-6) as Heaven', *New Testament Studies*, 45 (1999): 533–70. R. Jack McKelvey, 'The Millenium and the Second Coming', in *Studies in the Book of Revelation*, ed. Steve Moyise (Edinburgh: T&T Clark, 2001), 97. Dave Mathewson, 'A Re-Examination of the Millenium in Rev 20:1-6: Consummation and Recapitulation', *JETS*, 44/2 (2001): 251. Keith A. Burton, 'The Millennium: Transition to the Final Aeon', *Andrews University Seminary Studies*, 38/2 (2000): 213–14.

[6] Aune, *Revelation 17–22*, 1100.
[7] This reading differs from that of Malina and Pilch who write that 'John is located beyond the vault of the sky now, where there is no place for the earth and sky'. Malina and Pilch, *Social-Science*, 242. True, I have argued that John and/or the focalizer is unable to gaze upward through the sky-structure to view the Throne from an earthly position, an observation that could lend itself to Malina and Pilch's reading. However, their reading misses the significance of ἔφυγεν ἡ γῆ καὶ ὁ οὐρανός, which did not occur in previous experiences of the hyper-heaven. This verb phrase is not a passive description of the nature of a space; rather, it narrates a change to story-space. The change to story-space allows the focalizer/John to view the Throne.

In this way the scene is developed visually – beginning with the Throne and soon incorporating the people standing before it in undifferentiated space – but the chronology of the story is somewhat different. The chronological challenges of Rev. 20.11-15 are commonly discussed.[8] Most obviously, it would make little sense to say that all the dead stand in front of the Throne and face judgement (v. 12) and *subsequently* all the dead come out of the sea and Hades in order to face judgement (v. 13). Further, if ἔφυγεν ἡ γῆ καὶ ὁ οὐρανός (v. 11) indicates the erasure of sky, earth *and sea*, then the sea cannot subsequently hand over its dead (v. 13).[9] Charles argued that this passage 'betrays in its present form a hopeless confusion of thought, which can only be due to deliberate change of the text'.[10] He argued that both difficulties are resolved if v. 13 originally came before v. 12 and described the dead emerging not from ἡ θάλασσα but from τὰ ταμεῖα, that is, from the treasuries of the dead. I am instead persuaded by Beckwith's proposal that in v. 13 'the writer, in keeping with a common habit of his ... here turns back to a fuller statement' of events already described.[11] To expand on this proposal, the sea may cede its dead as it cedes its position, that is, simultaneously with the flight of sky, earth *and sea* from the face of the one sitting on the Throne. Further, Hades may cede its dead at the same time and, following a similar pattern, immediately undergo destruction. It is not only sky and earth that are erased in that moment but sky, earth, sea and under-earth – the entire sub-Throne cosmos.[12] Then at the eschatological moment of judgement all that is left of Revelation's story-space is undifferentiated space: there is only the Throne and the people who have no place to stand except in front of it.

Where ἡ γῆ and ὁ οὐρανός are paired they refer to spaces within the sub-Throne cosmos (Rev. 5.13; 6.13; 9.1; 10.6; 12.4; 13.13; 14.7; 18.1. See Figure 7.1).[13] It would make little sense for the Throne-space to flee from the Throne. Still, the other beings and objects in the Throne-space are not part of the narrative in Rev. 20.11-15. This does not mean that the four chimeric animals, the twenty-four elders and the myriads angels have been destroyed, only that they are not present within story-space at the narrative moment of judgement. At the moment of judgement there is only the Throne, the one sitting on it and the people standing in front of it.

---

[8] David E. Aune, *Revelation 17–22. Word Biblical Commentary*, vol. 52C (Nashville: Thomas Nelson, 1998), 1081.
[9] ἡ γῆ καὶ ὁ οὐρανός implicitly includes the sea (Rev. 5.13; 10.1-7; 12.12; 14.7; 21.1).
[10] R. H. Charles, *A Critical and Exegetical Commentary on the Revelation of St. John*, vol. 2. The International Critical Commentary (Edinburgh: T&T Clark, 1920), 194.
[11] Beckwith, *Apocalypse of John*, 748.
[12] See Sec. 5.3.
[13] In Rev. 18.1 the focalizer's gaze shows ἄλλον ἄγγελον καταβαίνοντα ἐκ τοῦ οὐρανοῦ. While the angel presumably has its origin in the hyper-heaven above the sky-structure, it can only be seen from earth once it has descended below the sky-structure. The focalizer's gaze shows an angel moving downward from the sky-heaven to earth.

7.2 Cosmos restructured

7.2.1 Story-space again

The stark scene of Rev. 20.11-15 was appropriate to the narrative moment but in Rev. 21.1 differentiated story-space returns. The focalizer remains coincident with the character John (καὶ εἶδον) in seeing the existent οὐρανός and γῆ. John's location within redifferentiated story-space is not explicitly marked in v. 1 so is assumed to be equivalent to his position immediately prior to Rev. 20.11-15, that is, on the plane of the earth. The earthly position is confirmed in v. 2 by his seeing the new Jerusalem καταβαίνουσαν ἐκ τοῦ οὐρανοῦ.[14]

In the redifferentiated story-space there are some notable absences. Sky and earth *and sea* fled from the face of the one sitting on the Throne, so the return of sky and earth might imply the return of the Mediterranean Sea. The narrator makes explicit, however, that the sea remains absent. By contrast, the continuing absence of Hades is understood from the manner of its departure in Rev. 20.14. Hades was thrown into the lake of fire, indicating either its absolute destruction or absolutely permanent incapacitation and removal from the cosmos.[15]

In addition, the abyss has disappeared from the narrative. The last occurrence of the abyss is in Rev. 20.7 where the satan is released from his prison. From this moment the abyss plays no role in the narrative and its continuing existence in story-space cannot be discerned. While the implied hearer may have assumed its continuing existence, two factors suggest that soon after Rev. 20.7 it ceases to exist. The first is the removal of associated cosmic locations, allowing the same possibility for the abyss: the adjacent under-earth region, Hades, is absolutely destroyed in Rev. 20.14; an associated cosmic region, the sea, is marked absent in Rev. 21.1. As noted in Chapter 5 the abyss has conflicting characteristics, being a bounded, lockable space controlled by God (Rev. 9.1-2; 20.1-3), yet also a deep, chaotic region associated with the sea.[16] This association with the sea can imply its absence in Rev. 21.1. The second factor suggesting the erasure of the abyss is the character of the cosmos in Rev. 21.1–22.5. Characterized by absolute peace and safety, the cosmos as it now exists is exclusive of threat and pain, and presumably of cosmic regions that are a source of threat and pain (Rev. 9.1-11; 11.7). With its absence from the narrative and its incompatibility with the present cosmos, the abyss is assumed to have disappeared along with Hades and the sea. Rev. 21.1–22.5 is therefore operating without an entire cosmic tier.

With the redifferentiation of story-space the Throne again has a location relative to other parts of the cosmos. As with the character John, the Throne's position is equivalent to its position prior to Rev. 20.11-15, in the highest cosmic tier. It has not moved into this position: it is in this position because of the redifferentiation

---

[14] As noted in Sec. 6.1.2, καταβαίνοντα/καταβαίνουσαν ἐκ τοῦ οὐρανοῦ occurs only when John is on earth (Rev. 10.1; 18.1; 20.1; 21.2, 10) and is suggestive of the hearer's ordinary viewing position as a human being on earth, looking upward to see something in the sky or coming down from the sky.
[15] See Sec. 7.3.
[16] See Sec. 5.2.4.

of story-space. The location of the Throne on which God is seated is confirmed in Rev. 21.2 by the narration of the new Jerusalem coming down ἐκ τοῦ οὐρανοῦ ἀπὸ τοῦ θεοῦ.

The narration of the new Jerusalem's descent begins a great cosmological restructuring that stretches the implied author's descriptive language. The descent of the new Jerusalem is narrated twice. This is not unique in Revelation – we have already seen the double narration of the woman's flight into the wilderness (Rev. 12.6, 14). The first narration of the new Jerusalem's descent begins in Rev. 21.2, with the focalizer coincident with John in an unspecified earthly location, gazing upward to see the city descending from above. The second narration begins in Rev. 21.10. Here the seer is taken to a viewing position atop a great mountain but still below the sky-structure. The focalizer is marked coincident with the character John not by the usual first-person verb of seeing but by the equivalent phrase ἔδειξέν μοι. From this location the angle of the focalizer's gaze is initially upward as the city begins to descend from above but may shift with the implied movement of the city all the way down to earth.

The vision is initially understood as the descent of a city (Rev. 21.2, 10) but it soon becomes apparent that the narrator is communicating the descent of God-space itself (Rev. 21.3, 22; 22.1-5). The city is coming down ἀπὸ τοῦ θεοῦ (Rev. 21.2, 10), yet God is within the city. This is where the implied author's descriptive language is stretched, as he attempts to describe the descent of God from God, or the descent of the God-space from the God-space to earth. Normally, an earthly position beneath the sky-structure limits the focalizer's perception and prevents the identification of the specific source of a voice from the Throne-space. The perception of a voice specifically from the Throne is now possible because the city that has just descended through the sky-structure has the Throne within it (Rev. 21.3, 22; 22.1-5).[17]

7.2.2 God-space merges with earth-space

The transition into undifferentiated space (Rev. 20.1-15) followed by the redifferentiation of space (Rev. 21.1) is a climactic moment in Revelation's narrative and worthy of the scholarly attention it has received, but from a cosmological perspective it is the descent of the new Jerusalem that is truly radical. This is because the descent of the new Jerusalem is not merely the downward movement of an object through story-space, rather, it is the merging of the God-space with the earth-space.

In the redifferentiated space of Rev. 21.1 the new sky and earth establish continuity with the spatial arrangement of Rev. 1.4–20.10. The appropriate space for human dwelling is earth, and high above the earth the sky-structure divides the space at its immediate underside from the space above, where the Throne is located. The descent of the new Jerusalem is also the descent of the Throne (Rev. 21.3-8, 22; 22.1-5) from the space above the sky-structure (Rev. 21.2, 10) – yet in Revelation the Throne does not move through space. In Chapter 4 I argued that the Throne is

---

[17] That the descent of the city is also the descent of the God-space is further indicated by its jasper radiance, connecting with the distinctive appearance of the one seated on the Thone in Rev. 4.2-3.

located above the sky-structure and is the primary existent defining both the centre and the surrounding space.[18] The crystalline sea that forms the lower boundary of the space is introduced not in its own right but in relation to the Throne (Rev. 4.6). Unlike equivalent spaces in *1 Enoch* and *2 Enoch* (*1 En.* 14.8-18; *2 En.* 25.4), neither ceiling nor horizontal boundaries mark a space in which the Throne can then be located: there is only the Throne that defines the centre and the space that extends outward from it. With the Throne as the primary existent, each new element becomes part of the space through relationship with the Throne. The four chimeric animals, the twenty-four thrones and the myriad angels are introduced through their spatial relationship with the Throne (Rev. 4.3, 6; 5.11) and developed through their responsive co-action with the Throne. We also saw the contrast between the way Revelation treats the Throne and the way Revelation locates all other objects and beings within spaces. Revelation's καὶ εἶδον descriptions initially define the stage and then locate objects, beings and events on that stage.[19] By contrast, Rev. 4.2 invites the hearer to see the Throne before locating the Throne ἐν τῷ οὐρανῷ. That is, the Throne is prior to the Throne-space. The narrative development of the space gives the sense that the Throne creates the space.

We also observed one key distinction between the Throne introduced in Rev. 4 and the very similar thrones of Ezek. 1.4-28 and *Apoc. Abr.* 17.1–18.14: Revelation's Throne does not move. Ezekiel and the *Apocalypse of Abraham* narrate movement and describe the wheels and chimeric beings that enable this movement. Revelation describes the chimeric beings but they, like the Throne, are unmoving.

In Revelation 21 the descent of the Throne cannot be locomotion through story-space; it can only be the radical rearrangement of story-space as the Throne-space merges with the earth-space. This has far-reaching implications: not only is the appropriate dwelling of humans now the same space as the God-space, but the earth-space is imbued with the characteristics of the God-space.[20]

We saw in Chapter 4 that Revelation's God-space allows only limited access to humans.[21] The God-spaces of the apocalypses show considerable variation in their accessibility to humans: at one end of the spectrum the *Ascension of Isaiah* shows a God-space accessible to many living humans in extra-ordinary experiences and to all the righteous dead, while at the other end of the spectrum *3 Baruch* (Greek) has a God-space that is not accessible to humans, whether living or deceased, righteous or unrighteous, in ordinary experiences or in extra-ordinary experiences. Revelation's God-space fell somewhere in the middle of this spectrum as it is ordinarily accessible only to a subset of the righteous dead and only temporarily, as a place of consolation while they await justice. In Revelation 21–22, however, all existing humans are fully alive in the earth-space which is now also the God-space. In a significant shift, the

---

[18] See Sec. 4.4.2.
[19] Ureña, *Narrative and Drama*, 72–3.
[20] The Animal Apocalypse describes God's throne set up for judgement on 'a pleasant land', which in this highly allegorical apocalypse is Israel (*1 En.* 90.20). Nickelsburg and VanderKam, *1 Enoch 2*, 403. In the Animal Apocalypse, and *1 Enoch* generally, God's throne does not define its own space; in some manner the throne has come to be in the Animal Apocalypse's earth-space.
[21] See Sec. 4.4.2.

God-space is now accessible to all righteous humans and that as a place of living fully. In fully living they look upon the face of God with joy (Rev. 22.4), an experience beyond any previous human experience, even that of Revelation's implied hearer whose virtual visionary experience showed them only the Throne and the radiance of the one sitting on it (Rev. 4.2-3).

Equally significant is the imbuing of the earth-space with the character of the Throne-space. In Chapter 4 I argued that as the space is defined by the Throne, so it is characterized by harmony with the Throne and by full recognition of the authority of the one who sits on the Throne.[22] This was seen in the responsive relationship between the Throne and each concentric circle around the Throne, and in the significant actions that begin with the Throne and are put into full effect through the obedience of the beings/objects in the space. In this way Revelation affirms the implied hearer's assumption of a God-space free of rebellion and further develops the concept, making God-space synonymous with Throne-space.

In Chapter 6 I argued that Revelation 12 is affirming of this characteristic of the Throne-space, locating its conflict and rebellion narratives in the sky-heaven and preserving the hyper-heaven as a space in which all beings, including the satan, acknowledge the authority of the Throne. While the god-space of Greek cultural stories was vulnerable to attack, but successfully defended by the Olympic gods and their allies, the concept affirmed and developed in Revelation is the inviolable God-space of the apocalypses.[23] By its very nature this God-space is inaccessible to beings who are in a state of rebellion against God. As the Throne-space merges with the earth-space, the place of human living takes on these characteristics. The cosmos-of-human-living is free from threat not merely because enemies have been defeated; it is free from threat because it is inherently inviolable and inherently exclusive of threatening elements. The safety of God's people is absolute.

This apocalyptic God-space is free of rebellion and also free of beings undergoing punishment for their former rebellion. Furthermore, as this merged space is now the totality of the cosmos, there is no place anywhere in the cosmos for rebellious beings. While God's people find comfort and life in this cosmos-of-human-living, 'the cowardly, the faithless, the polluted, the murderers, the fornicators, the sorcerers, the idolaters, and all liars' (Rev. 21.8) are in non-place, that is, the lake of fire.[24]

---

[22] See Sec. 4.4.2.

[23] Contrary to readings in which the dragon assaults the gates of heaven or attempts to pursue the child into the safe space, I argued that the dragon is left in position in the sky-heaven from Rev. 12.3-4 until 12.7 when its position comes under military assault.

[24] See Sec. 7.3.1. Rev. 21.27 is sometimes taken to mean that there are people practicing abomination and falsehood on the new earth. But as Murphy notes, 'The seer does not exactly claim that there *are* such sinners present at the end.' Murphy, *Fallen*, 426. As Rev. 21.27 contrasts the excluded group with those written in the book of life, it is better understood as a reaffirmation of Rev. 20.15. Bingham's comment is helpful: 'It may be thought from this sentence that in the *ultimate* there will still be this sort of people existing *in the universe*, free to do their wickedness, though prohibited from entering the Holy City. This will not be the case ... John is simply saying that this kind of evil person is presently prohibited and always will be.' Bingham, *Revelation*, 209.

7.3 Outside the cosmos: The lake of fire

Scholars have rarely considered the spatial location of the lake of fire. Some commentators understand ὁ οὐρανός and ἡ λίμνη τοῦ πυρός in similar ways, allowing only non-spatial meanings for both.[25] Where the location of the lake of fire is considered, one of three options is proposed: in front of the Throne, under the earth or 'no-place'.[26] I argue that 'no-place' is essentially correct but in a paradoxically spatial sense: it is outside the cosmos. Specifically, the lake of fire is beyond the horizontal extremities of the cosmos.

7.3.1 Locating the non-location

Revelation's cosmic tour is not comprehensive. It does not take the seer to the horizontal extremities of the cosmos, nor to the underworld.[27] The Book of Watchers takes its seer into the skies then to the extremities of earth and sky at every point of the compass. *2 Enoch* takes its seer vertically through seven/ten sky-layers and horizontally within the fourth sky-layer to the eastern and western extremities of the cosmos (*2 En.* 13–16). In *2 En.* 40.12 the seer claims to have been taken beneath the earth.[28] Some cosmic journeys are less comprehensive. The *Ascension of Isaiah* takes its seer vertically through the sky-layers then returns him directly to his starting point. Lying somewhere in the middle of this spectrum, Revelation's cosmic tour shows the spatial relations of most of its cosmic regions.

In Rev. 1.4–20.10 the greater cosmos is composed of hyper-heaven, sky-heaven, earth and under-earth. Revelation does not define a precise upper limit to the cosmos, and the hyper-heaven has no defined ceiling. Similarly, there is no precise lower limit to the cosmos, as is found in the second section of *2 Enoch* with its lower border made of solidified darkness, below which is nothing but nothingness. Nor is Revelation's cosmos given precise outer limits on the horizontal axis. While the 'four corners of the earth' may be understood as the extremities of the earth at the four compass

---

[25] Beale, *Revelation*, 319, 1029. A number of commentators place ὁ οὐρανός and ἡ λίμνη τοῦ πυρός into a heaven/hell theological paradigm, the lake of fire then defined as 'the experience of the absence of the presence of God' or similar. Witherington, *Revelation*, 245. See also Beale, *Revelation*, 760, 969. Fair, *Conquering*, 349–50, 53. Newton, *Pentecostal Commentary*, 264, 350. I find Witherington's statement misleading but it could be reframed: to be in the lake of fire is to be absent from the cosmos.

[26] In front of the Throne: Vinson, 'Sea of Glass', 134, 136. Under the earth: Aune, *Revelation 17–22*, 1066. 'No-place': McDonough, 'Revelation', 184. Friesen, *Imperial Cults*, 152–6.

[27] The Book of Watchers takes its seer beyond the horizontal extremity of earth and sky to see a terrifying place with a downward aspect but does not take him below the earth (*1 En.* 17.10–21.10). In the *Apocalypse of Abraham* the seer is standing on the seventh sky-layer and looks down at the airy surface on which he is standing, which becomes a kind of tapestry of moving images. In this he sees into under-earth regions (*Apoc. Abr.* 21.1-5; 24.6) but he does not travel into under-earth regions. In some recensions the third section of *2 Enoch* has the seer briefly recount his journey into the underworld, although the previous narrative of his journey did not include this detour (*2 En.* 40.12). Given the evidence that *2 Enoch* has undergone extensive editing, this detail probably dates to sometime after Revelation. Milik, *Books of Enoch*, 109, 112. Charlesworth, *The Pseudepigrapha and Modern Research, With a Supplement*, 104.

[28] A claim that does not accord with earlier narration of his journey and previous descriptions of the cosmic schema.

points, Revelation does not make it known whether the extremities of the earth are precisely identical with the extremities of the cosmos or if the cosmos extends a little further – perhaps incorporating an encircling Ὠκεανός or ending at the point where the sky is held in place by pillars. If Revelation's sky is dome-shaped, then the point where the dome of the sky rests on the plane of the earth would be a notable edge, but Revelation does not speak of this and we do not know whether Revelation's sky-structure is domed or flat. Of such possibilities Revelation says nothing; the outer edge of the greater cosmos is not defined.

The incomplete cosmic tour makes the lake of fire difficult to locate. The narrative logic that helped locate the Throne-space through the movements of the seer, and the shaft of the abyss through the completed movement of the star, makes no similar contribution to the location of the lake of fire. Likewise, the visual perspective that helped locate the shaft of the abyss on the earth, and the woman and the dragon at the underside of the sky-structure, makes no similar contribution to the location of the lake of fire. The lake of fire is first introduced in Rev. 19.21. There the focalizer is coincident with John, who has been on earth from Rev. 17.3, and from this position it gazes horizontally across the earth at the gathered armies. But when the beast and false prophet are thrown into the lake of fire, there is no indication of the direction of the focalizer's gaze to see this concluding event take place. The same is true in Rev. 20.10. In Rev. 21.8 the audiovisual focalizer hears the words 'their portion is in the lake burning with fire and sulphur' but again lacks visual perspective.

Let us then consider the three proposed locations for lake of fire. A position in front of the Throne is suggested by Richard Vinson, based on his argument that ἡ λίμνη τοῦ πυρός and the θάλασσα ὑαλίνη μεμιγμένη πυρί (Rev. 4.6; 15.2) are 'the same structure seen from different perspectives'.[29] He argues that this is also the location in which βασανισθήσεται ἐν πυρὶ καὶ θείῳ ἐνώπιον ἀγγέλων ἁγίων καὶ ἐνώπιον τοῦ ἀρνίου (Rev. 14.10).[30]

This argument, however, conflicts with the nature of the God-space. In Chapter 3 we noted a consistent characteristic of the God-spaces: they are not accessible to beings who are in a state of rebellion against God, nor to beings who are undergoing punishment for their former rebellion.[31] We have also seen that Revelation affirms and further develops this conception of the God-space.[32] By its very nature, Revelation's God-space excludes the possibility that people will be punished in front of the Throne.

Where then does the torment of Rev. 14.10 occur? Let us consider what is happening in the narrative. In Revelation 14 the narrator reports the words of three angels flying across the cosmos at the midpoint between earth and sky-heaven, the level at which

---

[29] Vinson, 'Sea of Glass', 134, 136.
[30] Vinson, 'Sea of Glass', 131. Many commentators argue that the torment occurs not in 'heaven' but in 'hell'. Gebhardt, *Doctrine*, 58–9. Elar, *Apocalypse*, 205–6. W. A. Grudem, *Systematic Theology: An Introduction to Biblical Doctrine* (Grand Rapids: Zondervan Academic, 2009), 1149. These are older scholars and theologians, but some recent scholars who do not use the word 'hell' nevertheless suggest a cosmic region dedicated to the purpose of eternal torment, including Beale, *Revelation*, 762. Aune, *Revelation 6–16*, 836. Koester, *Revelation*, 613–14.
[31] See Sec. 3.4.3.
[32] See Sec. 4.4.2 and Sec. 6.4.

large birds fly, and as such their messages speak to the entire earth. The first message speaks of God, the creator of all four components of the cosmos-of-ordinary-human-experience (sky, land, salt water, fresh water) and announces that the hour of his judgement has come. After the first angel has called attention to the entire cosmos-of-ordinary-human-experience, the second angel adds specificity: 'It fell, it fell, Babylon the Great.' The third angel brings the focus even closer, to each individual human who has participated in Babylon, announcing that just as they have participated in Babylon so they will participate in its negative fate in the day of judgement/wrath. This message is repeated in Rev. 18.1-8 where Babylon is destroyed by fire along with everyone who participated in it, and the smoke goes up εἰς τοὺς αἰῶνας τῶν αἰώνων (Rev. 19.3).[33] In this context, the third angel of Revelation 14 announces of each individual human βασανισθήσεται ἐν πυρὶ καὶ θείῳ ἐνώπιον ἀγγέλων ἁγίων καὶ ἐνώπιον τοῦ ἀρνίου. καὶ ὁ καπνὸς τοῦ βασανισμοῦ αὐτῶν εἰς αἰῶνας αἰώνων ἀναβαίνει. In a narrative and cosmological reading we recognize that the torment occurs on earth at a particular stage in the cosmic story.

Thus it is noteworthy that the torment occurs in front of the Lamb and the holy angels, but not in front of God.[34] In Revelation the Throne does not move from its position at the centre of the hyper-heaven, which is another way of saying that God does not move. On the other hand, the Lamb and the holy angels move freely between hyper-heaven and earth.[35] Thus torment in front of the Lamb and the holy angels, but not in front of the Throne, suggests an earthly location.

While the torment cannot occur in the hyper-heaven it fits its earthly location very well. The torment is caused by an act of judgement/wrath on Babylon, a city located on earth; if Babylon is destroyed in fire (strongly implied in Rev. 14 and confirmed in Rev. 18-19) it is hard to conceive of this event occurring anywhere other than earth. When an act of fiery destruction takes place on earth, it is natural to assume that the ensuing human suffering takes place on earth.[36] In fact, ancient authors understood that destruction of a city implies human suffering:

> No doubt, simply to say 'the city was stormed' is to embrace everything implicit in such a disaster ... If you expand everything which was implicit in the one word, there will come into view flames racing through houses and temples, the crash of falling roofs, the single sound made up of many cries, the blind flight of some, others clinging to their dear ones in a last embrace, shrieks of children and women, the old men whom an unkind fate has allowed to live to see this day ...[37]

---

[33] Sweet comments, 'The fate of the individual is depicted in terms of the fate of the city which has corrupted him.' Sweet, *Revelation*, 227.
[34] As Charles states, it is unlikely that 'the holy angels' is a periphrasis or circumlocution for God in this context. Charles, *Revelation*, vol. 2, 18. When Revelation speaks of being in God's presence, without using ὁ θεός, it uses ἐνώπιον τοῦ καθημένου ἐπὶ τοῦ θρόνου (Rev. 4.2, 9, 10; 5.1, 7, 13; 6.16; 20.11; 21.5) or simply ἐνώπιον τοῦ θρόνου (Rev. 1.4; 4.5; 7.9, 11, 15; 14.3; 20.12).
[35] For significant movement of angels see Rev. 7.2; 8.13; 10.1; 14.6-10, 17-19; 17.1-3; 18.1; 20.1; 21.10.
[36] It is a rather odd proposition to suggest that Babylon is destroyed by fire and sulphur but its inhabitants are removed to a different location in the cosmos to be tormented with separate fire and sulphur. Yet commentators imply exactly that when they suggest that the torment occurs somewhere other than earth.
[37] Quintilian, *Inst*, 8.3.67-9.

Rev. 14.9-11 announces in short form what is described elsewhere in Revelation: Babylon is destroyed when the Christ-figure and beings from the hyper-heaven descend to earth and wreak destructive judgement, leading to human suffering, notably of those who participated in Babylon (see Rev. 18.1-8; 19.1-3; 19.11-16). This concept is found in other Christian writings dating to the first century. 2 Thess. 1.5-12 speaks of an eschatological moment when the Lord Jesus appears from the sky with his forceful angels, in fire, wreaking destructive judgement on earth. In this eschatological moment, certain unrighteous people on earth undergo permanent destruction caused by the presence of the Lord Jesus (ἀπὸ προσώπου τοῦ κυρίου) and the glory of his might. Similarly, *Asc. Isa.* 4.1-19 speaks of the Lord Christ and his angels coming down from the ultimate heaven to drag Beliar/Nero into punishment, reprove the cities and the wilderness and burn the impious to nothing. The reader is directed to understand this as a vision concerning 'Babylon'.

In Revelation 14, when the Lamb and the holy angels descend to earth to enact destruction on the unrighteous city by fire and sulphur, the fire and sulphur also cause suffering to the individual human participants in Babylon. The destruction of the city is permanent, and the smoke from its fiery destruction becomes a smoke-signal declaring the judgement. This smoke-signal lasts as long as the ages last – in the context of Revelation's story about the cosmos, this means that it lasts until the end of the Millennium. Revelation 14 speaks of a destructive judgement in fire and sulphur, with 'eternal' smoke as a message to others. It is difficult to imagine how the torment could occur in the hyper-heaven where people could not see the smoke.

To conclude, in Rev. 14.9-11 the torment in fire and sulphur occurs on earth in the context of destructive judgement on the city – reminiscent of the destructive judgements on the city of Sodom and the kingdom of Edom[38] but through the agency of Christ and the holy angels, as in 2 Thess. 1.5-12.[39] The destruction is permanent, the resulting smoke functions as a smoke-signal that announces this destruction and suffering to the whole world, and this announcement of judgement is the final word εἰς αἰῶνας αἰώνων. It is the penultimate judgement immediately prior to the Millennium.

The second proposed location for the lake of fire is beneath the earth. Aune cites a number of references that purportedly point to this location. He writes, 'Fire in the underworld as a means of eternal punishment is first mentioned in Isa. 66.24 and frequently thereafter (*1 En.* 10.6, 13; Mt. 5.22; 13.42, 50; 18.9; 25.41; Mk 9.43, 48). It became natural to think of the underworld as the site for a river of fire (*2 En.* 10.2).'[40] However, none of those texts describe fire in the underworld.

---

[38] Compare 2 Pet. 2.6, which comments that just as Sodom was destroyed, so will unrighteous people be destroyed. See also Ezek. 38.22 and *Sib. Or.* 3.51-62,

> Then also implacable wrath will fall upon Latin men. Three will destroy Rome with piteous fate. All men will perish in their own dwellings when the fiery cataract flows from heaven. Alas, wretched one, when will that day come, and the judgement of the great king immortal God? Yet, just for the present, be founded, cities, and all be embellished with temples and stadia, markets and golden silver and stone statues so that you may come to the bitter day. For it will come, when the smell of brimstone spreads among all men. But I will tell all in turn, in how many cities mortals will endure evil.

[39] See also Lk. 10.12; 17.29-30.
[40] Aune, *Revelation 17–22*, 1066.

Isaiah 66.24 describes dead bodies piled up somewhere on the earth, not properly buried but burning and decaying.⁴¹ It does not describe an under-earth location. When *1 En.* 10.6 speaks of a fire it does not describe the location, and in the context of the Book of Watchers, and *1 Enoch* generally, it is unlikely that an underworld is in view. In describing cosmic locations that other texts might place in the underworld, *1 Enoch* holds back. It speaks of cursed valleys, of powerful sky beings trapped in the earth under a pile of rocks, of chasms and abysses at the edge of the earth and of fiery pits opening up in the earth (*1 En.* 10.4-5, 12; 18.10–22.14; 26.1–27.5; 54.1-6; 67.4-13; 90.24-27) but it stops just short of describing an underworld. In the Book of Watchers even the equivalent of Hades/Sheol is not exactly an underworld but cavities in a mountain at the edge of the earth (*1 En.* 22.1-4). Elsewhere in *1 Enoch* the picture for Sheol is ambiguous (*1 En.* 51.1; 56.8; 63.10). For humans standing on the earth, *1 Enoch* does not convey the sense that far beneath their feet there is another cosmic region of deceased humans and/or powerful nonhuman personages. It is unlikely that *1 En.* 10.6 speaks of fire in the underworld. More likely it connects with the non-place of *1 En.* 18.10–19.3 and 21.1-10 which does convey some sense of 'downness' but is located beyond the horizontal extremity of the cosmos rather than beneath the earth.

The other texts cited by Aune also do not show fire in the underworld. In *2 En.* 10.2 the river of fire is not in the underworld but in the skies. Matthew gives no hint of the location of its fire, nor does Mk 9.43, 48 (unless Mark is indicating the actual valley of Hinnom beside the earthly Jerusalem). The texts cited by Aune to show frequent mention of fire in the underworld do not, in fact, speak of fire in the underworld. The concept of a punitive fire *in the underworld* is not as ubiquitous as Aune suggests and it should not be assumed that Revelation's implied hearer takes 'lake of fire' as a reference to a subterranean location.

Aune presents a stronger case for a subterranean location when he discusses Egyptian sources but even this is inconclusive. He cites the Book of the Dead for the image of a lake of fire located in the underworld.⁴² Egyptian books of the dead often speak of underworld lakes, including a lake of fire. The image of a lake of fire is not found in the Hebrew scriptures or the Septuagint, in other apocalypses, early Christian writings, in Greek cultural stories or in Greek cosmological theorizing, so its presence in these Egyptian spell-books is noteworthy. It is possible that the real author of Revelation had some knowledge of this Egyptian tradition and incorporated this image into Revelation's cosmic picture. It is also possible that he created the image himself, influenced in part by the common images of furnaces, fire and sulphur, rivers of fire and his own image of the heavenly sea of glass mixed with fire (Rev. 15.2).⁴³ More

---

[41] John L. McKenzie, *Second Isaiah. Anchor Bible* (Garden City: Doubleday, 1968), 208. Joseph Blenkinsopp, *Isaiah 56–66, Achor Bible* (New Haven: Yale University Press, 1974), 317. John D. W. Watts, *Isaiah 34–66, Word Biblical Commentaries* (Nashville: Thomas Nelson, 2005), 941.

[42] Aune, *Revelation 17–22*, 1066.

[43] Woodington comments, 'The relevance of the Egyptian sources is debated ... Most commentators, however, have either ignored or dismissed this evidence because of the massive time gap between the Egyptian sources and Revelation. I concur with the majority viewpoint and find it extremely doubtful that John had these Egyptian texts in mind when he wrote the Apocalypse.' J. David Woodington, 'Crafting the Eschaton: The Second Death and the Lake of Fire in Revelation', *Journal for the Study of the New Testament*, 41 (2019): 502.

importantly, we do not have evidence that the implied hearer is familiar with Egyptian spell-books or their image of a lake of fire in the underworld. Given the significant chronological distance, and lack of evidence for the currency of the image, it seems improbable that the implied author would communicate with the implied hearer on the basis of a shared familiarity with these Egyptian traditions. We must conclude that without a prior association between a 'lake of fire' and the underworld, Revelation's implied hearer is not guided to locate the lake of fire beneath the earth.[44]

Woodington argues that John constructed the lake of fire himself by combining two Greek underworld notions, the fiery river Phlegethon and the Acherusian lake, commenting,

> Unlike Jewish thought, Greco-Roman mythology places a lake in the underworld. Notably, contemporary Jewish and Christian sources demonstrate an awareness of the Archerusian Lake and, even more importantly, a willingness to incorporate it into their eschatological visions (*Sib. Or.* 2.334-338; *Apoc. Mos.* 37.3; *Apoc. Pet.* 14; *Apoc. Paul* 22), indicating both the general prevalence of this notion at the time and its specific influence upon apocalyptic literature.[45]

It is indeed plausible that the implied hearer is familiar with the concepts of a subterranean river of fire and a subterranean lake ('where the souls of the dead must go'),[46] and is thus capable of understanding that the two are combined in Revelation to create a specifically subterranean lake of fire. But there are reasons to doubt this conclusion. First, in these Greek conceptions neither the lake nor the river of fire are places of punishment and/or destruction.[47] Further, the Jewish and Christian sources

---

[44] In *The Apocalypse, The Anti-Christ and the End*, Elar cited Josephus's *Discourse to the Greeks Concerning Hades* as evidence that a subterranean lake of fire was known to first-century Jews. Elar, *Apocalypse*, 260. However, it is now understood that the *Discourse to the Greeks Concerning Hades* was actually written by Hippolytus (c. 170–235 CE), and its 'lake of fire' is likely derived from Revelation itself.

Malina and Pilch state that the lake of fire is 'presumably' in the 'cosmic Abyss' (which they locate either in the southern part of the sky or in the sky of the southern hemisphere). They offer no evidence for this suggestion. Malina and Pilch, *Social-Science*, 233.

[45] Woodington, 'Crafting', 511.

[46] The heroes in Greek stories encountered the cosmic rivers, including the fiery river Phlegethon/Pyriphlegethon (Homer, *Odyssey* 10.513). Plato writes of the four cosmic rivers and describes the course of the river Acheron, which finally comes to the Acherusian Lake, 'where the souls of the dead must go'. This lake plays a very significant role in his depiction of the underworld and postmortem experiences. He also describes the course of Phlegethon/Pyriphlegethon, mentioning that at one point it too forms a lake:

> The third river flows out between these two, and near the place whence it issues it falls into a vast region burning with a great fire and makes a lake larger than our Mediterranean sea, boiling with water and mud … Then, after winding about many times underground, it flows into Tartaros at a lower level. This is the river which is called Pyriphlegethon, and the streams of lava which spout up at various places on earth are offshoots from it.

Plato, *Phaedo* 113b. We should note that this lake is very close to being a lake of fire, but it does not have a name nor any particular function, and does not appear to be well-known.

[47] In some conceptions both Phlegethon and the non-fiery Cocytus may play a role in carrying the souls of sinners to the place of their punishment, but the rivers themselves are neither the place nor

that incorporate an Acherusian lake do not place it in the underworld. The *Sibylline Oracles* and *Apocalypse of Peter* are unclear but the *Apocalypse of Moses* places it in the skies and the *Apocalypse of Paul* places it on the earth.[48] The *Apocalypse of Paul* is particularly interesting in this regard, as it appears to be influenced by Revelation but does not understand Revelation's lake of fire to be in any way related to the Acherusian lake. The *Apocalypse of Paul* has a city influenced by Revelation's new Jerusalem (*Apoc. Paul* 23-29) and locates its Acherusian lake beside this (*Apoc. Paul* 31). Its equivalent of the lake of fire is separate from its Acherusian lake, and this place is located not beneath the ground but beyond the western edge of the earth (*Apoc. Paul* 31). It appears unreasonable to expect Revelation's implied hearer to locate the lake of fire in the underworld on the basis of a connection with Phlegethon and the Acherusian lake.

Some further considerations speak against an under-earth location. An under-earth location does not accord with the narrative moments in which ἡ λίμνη τοῦ πυρός occurs. Of the six occurrences of this term, three occur while story-space is undifferentiated and lacking an under-earth space (Rev. 20.14-15) and one occurs when story-space is redifferentiated but still lacks an under-earth space (Rev. 21.8). Additionally, the narrative movements that remake/restructure the greater cosmos imply that the lake of fire is not part of the greater cosmos. There is 'a new heaven and a new earth', the hyper-heaven is merged with earth, the sea is no more and Hades is destroyed (thrown into the lake of fire). Revelation is describing the remaking/restructuring of the entire greater cosmos, from the highest level to the lowest. A lake of fire in the underworld would give the discordant picture of the remaking/restructuring of the entire greater cosmos except for one part of the underworld.

The more persuasive proposal is that the lake of fire is a non-place. McDonough writes that we are 'meant to see that the reprobate in the lake of fire are forever outside the renewed cosmos; they have, as it were, become eternally irrelevant. They are in a place that is No-Place'.[49] Similarly, Friesen writes that the lake of fire is difficult to locate on Revelation's tiered spatial schema: 'The lake of fire takes us to the limits of imaginative topography.'[50] This proposal accords with the lake of fire's function in the narrative, effecting either absolute destruction of the entity or absolute destruction of its cosmic relevance.

---

direct means of punishment. Plato, *Phaedo* 113b. Roman authors used Phlegethon in different ways; Virgil describes it as an encircling moat around the prison of the damned. Virgil, *Aeneid* 6.548.

Sib. Or. 2.331-338 appears strongly influenced by a Greek concept that Phlegethon may at some time carry the souls of sinners to the Acherusian lake in the hope of receiving forgiveness and release by those they wronged (Plato, *Phaedo* 114a). In the Sibylline presentation the wicked suffer fiery torment, in which the fiery river does play a role.

[48] In the *Sibylline Oracles*, the Acherusian lake is located on the Elysian plain (*Sib. Or.* 2.337-338). The same is true of the *Apocalypse of Peter*. Erik Peterson comments that in the *Apocalypse of Peter* the 'Elysian plain' is the land of Israel, and it is beside this that the Acherusian lake is found. Erik Peterson, 'Die Taufe im Acherusischen See', *Vigiliae Christianae*, 9/1 (1955): 19.

[49] McDonough, 'Revelation', 184.

[50] Friesen, *Imperial Cults*, 152-6.

The challenging concept of a non-place exists in ancient cosmological texts. Aristotle explored the concept of a non-spatial region above the heavens. Beyond the outermost sphere that is the absolute boundary of the cosmos there is neither space nor time but there is still existence. Entities can be spoken of as existing in non-place beyond the extremity of the cosmos (Aristotle, *De Caelo* 278b10–279a28). The Book of Watchers explores a non-place beyond the horizontal extremity of earth and sky. Its character as a non-place is explained not in the abstract terms of Aristotle but through the explicit lack of either a sky above or earth below to define it as a place (*1 En.* 18.10-15; 21.1-10). A fiery non-place lacking sky and earth may occur again in the Epistle of Enoch (*1 En.* 108.3).[51] Paradoxically, the non-places of *De Caelo* and *1 Enoch* exist in spatial relationship with the cosmos; in *De Caelo* the non-place is beyond the ultimate sky-structure while in *1 Enoch* it is beyond the horizontal extremity of earth and sky. Given this ancient context it is not entirely surprising to find that Revelation's narrative has a role for a non-place.

Though not taken up in subsequent scholarship, Charles was correct in his observation that 'to this conception is very nearly related the λίμνη τοῦ πυρός in our text. This λίμνη τοῦ πυρός appears, like all the places of punishment just described in Enoch, to be outside the bounds of heaven and earth'.[52] This is also the understanding of the author of the *Apocalypse of Paul*, which is heavily influenced by Revelation and has its equivalent of the lake of fire located beyond the western extremity of the earth (*Apoc. Paul* 31). By showing that in the early centuries of the era some real readers of Revelation developed the concept of an ultimate fiery destination beyond the edge of the earth, the *Apocalypse of Paul* adds weight to the suggestion that Revelation's implied reader understands Revelation in this way. Revelation's λίμνη τοῦ πυρός is a non-place with a paradoxical spatial relationship with the cosmos: it is outside. While the horizontal limits of Revelation's cosmos are not precisely marked, it appears that the lake of fire lies beyond them.

For this reason it makes sense for Rev. 21.5-8 to say that God's people, οἱ διψῶντες and οἱ νικῶντες, will participate in the πάντα καινά while those who have chosen not to be God's people have τὸ μέρος αὐτῶν ἐν τῇ λίμνῃ τῇ καιομένῃ πυρί. There is only inclusion in the cosmos or exclusion from the cosmos. To say that they inherit the lake of fire is another way of saying that they are excluded from the cosmos. In McDonough's words, they are 'eternally irrelevant'.[53]

---

[51] The textual variants each comment explicitly that there either is or is not a ground in that place. As the existence of the ground would not usually require comment, the variants that describe a lack of ground are probably more original. Isaac, '1 (Ethiopic Apocalypse of) Enoch', 88.

[52] Charles, *Revelation*, vol. 2, 138.

[53] For this reason it is not accurate to say, 'It seems that the wicked are still with us.' Barr, *Tales*, 264.

A comment that sometimes causes confusion is Rev. 22.15, which says in relation to the new Jerusalem, ἔξω οἱ κύνες καὶ οἱ **φάρμακοι** καὶ οἱ **πόρνοι** καὶ οἱ **φονεῖς** καὶ οἱ **εἰδωλολάτραι** καὶ πᾶς φιλῶν καὶ ποιῶν **ψεῦδος**. This verse is outside the narrative frame of Rev. 21.1–22.5 but is equivalent to Rev. 21.8, τοῖς δὲ δειλοῖς καὶ ἀπίστοις καὶ ἐβδελυγμένοις καὶ **φονεῦσιν** καὶ **πόρνοις** καὶ **φαρμάκοις** καὶ **εἰδωλολάτραις** καὶ πᾶσιν τοῖς **ψευδέσιν** τὸ μέρος αὐτῶν ἐν τῇ λίμνῃ τῇ καιομένῃ πυρὶ καὶ θείῳ. As such it continues the '*via negativa*' description that Boring observes in Rev. 21.1–22.5. Boring, *Revelation*, 216–18.

7.3.2 Experiencing the lake of fire

To be cast into the lake of fire means one of two things: absolute destruction of being or absolute exclusion from the cosmos. From the perspective of the cosmos these are the same thing but from the perspective of the individual entity there is a distinction. The distinction has significance as it relates to the two kinds of beings that experience the lake of fire: mortal and immortal.

The distinction between mortal beings and immortal beings is important in the apocalypses and in Greek cultural stories. It determines the kind of ending possible for a being, whether the ending results from the passing of time or defeat at the hands of an opponent. The assumption in Greek cultural stories is that humans must die but gods cannot. Yet gods often sought the destruction of other gods. Indeed, the development of the civilized cosmic order could only be achieved with the defeat of many older gods. This was achieved by imprisonment or emasculation. The primordial god Ouranos was defeated by his son, the Titan god Kronos. Kronos defeated his father Ouranos by castrating him, and in this way Ouranos faded into irrelevance as a power in the cosmos but did not cease to exist (Hesiod, *Theogony* 160-181; Apollodorus, *Library* 1.1.4).[54] Kronos then repressed the power of his own offspring by imprisoning them in his belly until one of his sons, the Olympian god Zeus, was able to defeat him in battle and release his siblings. Most of the Titan gods were then bound in Tartaros and in this way removed as cosmic powers but they did not experience death (Hesiod, *Theogony* 492-506; Apollodorus, *Library* 1.2.1). When the god Hephaistos was thrown from Olympos to earth this could result in permanent injury and deformity but not in death (*Homeric Hymn to Apollo* 316-321; Homer, *Iliad* 1.590-594; 18.395-405; Apollodorus, *Library* 1.3.5; Valerius Flaccus, *Argonautica* 2.82-97). While gods cannot die, humans *must* die, unless granted immortality as happened on very rare occasions.[55]

The distinction between two kinds of beings is found also in the apocalypses. The Book of Watchers (*1 En.* 1-36) distinguishes between earth-beings (humans) and sky-beings (angels/watchers). Most obviously, the natural state and native home of a sky-being is very different from the natural state and native home of an earth-being. Yet boundaries can be crossed. Indeed, the unacceptable crossing of these boundaries is the central theme in the Book of Watchers. But there is an even more fundamental difference between the sky-beings and the earth-beings: the earth-beings die but the sky-beings do not. The Book of Watchers does not consider the possibility that a sky-being could become like an earth-being in this regard.

We find earth-beings subjected to violent deaths, and when the death is unjust and human blood is spilt on the earth the lifeblood/soul may remain in the earth and cry out for justice (*1 En.* 9.1-3, 9-10; 22.1-7) as did the lifeblood of Abel in Genesis

---

[54] Robert Graves, *The Greek Myths* (Middlesex: Penguin, 1955), 39.

[55] In some accounts the mortal Tithonos was granted immortality but not perpetual youth, thus growing older and weaker until there was nothing left of him but a complaining voice. Although he wished to die, he could not (*Homeric Hymn to Aphrodite* 218-238). Richard Janko, 'Tithonus, Eos and the Cicada in the Homeric Hymn to Aphrodite and Sappho fr. 58', in *The Winnowing Oar: New Perspectives in Homeric Studies*, ed. Christos Tsagalis and Andreas Markantonatos (Berlin: De Gruyter, 2017), 283.

(Gen. 4.10). In this limited sense it could be said that the deceased human still has a kind of existence, though it is far less than life. But nowhere in the Book of Watchers is it even contemplated that a sky-being might die, whether naturally or violently, justly or unjustly. So when holy judgement is enacted against a sky-being this does not mean destruction of the being but destruction of their power and influence, and the experience of imprisonment and grief (*1 En.* 10.4-5, 11-13; 14.5). There are other beings in the Book of Watchers, most notably the enormous, hybrid offspring of the watchers. These are far more powerful than humans but they are ultimately subject to death. For these beings, holy judgement results in death (*1 En.* 10.9-15; 12.5-6; 14.6). Indeed, it is part of the punishment of the rebellious angels/watchers, who descended from sky to earth to procreate with human women, that they see their monstrous offspring killed – but it is beyond contemplation that they themselves might be killed.

This key distinction between sky-beings and earth-beings is carried through to the eschatological judgement. Sky-beings who have been bound in a deep, dark part of the earth are then led into the emptiness of fire, which they experience as imprisonment and torment. From the present time, condemned humans are also bound together with the sky-beings in this deep, dark part of the earth but in the eschatological judgement they experience the emptiness of fire very differently. In the emptiness of fire, sky-beings are imprisoned and tormented but earth-beings are burnt up and destroyed (κατακαυθῇ καὶ ἀφανισθῇ, *1 En.* 10.12-14).[56]

The distinction between mortal beings and non-mortal beings is found also in the Animal Apocalypse (*1 En.* 85–90). Human beings are represented allegorically as animals such as bovines and sheep, and the rebellious angels/watchers are represented allegorically as stars. In its ultimate eschatological judgement, the 'stars' are cast into a fiery abyss while the 'bad sheep' are cast into a separate fiery abyss. The result for the stars is not narrated explicitly but it is implied that they are now in an absolutely permanent and very unpleasant state. The result for the sheep is more explicit – they are burnt. Specifically, they are destroyed by the fire to the point where even their bones are burnt (*1 En.* 90.24-27). This is absolute destruction.[57] Like the Book of Watchers, the Book of Dream Visions assumes that human beings can be killed while

---

[56] Commenting on the Aramaic fragment 4QEn^c, Milik notes that the Aramaic חרר primarily means 'to burn' but also occurs in Aramaic contracts with the meaning 'to take proceedings'. Preferring the second meaning, he considers κατακαυθῇ to be a mistranslation of the Aramaic. Milik, *Books of Enoch*, 190. I would argue, however, that the primary meaning of חרר works perfectly well in this context and there is no reason to consider κατακαυθῇ a mistranslation. On the other hand, Milik's translation into English of 4QEn^c also has human beings destroyed, rather than tormented, in this passage: 'And everyone who is condemned, [will be lost from now on; with them they will be bound until annihilation of] their [generation]; at that time [of judgement] which I (God) shall judge, they shall perish for all [generations].'

Nickelsburg correctly notes that *1 En.* 10.14 'uses the watchers' temporary imprisonment and final judgement as a paradigm for the punishment of all sinners', but we should add that the final judgement has different consequences for sky-beings and earth-beings. Nickelsburg, *1 Enoch 1*, 224. Compare 1QS 4.13, 'And all the ages of their generations they shall spend in bitter weeping in the dark abysses until their destruction' (translation García Martínez).

[57] The entire being is obliterated, even the bones. The allusion to Ezekiel 37 communicates that there is no possibility of resurrection for these 'sheep'. Mark Adam Elliott, *The Survivors of Israel: A Reconsideration of the Theology of Pre-Christian Judaism* (Grand Rapids: Eerdmans, 2000), 80.

certain other beings cannot. Those that cannot be killed may instead be subjected to absolutely permanent loss of power and vitality through irreversible imprisonment and/or torment.[58]

This pattern is also found in a Christian apocalypse that is a near-contemporary with Revelation. The *Ascension of Isaiah* presents an eschatological judgement in which Beliar and his hosts are dragged into a deep cosmic region of torment called Gehenna or Perdition (*Asc. Isa.* 1.3; 4.14; 10.8), while recently resurrected humans are consumed by fire – that is, absolutely destroyed as if they had never existed (*Asc. Isa.* 4.18).

The assumption that defeat has different results for different kinds of beings is sustained in Revelation. Revelation explicitly communicates to the hearer that the lake of fire serves in the eschaton as a place of torment for the diabolical trinity (the dragon/serpent/devil/satan, the beast and the false prophet/second beast). These are categorized as the kind of being that, by its very nature, is incapable of utter cessation of existence. However, when Death and Hades are thrown into the lake of fire (Rev. 20.14) there is no narration of torment and it is unlikely that the implied hearer extrapolates from the diabolical trinity to conclude that Death and Hades also experience the lake of fire as ongoing torment.[59]

What then of humans? The implied hearer of Revelation assumes that there are fundamental differences between human beings, who are native to earth, and the powerful non-human personages, native to other cosmic regions.[60] Further, this implied hearer assumes that the enactment of holy judgement against humans is categorically different to the enactment of holy judgement against those powerful non-human personages that may not be subject to death. Revelation allows its implied hearer to maintain this assumption throughout the reading.

Beale presents a different argument for the ongoing existence of humans in the lake of fire. Commenting on Rev. 14.9-11, he argues that there is corporate representation in which individual humans are represented by the devil, beast and second beast, and therefore participate in their eternal torment in the lake of fire (Rev. 19.20; 20.10).[61]

---

[58] If we consider the Book of Parables, we note in *1 Enoch* 48 the eschatological judgement against unrighteous humans and in v. 9 the dual images of destruction: they burn up like grass in the fire and sink like lead in the water, 'and no trace of them shall any more be found'. Translation R. H. Charles, *The Book of Enoch, or, 1 Enoch* (Oxford: Clarendon, 1912). As human beings they are subject to destruction of the self.

[59] There appears to be near universal agreement among commentators that for Death and Hades, the lake of fire means utter destruction rather than tormented ongoing existence. Swete commented, 'The immersion of this symbolic pair ... can only mean the annihilation of the forces indicated'. Swete, *Apocalypse*, 270. See also Gebhardt, *Doctrine*, 290. Charles, *Revelation*, vol. 2, 145. Caird, *Commentary*, 260. Sweet, *Revelation*, 295. Bingham, *Revelation*, 192. Harrington, *Revelation*, 204–5. Labahn, '"Apokalyptische" Geographie', 140. Koester, *Revelation*, 781. The only exception of which I am aware is Woodington, 'Crafting', 513. However, some commentators take 'Death and Hades' as a metonymy standing for the unrighteous human dead. See Elar, *Apocalypse*, 267. Beale, *Revelation*, 1034–35. Aune, *Revelation 17–22*, 1103. But this is unlikely. In the narrative Hades hands over its dead – it is not cast into the lake of fire still holding its dead. Further, if Hades were a metonymy then it would stand for all the dead not only the unrighteous dead.

[60] Rodney Duke also discusses the importance of this distinction and the nature of the human in biblical texts. Rodney K. Duke, 'Eternal Torment or Destruction? Interpreting Final Judgment Texts', *Evangelical Quarterly*, 88/3 (2016): 245–8.

[61] Beale, *Revelation*, 762.

The problem with Beale's argument is this: while it would make sense for Revelation to present individual humans as participants in the beast, in fact it does not. Instead, Revelation presents individual humans as participants in the whore/Babylon. People are seduced by the whore/Babylon (Rev. 14.8; 17.1-5; 18.3, 9) and mourn its passing (Rev. 18.9-19). When it is destroyed, people share its fate (Rev. 14.8-11; 18.4) and Revelation calls its reader to come out of it lest they share its fate (Rev. 18.4). While people fear the beast and therefore worship it, they do not identify with it or mourn its passing, and Revelation does not call its hearer to come out of the beast. When the beast is thrown into the lake of fire, its followers suffer a different fate (Rev. 19.20-21).[62] The same is true of the satan/devil (Rev. 20.9-10). Given that individual humans are participants in the whore/Babylon, and not in the diabolical trinity, it is instructive to note that while the diabolical trinity are thrown into the lake of fire and suffer perpetual torment, the whore/Babylon is destroyed on earth by fire and martial attacks (Rev. 14.8-11; 17.16; 18.1-19.3). It would seem that individual humans do not participate in the perpetual torment experienced by the devil, beast and second beast, but in the perpetual destruction experienced by the whore/Babylon.

Revelation categorizes Hades, the whore/Babylon and humans as entities subject to death and destruction but the dragon, beast and second beast as beings that are incapable of utter cessation of existence. The dragon, beast and second beast experience the lake of fire as absolute exclusion and perpetual irrelevence to the cosmos. Hades and humans experience the lake of fire as utter cessation of existence. From the perspective of the cosmos these are the same thing.

7.4 Real cosmos replaced?

In the foregoing sections of this chapter I put aside the question that has troubled modern commentators: does Revelation indicate that the real cosmos will be destroyed? I argued above that the deletions in story-space were appropriate to the narrative moment of Rev. 20.11-15. In Caird's language, 'The first thing that John saw in heaven was a throne (iv. 2), surrounded by a heavenly choir … Now the choirs of heaven are silent, the created world fades into nothingness … the great white throne stands alone, with nothing to challenge, to qualify, or even to mediate its sole supremacy.'[63] But does this deletion in story-space indicate that the real cosmos will be erased? Over a hundred years ago Beckwith wrote of 'the question, frequently raised among earlier commentators, whether the new world is to be a renovation of that now existing, or a different one brought in in place of the old previously removed or destroyed'.[64] The question has been asked again by subsequent commentators and has

---

[62] 'The three ringleaders … suffer a punishment more severe than those whom they misled; whilst their dupes are at once consumed by fire from heaven, they are immersed in a fiery flood where their torture is increasing and perennial.' Swete, *Apocalypse*, 267.
[63] Caird, *Commentary*, 258.
[64] Beckwith, *Apocalypse of John*, 750.

not lost currency.⁶⁵ Contributions have been made by many scholars including N.T. Wright, Edward Adams and Mark. B. Stephens.

7.4.1 Existing scholarship

In Wright's many works he builds up an argument in which the theological significance of the cosmos is explained and its future determined on that basis. He describes a 'creational and covenantal monotheism'⁶⁶ in the Hebrew scriptures in which the physical universe is characterized as good, along with the 'linguistic convention' of using end-of-the-world language as a metaphor for dramatic theo-political events.⁶⁷ Wright reads the New Testament in that light and concludes that it consistently looks for transformation rather than destruction of the 'space-time universe'.⁶⁸ While the focus of his interest is on Mark 13 and parallels, he asserts that his finding is consistent in every text of the New Testament including Revelation.⁶⁹ Wright's proposal essentially precludes the possibility that Revelation may imagine an actual destruction of the cosmos.

Edward Adam's monograph reaches a very different conclusion regarding the language of cosmic destruction. Where Wright limits study to the Hebrew scriptures, Adams surveys also the extra-canonical apocalyptic literature and Graeco-Roman sources to discover what are the 'real cosmological option[s] for writers of this period'.⁷⁰ This then becomes the backdrop against which he reads Rev. 6.12-17 and 21.1. On this basis Adams concludes that John imagines the *'complete destruction* of the physical universe, followed by an act of re-creation' (emphasis in the original).⁷¹ Although, based on the wording of Rev. 21.5 and his survey of the cosmological options, Adams clarifies that this does not mean 'reduction to and creation out of non-being',⁷² but rather 'the first creation is taken back to its pre-created, chaotic state and a new creative

---

⁶⁵ Those who argue that 'the new world is to be a renovation of that now existing' include Caird, *Commentary*, 265. Boring, *Revelation*, 220. Richard Bauckham, *The Theology of the Book of Revelation* (Cambridge: Cambridge University Press, 1993), 49. Murphy, *Fallen*, 406. Beale, *Revelation*, 1040. Malina and Pilch, *Social-Science*, 244–5. Blount, *Revelation*, 376. Fair, *Conquering*, 357. Those who argue that there is to be 'a different one brought in in place of the old' include Hobbs, *Cosmic Drama*, 194. Beasley-Murray, *Revelation*, 307. Jürgen Roloff, *The Revelation of John: A Continental Commentary*, trans. John E. Alsup (Minneapolis: Fortress Press, 1993), 235. Osborne, *Revelation*, 730. Aune, *Revelation 17–22*, 1117. Koester writes, 'Interpreters often ask whether the new creation is a renewal of the first or a replacement of it. But these categories are inadequate.' Koester, *Revelation*, 803.

⁶⁶ N. T. Wright, *The New Testament and the People of God* (Minneapolis: Fortress Press, 1992), 252. Wright further argues that 'as good creational monotheists, mainline Jews were not hoping to escape from the present universe into some Platonic realm of eternal bliss enjoyed by the disembodied souls after the end of the space-time universe'. Wright, *New Testament*, 286.

⁶⁷ Wright, *New Testament*, 283.

⁶⁸ Wright, *New Testament*, 252, 286.

⁶⁹ This is the clear implication of many statements throughout his works, but it is also said explicitly in Wright, *Revelation*, 189.

⁷⁰ Edward Adams, *The Stars Will Fall from Heaven: Cosmic Catastrophe in the New Testament and its World*, Library of New Testament Studies, vol. 347 (London: T&T Clark, 2007), 238.

⁷¹ Adams, *The Stars Will Fall*, 238. Citing Aune, *Revelation 17–22*.

⁷² Adams, *The Stars Will Fall*, 238.

act takes place. The picture is indeed that of the renewal of creation, but the renewal is accomplished precisely by destruction and re-creation'.[73]

In his study, Mark B. Stephens investigates 'the issue of the continuity and discontinuity between this present creation and the new creation which is to come',[74] aiming to 'follow the thread of new creation throughout the entire work'.[75] He notes 'the archetypal worship of the living creatures, whose ... praise is exported and extended into the realm of earth. Similarly, within the compressed narrative of Chapter 5, creation is shown moving from a state of anguish (5:2-3) to a state of singing (5:13)'.[76] The whole of creation and its creatures rejoicing that the seven seals can now happen implies that the creation is going to be liberated rather than destroyed and replaced. Stephens ultimately concludes that John's 'articulation of cosmic renewal favours the "interventionist" model of final transformation (as seen in the Book of Watchers, Animal Apocalypse, the Parables of Enoch and *Sibylline Oracles* Book 3), as against the gradual renewal of the world we find in *Jubilees* (where there is no final assize)'.[77] Yet while

> there are numerous visions of judgement and destruction, in which nature apparently suffers along with humanity ... [this] is not to be interpreted as the systematic annihilation of creation. On the contrary, the destruction imagery depicts part of the process by which the present world order is judged and evil powers removed, in order that creation might be taken to its eschatological goal.[78]

Thus Revelation agrees with Romans 8 that 'the eschatological goal of creation is for it to be liberated along with humanity'.[79] His conclusion is perhaps similar to that of Hansen who suggests that in Revelation the material world is not completely destroyed but 'severely reorganized'.[80]

7.4.2 A narratological contribution

In this chapter we have seen how Revelation's story-space becomes undifferentiated in Rev. 20.11-15 and redifferentiated in Rev. 21.1. In the narrative of Rev. 20.11–22.5 God does not ennact the destruction of an earth and sky, nor does God create an earth and sky. Rather, God ennacts a moment of judgement, and the moment of judgement causes earth and sky not to exist for as long as that moment lasts (Rev. 20.11). When the moment of judgement is finished earth and sky again exist (Rev. 21.1).

---

[73] Adams, *The Stars Will Fall*, 238.
[74] Mark B. Stephens, *Annihilation or Renewal?: The Meaning and Function of New Creation in the Book of Revelation*, Wissenschaftliche Untersuchungen zum Neuen Testament 2 Reihe, vol. 307 (Tübingen: Mohr Siebeck, 2011), 1.
[75] Stephens, *Annihilation or Renewal?*, 11.
[76] Stephens, *Annihilation or Renewal?*, 190.
[77] Stephens, *Annihilation or Renewal?*, 259.
[78] Stephens, *Annihilation or Renewal?*, 258.
[79] Stephens, *Annihilation or Renewal?*, 259.
[80] Hansen, *Silence*, 66, 95.

The moment of judgement also means that earth and sky cannot have the characteristic of 'conflicted space' that they had prior to the moment of judgement. For this reason John sees 'a new heaven and a new earth; for the first heaven and the first earth had passed away'. When sky and earth again exist they must also be different in character. There are two narrative shifts at work:

1. the moment of judgement means that earth and sky cannot exist for as long as the moment lasts but must exist again as soon as the moment passes; and
2. an effect of the judgement is that any earth and sky must be of character consistent with God's authority over everything.

Earth and sky exist again because judgement is complete; earth and sky have a different character because judgement is complete. As Rev. 21.1 does not narrate any direct action to achieve the existence or changed character of earth and sky it appears that this results simply from the passing of the narrative moment of judgement.

It is only in Rev. 21.5 that we discover an action performed on earth and sky. This action is revealed through the direct speech of the one sitting on the Throne: ἰδοὺ καινὰ ποιῶ πάντα. This construction indicates that God is causing all things to conform to the adjective.[81] God is not causing new things to exist; that would be expressed as ποιῶ τὰ πάντα τὰ καινά. Rather, God is causing things to conform to the characteristic implied by καινός.

This meaning is suggested also by the verb choice. While Revelation does use ποιέω with the meaning of 'cause to exist', it does so only twice (Rev. 14.7; 22.20). In all other instances it indicates doing an action, causing an event to happen or causing an entity to have a certain characteristic (including the characteristic of performing an ongoing action). Thus Rev. 1.6 and 5.10 refer to the act of causing people to be priests, not causing them to exist. Similarly, when the second beast ποιεῖ τὴν γῆν καὶ τοὺς ἐν αὐτῇ κατοικοῦντας ἵνα προσκυνήσουσιν τὸ θηρίον τὸ πρῶτον it is not causing the earth and its inhabitants to exist but causing them to have the characteristic of worshipping the first beast (Rev. 13.12). Where Revelation uses κτίζω it refers to God's act of causing all things to exist (Rev. 4.11; 10.6) but where Revelation uses ποιέω it more commonly indicates causing an entity to conform to a characteristic. The use of this verb in Rev. 21.5 strengthens the sense that God is conforming all things to the characteristic καινός, not causing all things to exist.

The characteristics that may be implied by καινός are freshness, dynamism and purpose, in continuity and contrast with what went before.[82] In the context of Revelation's narrative movement, it suggests that earth and sky and everything in them now have the characteristic of being consistent with God's authority over all things and God's desire to end death, grief, crying and suffering (Rev. 21.4). This state now

---

[81] Beale writes that this is an example of the predicate accusative, thus indicating 'I will make all things as new'. Beale, *Revelation*, 1054. A. T. Robertson, *A Grammar of the Greek New Testament in the Light of Historical Research* (London: Hodder and Stoughton, 1919), 480.
[82] Henry George Liddell et al., *A Greek-English Lexicon* (Oxford: Clarendon Press, 1968). R. A. Harrisville, 'The Concept of Newness in the New Testament', *Journal of Biblical Literature*, 74 (1955): 69, 79.

characterizes τὰ πάντα, that is, ὁ οὐρανός καὶ τὰ ἐν αὐτῷ καὶ ἡ γῆ καὶ τὰ ἐν αὐτῇ (Rev. 4.11; 10.6).

If Rev. 21.5a gives an active role to God in Rev. 21.1a then the role is causing newness in this sense. The chiastic structure noted by Aune suggests that this may be the case. Aune presents this chiastic structure:

a	new [καινός] heaven and the new [καινή] earth (v. 1a)
b	first [πρῶτος] heaven, earth, and sea have passed away [ἀπῆλθαν] (v. 1b)
c	the sea exists no longer [οὐκ ἔστιν ἔτι] (v. 1b)
d	the holy city descends from heaven (v. 2)
d'	God dwells with people (vv. 3–4a)
c'	death exists no longer [οὐκ ἔσται ἔτι] (v. 4b)
b'	former things [τὰ πρῶτα] have passed away [ἀπῆλθαν] (v. 4b)
a'	God creates everything new [καινά] (v. 5a)[83]

The parallel between v. 1a and v. 5a allows that God may have an active role in causing the newness that now characterizes earth and sky. But no being has caused earth and sky to come into existence again after the moment of judgement in Rev. 20.11-15. Earth and sky exist again because the narrative moment that prevented their existence has now passed.

7.4.3 This earth and this moment

In Revelation's narrative we have seen deletions in story-space (Rev. 20.11-15) and the redifferentiation of story-space (Rev. 21.1–22.5). But the deletions and redifferentiation appear to result from the narrative moment and the passing of the narrative moment, rather than actions performed in relation to earth and sky. For this reason it is difficult to make the inference that the real earth and sky are being destroyed and replaced. I do argue that the experience of Revelation's story-space is meant to shift the hearer's pecerption of the real cosmos. Further, the hearer is meant to understand from the changes in story-space that there will be changes to the structure and character of the real cosmos. But the deletions in story-space and redifferentiation of story-space communicate little about any real process by which the real earth and sky may be made absent and then present.

We have seen in the narrative the presence then absence then presence of spaces and structures. We have not seen any discussion of matter or materiality. For this reason, Wright's framing of the issue can be unhelpful, as his discussion of 'the space-time universe' is not just about space and time. Rather, 'space-time universe' connects the discussion with modern scientific cosmology in which the universe comes into existence as space-time and matter-energy, and may go out of existence in the same way.[84] When Wright opposes the idea of the universe going out of existence, he has this

---

[83] Aune, *Revelation 17–22*, 1114.
[84] Barry Wood, 'Imagining the Unimaginable: Narratives of the Big Bang: Time, Space, Matter, Energy', *Journal of Big History*, 2/1 (2018): 1–13.

sense in mind. This explains Wright's frequently posed dichotomy between a 'space-time universe' and a 'Platonic realm' in which there is no matter.[85] But the narrative of Rev. 20.11–22.5 is not concerned with the matter and materiality of the cosmos but with the presence, absence and presence of spaces and structures. Swete pointed towards this in 1906 when he wrote, 'It is only the external order of the world which is to be changed and not its substance or material; so e.g. Irenaeus. v. 36 I: οὐ γὰρ ἡ ὑπόστασις οὐδὲ ἡ οὐσία τῆς κτίσεως ἐξαφανίζεται … ἀλλὰ τὸ σχῆμα παράγει τοῦ κόσμου τούτου.'[86] So Wright's dichotomy is a false one. In discussing the possibility that Revelation communicates the destruction of the real cosmos, we are not discussing the possibility that it communicates the end of an entire space-time matter-energy universe. We are instead discussing the possible destruction of cosmic structures and the spaces created by those structures. Wright's assertions cannot validly preclude Hansen's judgement that the material world is 'severely reorganized'.[87]

The deletions in story-space and redifferentiation of story-space communicate little about any real process by which the real earth and sky may be made absent and then present. But we can observe that earth's absence from story-space in Rev. 20.11 is the effect of the narrative moment of judgement and earth's presence again in Rev. 21.1 is the effect of that narrative moment passing. So there is one inference we can make from story-space to the real cosmos: the γῆ of Rev. 21.1 is the same entity that is called by that name in Rev. 1.4–20.10. It is this earth that is given the characteristic of newness.

Finally, let us note the relative significance of this issue. The question of whether 'the new world is to be a renovation of that now existing, or a different one brought in in place of the old previously removed or destroyed' is of particular currency in the historical moment in which I write, as humankind continues the wilful destruction of τὸν οὐρανὸν καὶ τὰ ἐν αὐτῷ καὶ τὴν γῆν καὶ τὰ ἐν αὐτῇ καὶ τὴν θάλασσαν καὶ τὰ ἐν αὐτῇ. It is not only those who approach Revelation as Holy Scripture who want to know its attitude to this earth.

Within Revelation's narrative the most radical cosmic shift is not the presence then absence then presence of earth, nor even the newness of the earth that makes it fresh and fit for God's purposes. The most radical cosmic shift occurs not in Rev. 21.1 but in Rev. 21.2. The merging of the Throne-space with the earth-space in Rev. 21.2 means that the earth-and-sky cosmos is inherently, absolutely, eternally safe – a space of fully living in which the earth-dwellers are nourished by the river and the tree and may look upon God's face with joy.

7.5 Conclusion: Cosmos anew

This chapter has examined the cosmic changes that occur in Rev. 20.11-15 and 21.1–22.5 from the same narratological perspective that guided the examination of cosmic

---

[85] Wright, *New Testament*, 286. N. T. Wright, *Jesus and the Victory of God* (Minneapolis: Fortress Press, 1996), 283.
[86] Swete, *Apocalypse*, 268.
[87] Hansen, *Silence*, 66, 95.

story-space in Rev. 1.4–20.10. The presence then absence then presence of earth and sky (Rev. 20.11; 21.1) was seen to result not from the direct actions of any actor but from the narrative moment that required their absence (Rev. 20.11-15) and the passing of that narrative moment.

In the redifferentiated space of Rev. 21.1 the new sky and earth establish continuity with the spatial arrangement of Rev. 1.4–20.10. That the earth and sky are 'new' (fresh, dynamic, fit for purpose) results from the recent moment of judgement and from God's direct action of causing everything to have this quality. But the greatest cosmic change is more radical still: the descent of the new Jerusalem is the merging of the God-space with the earth-space. As a result of this merger the God-space is now accessible to all existing humans as a space of fully living, and the earth-space is inherently, absolutely, eternally safe.

This means that some things are negated: specifically, those beings who do not give up practices that are destructive to earth and sky and to those who dwell in them. These beings are cast out of the cosmos, that is, into the lake of fire. The lake of fire is non-existence or non-participation in the cosmos, which is very nearly the same thing. Paradoxically, this non-space has a spatial relationship with the cosmos; the implied hearer understands that it is beyond the horizontal limits of earth and sky. For the ancient person, it is this paradoxical spatial relationship with the cosmos that gives it its character as non-place.

Finally, this chapter returned to the question of whether Revelation's narrative communicates that the real cosmos will be destroyed. We observed how Revelation's story-space expands from the initial scene of action on an Aegean island to become co-extensive with a cosmos of four spatial levels, but in Rev. 20.11-15 story-space becomes undifferentiated. This fit the narrative moment in that people had no space in which to be distant from the Throne and nowhere to stand except in front of the Throne. While the experience of cosmic story-space is meant to shift the hearer's perception of the real cosmos, how these changes in story-space relate to the process of change in the real cosmos is not a simple question. Because the presence then absence then presence of earth and sky resulted from the narrative moment and the passing of the narrative moment, and not from the actions of an actor, we could not draw the inference that Revelation expects the real cosmos to be destroyed and replaced. From this narratological perspective, it appears that the earth of Rev. 21.1 is the same entity called earth in Rev. 1.4–20.10.

8

The ideological import of the cosmic structure

This chapter examines the ideological significance of the tiered cosmic structure in which Revelation's narrative operates. The virtual experience of Revelation's cosmic story-space is contrasted with the experience and ideology of space within the dominant imperial culture. This draws on work by Steven Friesen and Wei Hsien Wan on spatial experience and spatial ideology in the Roman imperial cults of Asia Minor and neighbouring Anatolian provinces,[1] connecting this with the basic cosmic schema and assumed place of gods in Greek cultural stories and worship practices. While the spatial ideology of empire makes Rome the centre of the earth and established also in the god-space, I argue that Revelation locates empire within its spatial schema in such a way that it is de-centred, relativized, and negatively characterized.

I build on the existing scholarship on Revelation's 'symbolic universe', 'worldview' or 'rhetorical cosmology',[2] but with a focus on the complementary roles played by the sky-heaven and the hyper-heaven. In the sky-heaven pagan imperial culture is exposed as draconian. The narrative thus demands nonparticipation in its social and economic practices, while the hyper-heaven makes such nonparticipation a viable option. In this way Revelation conveys a very different understanding of appropriate action in cosmic context.

8.1 Imperial space: Architecture, ritual, myth

In recent decades the field of spatial theory has shown that human perception and experience of space is socially constructed, shaped by practices and conceptions regarding the physical/social order.[3] Of this understanding of space Wan writes, 'Rather than being the passive stage on which human activity takes place, it is transformed into a dynamic element of social life itself—caught up in, forming, and being formed by our interactions with one another.'[4] From the perspective of spatial theory we see

---

[1] Friesen, *Imperial Cults*. Wan, *Contest*.
[2] In particular: Schüssler Fiorenza, *Revelation*. Friesen, *Imperial Cults*. DeSilva, *Seeing*. Hansen, *Silence*.
[3] Early work on this was done by Henri Lefebvre. Lefebvre, *La production*. English translation: Lefebvre, *Production*. See also Kitchin, and Hubbard, *Key Thinkers on Space and Place*.
[4] Wan, *Contest*, 35.

how the Roman Empire shaped spatial experience by incorporating new territories into empire, reorganizing occupied territory into provinces, and building new roads that made certain locations experientially closer.[5] Architectural projects shaped the experience of space within cities, with porticoes and colonades that defined the boundaries of public spaces, influencing the use of space and movement within and between spaces.[6] The construction of imperial temples and sanctuaries in the most prominent locations 'redefined the local topography' and emphasized 'the looming and pervasive presence of Rome over the lives of the city's inhabitants'.[7] It was not only architectural projects that affected the experience of space. Seasonal festivals organized around the recognition of Roman power meant that 'the ways people moved in and experienced urban spaces were now reconfigured'.[8]

As the experience and conception of space are socially constructed, so they interact with ideology.[9] Ideas about spatial reality exist in reciprocal relationship with ideas about the social order.[10] Spatial practices and conceptions define centre, periphery, and border, making particular power structures and cultural practices normative.[11] In Asia Minor and neighbouring provinces, the spatial conceptions of pagan imperial culture included three key elements: Rome/Caesar as the centre of spatial reality; the empire of peace extending across the whole earth; and the god-space high above the earth in which Rome/Caesar is also present.

It is not unusual for a civilization to define space in relation to itself. Ancient Greek culture considered Delphi to be the centre not only of the Greek-speaking world but of the whole earth,[12] and the further one travelled from the centre of Greek civilization the more disordered reality became.[13] Likewise, Judeans considered Jerusalem the centre of the earth.[14] It is therefore not surprising that Romans considered Rome the centre of the earth. What is distinctive about the Rome-centred view of space is that it could be enacted throughout a vast empire stretching both east and west of the centre. Wan writes of the 'obsession with space' that characterized the Augustan period:

> The energetic nexus between imperial politics and geography gave birth to a feverish increase in partial and global censuses and the publication of cadastral

---

[5] Wan, *Contest*, 39.
[6] Wan, *Contest*, 151.
[7] Friesen, *Imperial Cults*, 124. Wan, *Contest*, 133.
[8] Wan, *Contest*, 154.
[9] Spatial conceptions are 'human constructs that are socially contested.' Jon L. Berquist, 'Critical Spatiality and the Construction of the Ancient World', in *'Imagining' Biblical Worlds: Studies in Spatial, Social, and Historical Constructs in Honor of James W. Flanagan*, ed. David M. Gunn and Paula M. McNutt, JSOTSup (London: Sheffield Academic, 2002), 15.
[10] Wan, *Contest*, 26.
[11] 'Reality revolved around the imperial city. Asia was defined as "provincial", subsidiary, dependent.' Friesen, *Imperial Cults*, 125.
[12] Herbert William Parke, *A History of the Delphic Oracle* (Oxford: Basil Blackwell, 1939), 6.
[13] The mythical Amazons, for example, lived at the fringe of the human-inhabited earth. This was a tribe of unwomen who lived in the manner of men, contrary to civilized cosmic order. P. Walcot, 'Greek Attitudes Towards Women: The Mythological Evidence,' *Greece and Rome* 31/1 (1984) 37-47.
[14] *Jub.* 8.19. And in our own time it is Australia and New Zealand, not the British Isles or North America, that are called the Antipodes.

books and maps in various regions, as well as the establishing of road itineraries. The world to be conquered also had to be known, measured, and drawn. At the center of the new imperial geography lay the city of Rome, with her imperial provinces both East and West conceived as dependent peripheries.[15]

This spatial conception was enacted in the construction of roads that facilitiated movement between centre and periphery and the economic systems that brought goods by road or by sea from the periphery to the centre.[16] Further, this conception of space was symbolically enacted in the rituals that bound the provinces to the capital. In Asia Minor and neighbouring provinces, imperial cults existed as 'a complex of symbols that was to some extent shared by its collaborators (the emperor, the Senate, Roman and local government officals, local elites, non-elite participants, etc.) and regarded by them as efficacious responses to Roman presence in Anatolian territory'.[17] Imperial cults situated the city and province in relation to Rome as capital and centre,[18] and in relation to Rome as empire of peace existing across the entirety of land and sea. Thus the imperial temple at Aphrodisias depicted all fifty ἔθνη as participants or subjects of empire,[19] as well as Augustus accompanied by Land and Sea: 'Land places a cornucopia in his right hand and Sea offers him the rudder of a ship. The message is clear: Augustus' rule has brought prosperity and peace, fertility to the land, and navigability to the seas.'[20] On the top level of the north portico the reliefs depicted the empire as the ordering presence not only in relation to the sea and the land that surrounds the sea, but in relation to the earth and the ocean-river that encircles the earth: 'an enthroned Nero coronated by his mother, with Day and Evening/Night as well as Ocean and Earth bearing witness to the reach of his power'.[21]

Imperial cosmology left some abiguity as to whether Rome existed as the ordering presence over the whole οἰκουμένη or over the entire plane of the earth. Dionysius of Halicarnassus wrote:

> But Rome rules every country that is not inaccessible or uninhabited, and she is mistress of every sea, not only of that which lies inside the Pillars of Hercules but also of the Ocean, except that part of it which is not navigable; she is the first and the only State recorded in all time that ever made the risings and the settings of the sun the boundaries of her domain.[22]

---

[15] Wan, *Contest*, 131–32. Citing Claude Nicolet, *Space, Geography, and Politics in the Early Roman Empire* (Ann Arbor: University of Michigan Press, 1991), 8, 95.
[16] Howard-Brook and Gwyther, *Unveiling*, 99.
[17] Wan, *Contest*, 52.
[18] 'Asia's provincial cults particularly dealt with cosmology: the maintenance and nourishment of the province's relationship with Rome and with the centers of authority within the imperial city.' Friesen, *Imperial Cults*, 54.
[19] Wan, *Contest*, 141. Friesen, *Imperial Cults*, 86–90.
[20] Wan, *Contest*, 142. Friesen shares this understanding of the symbolism but identifies the figure as Claudius. Friesen, *Imperial Cults*, 92.
[21] Wan, *Contest*, 139.
[22] Dionysius of Halicarnassus, *Roman Antiquities* 1.3.3. Translation Earnest Cary, Loeb Classical Library. Cited in Wan, *Contest*, 131.

If there was a border to the Roman Empire then any space beyond the borders 'was chaos, peopled by weird people living in an uncustomary way'.[23] In these deeply ideological ways Roman imperial cosmology defined centre, periphery, and border.

Through architecture, ritual, and myth the imperial cults legitimated the rule of the imperial capital over the provinces 'by "re-describing" the order of things—that is, re-framing the status quo (i.e. of Roman occupation) within a broader cosmic order'.[24] This cosmic order identified the centre of reality not only with Rome but with the Roman emperor: 'Power radiated, as if in concentric circles, from the body of the emperor to the bodies of his kin (fictive or real) and outward, beyond the city of Rome to the Empire's furthest-flung territories.'[25] The emperor's role in cosmic ordering extended not only horizontally across the plane of the earth but also vertically, binding human-space with god-space: 'the imperial cults emphasized the emperor's role as mediator between the Empire and the divine realm, and thus as a guarantor of the stability of the cosmic order'.[26]

Further, Rome and Roman emperors were themselves present in the god-space. While Graeco-Roman myth located gods throughout the cosmos, the distinctive god-space was located in the skies, existing in vertical spatial relationship with earth.[27] In the god-space high above the earth, Rome is present in the person of the emperor, either in post-mortem divinised form in the Roman sense (that is, as *divus* but not as *deus*) or as gods in the Asian Hellene sense (as θεοί),[28] or assimilated with traditional gods such as Zeus.[29] While divinization in the Roman sense was more important in Rome itself, 'the imagery of the emperor ascending to heaven in the chariot of the sun was also well known in Asia ... and it affirmed a special geography of the afterlife for deserving emperors: they entered the realm of the Olympians'.[30] Whether as city or as emperor, Rome is the centre of the earth and established also in the heavens.[31]

Roman imperial cosmology allowed the most basic of existing spatial conceptions to remain. It was fully compatitible with looking out across a broad earth stretching from

---

[23] John Helgeland, 'Time and Space: Christian and Roman,' *Aufstieg und Niedergang der römischen Welt*, 23/2 (1980): 1299. In the symbolism of the imperial temple at Aphrodisias 'there is even the suggestion that the edges of the Roman world are the edges of human civilization.' Friesen, *Imperial Cults*, 90.

[24] Wan, *Contest*, 60. 'The provincial temples served as crucial symbols of the cosmology that supported imperial rule.' Friesen, *Imperial Cults*, 55.

[25] Wan, *Contest*, 135.

[26] Wan, *Contest*, 61. See also Kahl, *Galatians Re-Imagined: Reading with the Eyes of the Vanquished* 143.

[27] Olympos 'was more often in some indefinite area of the sky than on the mountain in Thrace'. Wright, *Cosmology*, 38.

[28] Friesen, *Imperial Cults*, 75.

[29] As, for example, 'Emperor Caesar Hadrian Sebastos Zeus Olympios.' Friesen, *Imperial Cults*, 75–76, 117. 'The emperors joined the ranks of the divine and played their own particular role in that realm.' Steven J. Friesen, *Twice Neokoros: Ephesus, Asia, and the Cult of the Flavian Imperial Family* (Leiden: Brill, 1993), 75.

[30] Friesen, *Imperial Cults*, 130. 'The transfer of the god-king from earth to Olympus did not require the manufacture of altogether new machinery. The Attic vase painters knew how Hercules, Dionysus, and Ganymede reached the divine abode.' William Scott Ferguson, 'Legalized Absolutism en Route from Greece to Rome,' *The American Historical Review* 18/1 (1912): 32.

[31] In addition to the divinised or deified emperor, the city of Rome is represented on coins and temple reliefs as the goddess Rome, often alongside other gods. J. Nelson Kraybill, *Imperial Cult and Commerce in John's Apocalypse* (Sheffield: T&T Clark, 1996), 138.

east to west, with looking down at the ground and knowing that there is a space below, and looking up at a material sky-structure and knowing that there is a space above. As imperial cults were 'an imperialist elaboration within Greco-Roman polytheism' so the cosmology of the cult was an imperialist elaboration within a basic spatial schema.[32] Rome is the centre of the earth and established also in the skies, and the cosmos is well-ordered and bountiful because the presence of Rome/emperor extends over the whole earth.[33]

In these cosmological conceptions we see the reciprocal relationship between ideas about cosmology and ideas about the social order. Roman presence in Asia Minor enacted a perception and experience of space that reinforced pagan imperial practices and conceptions.[34] In cosmic context the only appropriate power structures are those of pagan empire, and the only appropriate cultural practices are those consistent with and supportive of pagan empire. Anything contrary to this would disrupt the peace and wellbeing of the cosmos and human life within it. On the other hand, anything contrary to pagan empire is scarcely possible, as the Roman order is characterized by victory, peace, and perpetuity. To the extent that people were influenced by pagan imperial cosmology, the possibility that current power structures and cultural practices could end, or that such an end could be good, was almost beyond conception.

8.2 Alternative spatial construction

Revelation's story-space initially reaches from mainland Asia Minor to an Aegean island called Patmos (Rev. 1.4-9). The implication of Rev. 1.9 is that John's faithfulness to the word of God has caused him to be pushed into a peripheral space which then serves at the appropriate space for the prophetic experience.[35] While the island called Patmos is periphery in relation to Asia Minor, the earth-space has no centre in relation to which Asia Minor is periphery.

Rome is experienced in the earth-space, but not as centre. Throughout Revelation there are allusions to Rome/Babylon as empire but the location of the city within Revelation's earth-space is unspecified.[36] The city of Rome is first experienced in overt

---

[32] Friesen, *Imperial Cults*, 4. For highly educated Greeks and Romans who adopted a spherical model of the cosmos, Roman imperial cosmology could serve as an elaboration of that schema. The spherical earth had an οἰκουμένη in the northern hemisphere, of which Rome and its empire could be the centre and extent. The emperor's presence in the god-space could place him in or beyond the eighth sky-sphere.

[33] The emperor's presence was felt to extend throughout the empire, manifested in images and in cultic celebrations. 'Even outside designated cultic spaces, these images were not merely ornamental or didactic, but objects that manifested the emperor's presence.' Wan, *Contest*, 60, 152.

[34] Wan, *Contest*, 26. '*Weltbild* and *Weltanschauung* are inextricably and substantially intertwined.' Pennington, and McDonough, *Cosmology*, 4.

[35] Peripheral spaces are appropriate for a prophetic experience (Rev. 17.3; 21.10; Hermas, *Vis.* 1.1.3; 2.1.1). 'The wilderness is the realm where mysteries are explained in the spirit.' Friesen, *Imperial Cults*, 156.

[36] The second trumpet (Rev. 8.8-9) alludes to the oracle against Babylon in Jer. 51 while the sixth trumpet and sixth bowl (Rev. 9.13-19; 16.12-16) suggest destruction of the Roman empire by forces from beyond its border. The Roman empire is also experienced intruding into Asia Minor in Rev. 13.1-8. These narratives do not locate the city of Rome/Babylon.

visionary form as the Great Whore Babylon-Roma in indeterminate peripheral space (Rev. 17.3-18).[37] The pre-emptive dirge for the fallen city acknowledges that it functions as the economic centre, drawing goods to itself by road or by sea (Rev. 18.11-19), but the experience of the city first in peripheral space, and then through the speech of angels from heaven and human mourners who stand far off (Rev. 18.17), denies the city true centrality.

The Roman empire is experienced as a presence in Asia Minor, but not a stabilizing presence. Rather than permeating the whole earth-space, the empire enters into the local space from the outside, as an intruder (Rev. 12.18–13.1). The beast that is the empire has its origins both in the sky-heaven and in the sea: its form and power come from the sky-being who was seen disrupting the cosmic order in the sky (Rev. 12.4) but the beast is seen emerging from the sea (Rev. 13.1), connoting the primordial watery threat to cosmic order (see also Rev. 11.7). These connotations are emphasized as the focalizer's gaze shows first the sea and then the beast coming from it (καὶ εἶδον ἐκ τῆς θαλάσσης θηρίον ἀναβαῖνον). As the empire intrudes into Asia Minor, and into the territory of every ἔθνος, it does so as an anti-cosmic force. Contrary to Roman spatial ideology, empire has not tamed the sea. Rather, empire is the anti-cosmic chaos of the primordial sea now spread past the sand and onto every land (Rev. 12.18–13.1; Jer. 5.22).[38]

When emphasizing the beast's power Revelation acknowledges its power over ὅλη ἡ γῆ (Rev. 13.3), but when the beast's vulnerability is emphasized so are its horizontal limits; empire is not truly present over ὅλη ἡ γῆ but only over ἡ οἰκουμένη ὅλη (Rev. 16.12-16). At the extremities of the earth are untamed forces that are a genuine threat to the supposed *Pax Romana* (Rev. 7.1-3; 9.13-19; 16.12-16. See also Isa. 13.4-5). While imperial ideology sometimes acknowledged a spatial border, making this the border of human civilization and speaking dismissively of the regions beyond, Revelation emphasizes the spatial border (the great river Euphrates) as a real marker of empire's limitation and vulnerability. The regions beyond the Euphrates are not dismissed but emphasized as representing a real and present threat to the supposed victory, peace, and perpetuity of empire. This is tied to the apocalyptic concept that within the present cosmos, perhaps at its horizontal extremities, there already exists the means of destroying the forces of cosmic disorder (Rev. 7.1; 9.14).[39]

The contrast with the spatial ideology of pagan empire is especially striking as the virtual cosmic tour moves beyond the human-proximate cosmos of earth and sky-heaven. After the hearer passes through the sky-structure and becomes present in the hyper-heaven, three charateristics of this space are soon apparent: the way the space

---

[37] The beast of Rev. 13.1-8 and 17.3-18 is the empire, including its βασιλεῖς and ἔθνη. The whore/Babylon of Rev. 17.3-18 and 18.2-24 is the city of Rome.

[38] In the Hebrew scriptures the cosmos is created through divisions and boundaries, including the boundary between sea and land (Gen. 1.6-10; Ps. 104.5-9). Should the primordial deep burst forth and breach the boundary between sea and land then the cosmos would be partially undone (Gen. 7.11). But the sand marks the boundary that the sea cannot cross: 'I placed the sand as a boundary for the sea, a perpetual barrier that it cannot pass; though the waves toss, they cannot prevail, though they roar, they cannot pass over it' (Jer. 5.22; see also Job 38.10; Ps. 104.9; Prov. 8.29). The crossing of cosmic boundaries is the central theme of the Book of Watchers.

[39] See also Sec. 3.5.

is defined, what is present, and what is absent. Revelation's God-space is not just an awesome space in which divinity is present, but a space created by God's Throne.[40] Space extends outward from this centre and beings exist in concentric circles around it.[41] The space does not allow beings within it except as they exist in relationship with the Throne as centre and as seat of ultimate authority. While Revelation's earth-space has no centre, its God-space is defined by the Throne as centre. As all sub-Throne regions respond to the Throne-space and acknowledge the Throne, it becomes the centre or apex of all spatial reality.[42] All earthly locations are equally defined in relation to the centre of reality which is not on earth but in the hyper-heaven.

Necessarily absent from this God-space are Rome and the traditional gods. The hearer is shown a God-space marked by the conspicuous absence of the goddess Rome, the god Augustus and other emperors, assimilated deities such as Zeus Caesar Olympios Sebastos,[43] and traditional gods in the role of patron deity. Besides the one sitting on the Throne, there is no being towards whom worship and allegiance can be directed.[44] Rome may be a significant power on earth but it is not present in the hyper-heaven.[45]

What we do see established in the hyper-heaven is not the empire but God's βασιλεία, that is, people from every φυλή καί γλῶσσα καί λαός καί ἔθνος now existing as the βασιλεία καί ἱερεῖς τῷ θεῷ (Rev. 1.6; 5.10).[46] The followers of Jesus understood as temple occurs in Rev. 3.12 where it is promised that the one who perseveres through difficult circumstances will become a pillar in the temple of God. As the collective becomes the temple, individual followers become parts of the temple and worshippers within the temple. The blurred line between these two images (the individual as part of the temple and as worshipper within the temple) explains the promise that 'the one who conquers will be a pillar in the temple and will never go out of it' (Rev. 3.12).[47] The mixed image also connects Rev. 3.12 with Rev. 7.15, where those who have persevered are now within the heavenly temple day and night.

The motif is given 'expanded visual form' in Rev. 11.1-2,[48] where John is told to 'measure the temple and the altar and those who worship in it'. As Charles observed, ὁ ναός and ὁ θυσιαστήριον and οἱ προσκυνοῦντες ἐν αὐτῷ are used together to form

---

[40] See Sec. 4.4.2.
[41] Compare with the spatial ideology in which power radiates from Rome/emperor 'as if in concentric circles'. Wan, *Contest*, 135.
[42] See Sec. 5.3.
[43] Friesen, *Imperial Cults*, 76. See also Wan, *Contest*, 54.
[44] Not even intermediate patron relationships are allowed (Rev. 19.10; 22.8-9).
[45] There is a sense in which one aspect of Rome was present in the hyper-heaven as the accuser (see Sec. 6.3.3) but this being was a mere functionary of God's court and its only action was petitioning God for God's negative verdict on people. It did not have its own power or the power to serve as patron deity for imperial power.
[46] Keith Dyer writes, '*basileia* is not equivalent terminology for the Roman *imperium* in the first century, and in preferring the former term, John resists, re-defines, relativizes, and rejects the language of empire as he describes a vision of an alternative and transforming reality.' Keith Dyer, 'Beastly Hybridity: Leviathan, Behemoth, and Revelation 13,' *St Mark's Review* 239, 1 (2017): 96.
[47] The same mixed image occurs in 1 Pet. 2.5: 'like living stones, let yourselves be built into a spiritual house, to be a holy priesthood, to offer spiritual sacrifices acceptable to God through Jesus Christ'.
[48] Koester, *Revelation*, 495.

one idea,[49] that is, the people of God.[50] The temple is measured/protected but part of it is trampled along with the holy city for three and a half years.[51] This experience of the people of God, here as the temple in the holy city, is narrated again in Rev. 12.13-17, there as the woman in the wilderness. The woman is the people of God as a collective while her children are individuals.[52] As a collective the people of God cannot be destroyed, but individual followers of Jesus are not protected from lethal violence (Rev. 12.17). Whether as the temple or as the woman, the earthly followers of Jesus are both protected and unprotected, that is, protected on earth as a collective but unprotected on earth as individuals.

The protected status of the collective has a spatial dimension. The people of God on earth is established also in the hyper-heaven, specifically seen in the hyper-heaven as the temple. While the heavenly temple language lacks visual clarity, the hearer understands that the hyper-heaven either contains a temple or *is* a temple (Rev. 6.9; 7.15; 8.3, 5; 9.13; 11.1, 19; 14.15, 17, 18; 15.5, 8; 16.1, 7, 17).[53] The people of God understood as temple connects with the presence of a temple above the sky-structure. The βασιλεία καί ἱερεῖς τῷ θεῷ that the Lamb has made, of people from every φυλή καί γλῶσσα καί λαός καί ἔθνος (Rev. 5.9-10), is established in the hyper-heaven and so protected also on earth. The empire is conspicuously absent from the God-space – the alternative to empire is present.

8.3 Complementary sky-spaces

Revelation's concern about idolatry in general (Rev. 2.14, 20; 9.20; 21.8; 22.15) is sufficiently addressed by the absence of traditional gods from the God-space, but worship and allegiance given specifically to Rome requires far more extensive treatment.[54] In the foregoing discussion we have noted Rome's conspicuous absence from the God-space, but that does not mean that Rome is absent from the heavens – the 'divinity' equivalent to Rome is seen in the sky-heaven (Rev. 12.3-9).[55] As noted above, in imperial ideology there are several ways in which Rome may have an equivalent divinity: the city Rome seen as the goddess Rome, Rome in the person of a divinised or deified emperor, Rome in the person of the emperor assimilated with a traditional deity and traditional gods acting in the role of patron deity. While Revelation's sky-dragon is a primitive reality in the cosmos, and far more than a representation of the

---

[49] Charles, *Revelation*, vol. 2, 277.
[50] For the temple as people of God see Koester, *Revelation*, 484. Charles, *Revelation*, vol. 2, 274.
[51] For measuring as protection see Aune, *Revelation 6–16*, 603–04. Charles, *Revelation*, vol. 2, 275.
[52] For the woman as the people of God see Koester, *Revelation*, 542. Charles, *Revelation*, vol. 2, 315.
[53] See Sec. 4.4.1.
[54] The *Apocalypse of Abraham* refutes idol worship (*Apoc. Abr.* 1–8) through a journey into the skies (*Apoc. Abr.* 9–22), showing that beside the one creator God of Israelite tradition there is nothing in the skies worthy of worship (*Apoc. Abr.* 19.4). Revelation makes a similar move, as hyper-heaven is defined by the Throne and the one sitting on it, with no other being in the cosmos worthy of worship.
[55] That is, the 'divinity' equivalent to Rome's imperial power and military might.

Roman Empire, even so it is empire's equivalent 'divinity' in the sky-heaven. Empire is present in the sky-heaven as the sky-dragon.[56]

This spatial move has implications for the nature of imperial power. First, it acknowledges the real power of the Roman Empire. Within the frame of the cosmos-of-ordinary-human-experience the empire is practically invincible and this is how empire is experienced in its earthly presence: 'Who is like the beast and who can fight against it?' (Rev. 13.4). Above the earth, the sky-heaven is still within the cosmos-of-ordinary-human-experience but is a higher space whose native beings are an order of magnitude brighter and stronger, so empire's presence also in this space is an indication of its great power. Even within the sky-heaven empire is an exceptionally powerful being, exercising its destructive power over many other sky-beings (Rev. 12.4). But within the frame of the greater cosmos empire is relatively weak. Although it is the most powerful native being of the sky-heaven, empire remains an order of magnitude weaker than the most powerful beings of the hyper-heaven (Rev. 20.1-3).[57]

Second, empire's presence specifically in the sky-heaven allows it to be exposed as a force of cosmic disorder in conflict with true cosmic order. While Revelation's hyper-heaven is a space of true cosmic order, its sky-heaven is the conflicted lower sky-space known in apocalyptic literature.[58] As the underside of the sky-structure, Revelation's lower sky-space is most nearly equivalent to the underside of the firmament in the *Ascension of Isaiah*. This is the space of Satan/Sammael and his powerful armies (*Asc. Isa.* 7.9) and the space from which Nero-Beliar descends (*Asc. Isa.* 4.2).[59] In Revelation the space at the underside of the sky-structure is home to beings who are part of the cosmic order (the stars, Rev. 12.1-4), but as a conflicted space it is also a space in which empire can be exposed as anti-cosmic. Thus it is seen in the sky-heaven first as chaos monster, engaging in acts of destruction against cosmic order (Rev. 12.4), then as military chief, leading armies of rebellious powerful beings in military conflict with the powerful beings who serve God's cosmic order (Rev. 12.7-9). Empire seen as monster of chaos contrasts sharply with empire seen as god of civilization in idealized human form.[60]

It is Revelation's sky-heaven that resembles the 'heaven' that Wink describes. For Wink, 'heaven' is the metaphorical 'place' in which the spirituality of everything is 'located', and seeing an earthly entity in its heavenly aspect can give a clearer picture of its true nature.[61] Thus for Wink, heaven functions as a 'place' of conflict inextricably bound to earthly conflict. Differing somewhat from Wink, I note that in Revelation's story-space the sky-heaven is a place that exists in spatial relationship with the earth.

---

[56] By contrast, the sea-beast is less than the sky-dragon and almost identical with the Roman Empire.
[57] In several apocalypses the lower skies are lesser in glory in comparison with the higher skies, and likewise the beings of the lower skies are lesser in glory, power, and authority in relation to the beings of the higher skies. See *Asc. Isa.* 7-9; *Apoc. Abr.* 19.5-9.
[58] See Sec. 3.4.3.
[59] In *Asc. Isa.* the earth and the lowest sky-space comprise the cosmos-of-ordinary-human-experience (*Asc. Isa.* 4.18). They mirror each other in their conflicted nature (*Asc. Isa.* 7.10).
[60] Wan, *Contest*, 141.
[61] Wink, *Naming*, 119.

But seeing the empire in the sky-heaven does give a clearer picture of its true nature and its conflict with cosmic order.

As a native being of the sky-heaven the dragon is roughly equivalent to the stars, and as a rebellious being of this space it is roughly equivalent to those stars in the Astronomical Book (*1 En.* 72–82) that deviate from true cosmic order (*1 En.* 80.4-7). While the Astronomical Book urges its reader to live in accord with the cosmic order as seen in the orderly movements of the sun, moon, and stars (*1 En.* 82.1-9), it also warns of a time when stars will deviate from the true cosmic order. When this happens people should not follow the stars in their anti-cosmic behaviour but continue living in accord with the true cosmic order.[62] In Revelation's conflicted sky-heaven pagan imperial culture is exposed as draconian, the narrative thus demanding nonparticipation in its false cosmic order. Yet its power and domination of earth-space is such that 'who can fight against it?' This is where the hyper-heaven plays its complementary role in the ideological construction of space. Revelation's hyper-heaven resembles the 'heaven' that Gwyther describes, the aspect of reality in which 'God lives and reigns'.[63] Differing somewhat from Gwyther, I note that in Revelation's story-space the hyper-heaven has a spatial aspect and exists in spatial relationship with the earth and sky-heaven. Similar to Gwyther's 'heaven' the hyper-heaven is the space where God lives and reigns, 'the source of the transformative possibilities that God presents' for τὰ πάντα.[64] In Minear's terms, this heaven is 'above the above' and 'the source of all God's creative acts'.[65] It serves to make nonparticipation in pagan empire (that is, participation instead in the βασιλεία καί ἱερεῖς τῷ θεῷ) a real and viable option.

8.4 Appropriate action in cosmic context

Revelation's cosmic tour displays the lack of conformity between the cosmos-of-ordinary-human-experience and the true order of the greater cosmos, a lack of conformity that must ultimately be resolved. The existence of the hyper-heaven, in contradistinction to the false ordering of earth and sky-heaven, is a present cosmic guarantee of the final cosmic transformation that creates a new space for human life exclusive of draconian elements. This gives a very different cosmic context to present life. To live in accord with the falsely ordered cosmos is to live in accord with a fading reality. Although it is difficult in the present time, to live in accord with the true cosmic order is to participate in a reality that exists in a higher cosmic space and must ultimately exist in all cosmic space.

---

[62] 'The charge that sinners will misconstrue astronomical data culminates in the prediction that they will take the stars to be gods.' Nickelsburg, and VanderKam, *1 Enoch 2*, 529.
[63] Howard-Brook and Gwyther, *Unveiling*, 122.
[64] It is Wink who wrote of heaven, 'It is where God is enthroned and thus is the source of the transformative possibilities that God presents to every actual entity.' Wink, *Naming*, 119. As noted in 1.2.2 Dynamic Cosmology, this aspect of Wink's heaven stands in tension with his general presentation of heaven as an inner dimension of earthly realities and earthly conflict. It is closer to the way heaven is primarily presented by Gwyther. Gwyther, 'New Jerusalem Versus Babylon'.
[65] Minear, 'The Cosmology', 32.

We have seen that in Revelation's cosmic story-space the Roman Empire is a presence that looms large but is also relativized by the larger cosmic context and by where it is spatially located within that cosmos. This alternative experience of space is significant within the plane of the earth, as Rome defines neither centre nor periphery and is further limited by its border. The extremities of the earth and the region beyond the Euphrates are a real threat to the supposed victory, peace, and perpetuity of Roman rule, and thus empire's border is a symbol of its limitation and vulnerability. Empire is limited also on the vertical axis. It was present in the elevated space of sky-heaven but conspicuously absent from the hyper-elevated space.

We have seen how the nature of empire's presence in space also characterized it negatively. Rather than permeating the οἰκουμένη as a civilizing presence, it enters as an intruder. Rather than taming the chaotic sea, it is characterized by its origin in the chaotic sea, and is seen as an anti-cosmic force crossing the sand-boundary as it intrudes into the surrounding spaces of the land. The negative characterization is there also in its vertical aspect, as empire has its origins also in the conflicted lower sky-space known in apocalyptic cosmology, where it is seen in its true draconic form.

This creates critical distance between the hearer and the dominant social and economic practices that centre Rome – that is, Rome as city, Rome as emperor, and Rome as power-structure. As empire is relativized and negatively characterized so its practices are relativized and negatively characterized – practices that are foundational for the social order, including those of cult and economy.

Revelation's particular focus on imperial cult is not a focus on 'religion' in a modern compartmentalized sense. The imperial cults gave form to social life by shaping how people experienced work, rest, and entertainment, and by reconfiguring existing networks of social relations.[66] Imperial cults existed in their own dedicated spaces, strategically situated to dominate the topography,[67] and in the spaces of commerce, civic life, and the traditional cults.[68] They 'provided the context in which inhabitants of towns spread for hundreds of miles throughout the Empire could celebrate their membership of single political order and their place within it'.[69]

The imperial and traditional cults were very much part of the food economy. They played a role in civic events involving the sharing of meals and distribution of food,[70] and in the trade associations and private gatherings where meals were shared. Such gatherings were contexts in which business and social relationships were maintained.[71] Meat sold in markets commonly came from cultic practices involving ritual slaughter and the sharing of a portion with the gods.[72] Imperial cults were also embedded in the means of economic exchange. As noted in Mt. 22.20, coins were frequently stamped

---

[66] Wan, *Contest*, 50, 155.
[67] Friesen, *Imperial Cults*, 124. Wan, *Contest*, 133.
[68] Friesen, *Imperial Cults*, 62, 68, 95–101. Wan, *Contest*, 137–8.
[69] Wan, *Contest*, 61.
[70] Koester, *Revelation*, 99. Friesen, *Imperial Cults*, 105.
[71] Koester, *Revelation*, 99. Aune, *Revelation 1–5*, 186.
[72] Koester, *Revelation*, 288. Joseph A. Fitzmyer, *First Corinthians*, Anchor Bible (New Haven: Yale University Press, 2008), 331.

with the image of Caesar and associated cultic imagery.[73] A key place of exchange, the agora, typically included an imperial cult within it.[74] In addition, imperial temples were often placed strategically in relation to the agora such that they dominated the space and imbued it with Roman presence.[75] The negative characterization of the imperial economy occurs not only in relation to its cultic practices, as if they could be separated, but also in relation to its centring of Rome in the transfer of goods from the provinces to the capital (Rev. 18.11-19). This system could lead to hardship,[76] yet participation in the Rome-centred economy was a way for empire's subjects to earn a living and perhaps gains wealth.[77]

Some Christian leaders apparently tried to negotiate the Christian's place in the existing social order (Rev. 2.14, 20. See also 1 Cor. 8.1-13; 10.14-21). Revelation takes a different approach. In Revelation's story-space, the empire's exposure in the conflicted sky-heaven demands nonparticipation in these foundational social practices. The hyper-heaven makes nonparticipation a viable option and the alternative a genuine possibility. Its existence as the highest cosmic space – defined by God's Throne, so characterized by absolute safety and perfect coaction with the one who sits on the Throne – defines the true order of the cosmos and serves as the source of transformative possibilities for τὰ πάντα.[78] To live in accord with the true cosmic order is to participate in a reality that exists in a higher cosmic space and must ultimately exist in all cosmic space.[79] In contrast to the spatial ideology enacted in the empire's eastern provinces, Revelation creates an alternative experience of space, and an alternative cosmic context, that enables an alternative to negotiating one's place in the cosmos as defined by empire.[80]

The way of living enabled by Revelation's cosmos includes worshipping along with all creation, participating in an alternative community, and persisting in right action. To worship truly is to participate in the cosmos as it is meant to be. In false worship, allegiance is given to a false ordering of the cosmos, based in the sky-heaven and out of step with the true order of the greater cosmos. In Revelation the earth and sky-heaven are conflicted space. In the experience of Rev. 5.6-14 the proper recognition of the hyper-heaven is emphasized as whole sub-Throne cosmos is heard responding to the

---

[73] 'Because of the offensiveness of a human image on a coin, it would be most appropriate for Jews to be rid of such a coin.' Donald Alfred Hagner, *Matthew 14–28*, Word Biblical Commentary (Dallas: Word Books, 1995), 636. See also Martin Hengel, *The Zealots: Investigations into the Jewish Freedom Movement in the Period from Herod I until 70 A.D.*, trans. David Smith (Edinburgh: T&T Clark, 1989), 190–95. Caesar's cultic image on coins is at least one connotation of Rev. 13.17. See Kraybill, *Imperial Cult*, 138. Adela Yarbro Collins, 'The Political Perspective of the Revelation to John,' *Journal of Biblical Literature* 96/2 (1977): 253.

[74] Friesen, *Imperial Cults*, 68, 95–101. Wan, *Contest*, 137–8.

[75] Wan, *Contest*, 133–4.

[76] Howard-Brook and Gwyther, *Unveiling*, 96–101.

[77] Koester, *Revelation*, 93.

[78] Wink, Gwyther and others depict an ambivalent heaven, a heaven that is conflicted but also the true form of the cosmos and the source of positive change. In contrast, I describe a consistent hyper-heaven that is unambiguously the standard for the whole cosmos and the source of positive change.

[79] See Sec. 7.2.

[80] This is, perhaps, similar to Mt. 6.25-33: 'Do not worry about what you will eat or what you will wear … but seek first the kingdom and righteousness of God and these things will be given to you as well.'

Throne-space in a cosmic liturgy centred around the Throne. This becomes a cosmic context around the worship practices of the ἐκκλησίαι. Through participation in the worship practices of the ἐκκλησία the hearer participates in the cosmos as it is meant to be.[81]

Those who participate in true worship are not ἔθνη subjugated to empire but people from every φυλή καί γλῶσσα καί λαός καί ἔθνος now existing as the βασιλεία καί ἱερεῖς τῷ θεῷ (Rev. 1.6; 5.10). The βασιλεία of God is more real than the *imperium*. In this βασιλεία of people from all tribes, langauge-groups, peoples, and nations, none has dominance over another. This has implications for the social and economic relationships between those who come together in the ἐκκλησίαι. That worship/ allegiance is given only to God and directly to God, not through intermediary patron-client relationships (Rev. 19.10; 22.8-9), implies that those within the ἐκκλησία instead relate as 'fellow servants'. The call to return to works of love (Rev. 2.4-5) assumes the kind of relationships in which people are committed to the wellbeing of others and practice acts of service.[82] It gives a distinct context for the sharing of food in the ἐκκλησίαι.[83]

Revelation's cosmos allows its hearer to persist in these practices (ὑπομονή) and other correct actions in spite of the consequent hardships (θλῖψις) (Rev. 1.9; 2.2-3, 19; 3.10; 13.10; 14.12). Correct action is further defined as refraining from murder, fornication, sorcery, idolatry, deceit, and theft (Rev. 9.21; 21.8; 22.15),[84] that is, respecting a person's life, respecting people's dependence in the necessities of the life and the ways in which these are shared, giving allegiance only to what is good, and practicing truthfulness – even when this leads to hardship. Revelation's cosmos is a structure around the calls to endure and the *makarisms* for those who are faithful even unto death (Rev. 1.3; 14.12-13; 16.15; 19.9; 20.6; 22.7). The hearer has a broader perspective on the current hardships associated with this way of living, understanding that their way of living is a participation on the true order of the greater cosmos – the reality that exists in the highest cosmic space and must ultimately exist in all cosmic space.

---

[81] Where the hearer is an early real hearer who participates in the experience of the implied hearer. The experience of the implied hearer is the experience towards which Revelation pulls its real hearer. Barr, *Tales*, 26. See also Hongisto, *Experiencing*, 187–91.

[82] Koester, *Revelation*, 262, 69. See also Blount, *Revelation*, 51.

[83] Revelation assumes that its hearer has knowledge of the life of the ἐκκλησία and very little is said explicitly. It is likely that Revelation's ἐκκλησίαι met on the first day of a seven-day week (Rev. 1.10; Acts 20.7; *Did.* 14.1) for practices common to many Christian ἐκκλησίαι. Koester, *Revelation*, 86. This would include reading scriptures, singing hymns, and praying (Rev. 5.8-14; 8.3-4; 15.2-4), and probably also the sharing of food, including bread and wine (see Mt. 26.26-29; Mk 14.22-25; Lk. 22.14-20; 24.30-35; Acts 20.7; 1 Cor. 10.16-17; 11.20-34; *Did.* 14.1). Note also Pliny the Younger, *Ep. Tra.* 10.96.7: 'They had met regularly before dawn on a fixed day to chant verses alternately among themselves in honour of Christ as if to a god … After this ceremony it had been their custom to disperse and reassemble later to take food.' Translation, Betty Radice. Jeffrey Henderson, ed., *Pliny: Letters and Panegyricus: With an English Translation by Betty Radice*, Loeb Classical Library (Cambridge: Harvard University Press, 1969).

[84] 'to bind themselves by oath … to abstain from theft, robbery and adultery, to commit no breach of trust and not to deny a deposit when called upon to restore it'. Pliny the Younger, *Ep. Tra.* 10.96.7. Translation, Henderson, *Betty Radice*.

8.5 Conclusion: Living in the cosmos

This chapter has shown how Revelation's cosmology has ideological import in the context of the dominant imperial culture. That culture enacted a spatial ideology that defined centre, periphery, and border in particular ways: on the horizontal axis Rome was the centre of the earth and the ordering presence throughout the earth; on the vertical axis it was present also in the god-space. The reciprocal relationship between ideas about spatial reality and ideas about the social order means that within this spatial ideology it would be almost beyond conception to imagine that current power structures and cultural practices could, or should, end.

A reading of Revelation is an alternative experience of space, tied to an alternative conception of the physical/social order. Revelation's cosmic story-space extends beyond the cosmos-of-ordinary-human-experience and relativizes the reality of empire. On the earth, Rome is denied centrality and has no specified location – the city/goddess Rome is experienced in indeterminate, peripheral space, but its presence is felt in Asia Minor as an intrusion of chaos. Above the earth it was seen as a presence in the sky-heaven in its true draconic form, the narrative thus demanding nonparticipation in its practices on earth. Above the cosmos-of-ordinary-human-experience, Revelation's hyper-heaven defined the true cosmic order. Correct action is thus defined and enabled: nonparticipation in empire is not only a demand but also a viable option, as the hearer is invited to instead participate in the reality that exists in the highest cosmic space and must ultimately exist in all cosmic space.

9

Conclusion

Many apocalyptic texts feature a journey into the skies, in which the seer learns the true order of the cosmos. Their cosmic tours and cosmological descriptions serve particular purposes, calling the reader to awe before the one creator God of Israelite tradition, to a life ordered by certain organizing principles and to perseverance in these practices in spite of the oppressive, destructive and deviant forces that dominate human existence. This observation became the impetus for reading Revelation's story of a journey into the skies, applying a visual-narrative reading strategy to observe the cosmic story-space in which the narrative operates and its theological and ideological significance in the historical context.

Previous scholarship has generally assumed a three-tiered cosmic structure in Revelation, consisting of heaven, earth and the underworld. Yet the upper tier is often not allowed to be truly *heaven*. Instead, scholars have often argued that Revelation uses οὐρανός in two distinct senses. The first denotes the physical sky above the earth, the sky that is perceptible to the senses, with its sun, moon, stars and birds.[1] The second sense of οὐρανός points towards something else that is more difficult to define: it is a metaphorical 'place' that is 'spiritual' and 'beyond space and time'.[2] This is the 'place' that is truly 'heaven'. If some parts of Revelation appear to blur the distinction between the two senses of οὐρανός, that is because the sky is being used as a metaphor for heaven.[3] While οὐρανός in the second sense is understood to be the 'place' in which God is enthroned and God's will is done,[4] this is qualified by the observation that 'heaven' also includes conflict between 'spiritual beings'.[5]

This study has framed the issue differently. While previous scholarship has assumed a three-tiered cosmic structure, the visual-narrative reading showed that Revelation's narrative operates in a cosmic story-space consisting of four spatial levels, with the

---

[1] For example, Gebhardt, *Doctrine*, 43. Caird, *Commentary*, 62. Witherington, *Revelation*, 115, 67. Jordaan, 'Cosmology', 3.
[2] For example, Gebhardt, *Doctrine*, 43, 50. Caird, *Commentary*, 62. Sweet, *Revelation*, 16. Wink, *Naming*, 119. Beale, *Revelation*, 319. Jordaan, 'Cosmology', 4.
[3] Jordaan, 'Cosmology', 3.
[4] Gebhardt, *Doctrine*, 50. For example, Wink, *Naming*, 119. Gwyther, 'New Jerusalem Versus Babylon', 48. McDonough, 'Revelation', 182. Jordaan, 'Cosmology', 3, 5.
[5] For example, Gebhardt, *Doctrine*, 50-1. Swete, *Apocalypse*, 150. Caird, *Commentary*, 62. Wink, *Naming*, 119. Resseguie, *Revelation Unsealed*, 85-6. Beale, *Revelation*, 319, 625. Gwyther, 'New Jerusalem Versus Babylon', 50. Witherington, *Revelation*, 167, 170. McDonough, 'Revelation', 182. Jordaan, 'Cosmology', 3. Koester, *Revelation*, 562. Newton, *Pentecostal Commentary*, 227.

hyper-heaven sitting above the sky-heaven, earth and abyssal depths. Thus, as with previous scholarship, I recognize more than one sense of οὐρανός, but the distinction is not between the physical sky and the spiritual heaven – that distinction depends too heavily on a blend of modern scientific cosmology and traditional Christian theology.[6] Instead, the senses of οὐρανός relate to the sky-heaven and the hyper-heaven. I have argued that ancient conceptions of the heavens, and the narrative moves within Revelation, point towards οὐρανός as (1) the sky-structure, (2) the space immediately below the sky-structure and (3) the space above the sky-structure.[7] Revelation's lower sky-space and upper sky-space both exist in spatial relationship with the earth, both have dynamics within them that relate to certain realities on earth and both are inhabited by powerful beings appropriate to the space.

The hearer experiences a sky-heaven characterized by archetypal conflict between powerful sky-beings, existing as another aspect of the conflicted earth and the powerful forces experienced in daily life. Through the experience of the sky-heaven, earthly realities are seen more clearly and more truly. Above the sky-structure, the hyper-heaven is experienced as a harmonious space in which all beings exist in spatial and functional relationship with the Throne of God. Contrary to previous Revelation scholarship, the heaven in which God is enthroned is experienced as a consistently harmonious space inherently exclusive of rebellious elements. Thus the hyper-heaven *unambiguously* sets the standard for the whole cosmos and *unambiguously* serves as the source of transformative possibilities for everything that exists. The upper sky-space and the lower sky-space are both deserving of the name 'heaven' as both are far more than 'just the sky'. The hyper-heaven is the God-space known in apocalyptic literature, in contrast with the conflicted lower heavens.[8]

This spatial experience contrasts with the spatial ideology enacted in the imperial province of Asia Minor. As ideas about the spatial order exist in reciprocal relationship with ideas about the social order, so the empire enacted a spatial ideology in which Rome is the centre of the earth-space and established also in the god-space. Thus empire gives order to the cosmos. The Roman Empire is characterized by victory, peace and perpetuity, making it almost impossible to conceive of the end of empire or to imagine that such an end could be good. In the cosmos as ordered by Rome the only appropriate power structures are those of the Roman Empire, and the only appropriate social and economic practices are those consistent with and supportive of eternal Roman rule.

A reading of Revelation in the ἐκκλησίαι gave an alternative experience of space, tied to an alternative conception of the physical/social order. The cosmic

---

[6] See also Howard-Brook and Gwyther, *Unveiling*, 127.
[7] Revelation's use of οὐρανός in these three senses is similar to Aristotle's use of οὐρανός for (1) the sky-structure, (2) the space immediately below the sky-structure and (3) the entire cosmos, that is, the entire cosmos contained within the spherical sky-structure. Aristotle, *De Caelo*, 278b10-20.
[8] It may be fruitful to examine whether this cosmic structure is assumed in other early Christian narratives. In private communication, Rev Alison Sampson suggested that the lower and upper sky-spaces may be at play in Luke when those following Jesus cry out 'ἐν οὐρανῷ εἰρήνη καὶ δόξα ἐν ὑψίστοις' (Lk. 19.38). There can be peace in the conflicted γῆ and οὐρανός when the humans and even stones of the earth respond to the ὕψιστοι (Lk. 2.14; 19.38-40), leading to a reconciliation of the whole cosmos.

tour takes the hearer beyond the cosmos-of-ordinary-human-experience to see the broader cosmological frame. Thus the reality of empire is relativized and negatively characterized. On the earth, Rome is denied centrality and is instead experienced in indeterminate, peripheral space, while Roman presence in Asia Minor is experienced as an intrusion of chaos. The empire's vulnerability is exposed by the reality of its border and the regions beyond its reach. Above the earth, empire was seen as an anti-cosmic force in the sky-heaven and conspicuously absent from the hyper-heaven. Revelation's hyper-heaven defined the true cosmic order, absent of empire. Present instead is the βασιλεία καί ἱερεῖς τῷ θεῷ, composed of people from all tribes, language groups, peoples and nations, in which none has dominance over another. In this way the experience of the sky-heaven demands non-participation in the social, cultic and economic practices of empire, while the experience of the hyper-heaven makes such non-participation a viable option. Through the experience of the hyper-heaven, the hearer is invited to participate in the true order of the cosmos, the reality that exists in the highest cosmic space and must ultimately exist in all cosmic space.

Bibliography

Aalen, Svere. 'St. Luke's Gospel and the Last Chapters of 1 Enoch'. *New Testament Studies*, 13 (1966): 1–13.

Adams, Edward. 'Graeco-Roman and Ancient Jewish Cosmology'. In *Cosmology and New Testament Theology*. Edited by Jonathan T. Pennington and Sean M. McDonough, 5–27. London: T&T Clark, 2008.

Adams, Edward. *The Stars Will Fall from Heaven: Cosmic Catastrophe in the New Testament and Its World*. Library of New Testament studies, vol. 347. London: T&T Clark, 2007.

Andersen, F. I. '2 (Slavonic Apocalypse of) Enoch'. In *The Old Testament Pseudepigrapha*. Edited by James H. Charlesworth, vol. 1, 91–222. Garden City: Doubleday, 1983.

Arndt, William, Frederick W. Danker and Walter Bauer. *A Greek-English Lexicon of the New Testament and Other Early Christian Literature*. 3rd edn. Chicago: University of Chicago Press, 2000.

Aune, David E. 'Apocalypse Renewed: An Intertextual Reading of the Apocalypse of John'. In *The Reality of the Apocalypse: Rhetoric and Politics in the Book of Revelation*. Edited by David L. Barr, 43–70. Atlanta: SBL, 2006.

Aune, David E. *Revelation 1–5*. Word Biblical Commentary, vol. 52A. Nashville: Thomas Nelson, 1997.

Aune, David E. *Revelation 6–16*. Word Biblical Commentary, vol. 52B. Nashville: Thomas Nelson, 1998.

Aune, David E. *Revelation 17–22*. Word Biblical Commentary, vol. 52C. Nashville: Thomas Nelson, 1998.

Bal, Mieke. *Narratology: Introduction to the Theory of Narrative*. Translated by Christine Van Boheemen. Toronto: University of Toronto Press, 1985.

Barker, Margaret. *The Revelation of Jesus Christ: Which God Gave to Him to Show to His Servants What Must Soon Take Place (Revelation I.I)*. Edinburgh: T&T Clark, 2000.

Barnett, Paul. *Apocalypse Now and Then: Reading Revelation Today*. Sydney: Aquila Press, 1989.

Barr, David L. 'The Story John Told: Reading Revelation for its Plots'. In *Reading the Book of Revelation: A Resource for Students*. Edited by David Barr, 11–24. Atlanta: Society of Biblical Literature, 2003.

Barr, David L. *Tales of the End: A Narrative Commentary on the Book of Revelation*. Santa Rosa: Polebridge Press, 1998.

Bauckham, Richard. *The Fate of the Dead: Studies on Jewish and Christian Apocalypses*. Supplements to Novum Testamentum, vol. 93. Boston: Brill, 1998.

Bauckham, Richard. *The Theology of the Book of Revelation*. Cambridge: Cambridge University Press, 1993.

Bautch, Kelley Coblentz. *A Study of the Geography of 1 Enoch 17–19: No One Has Seen What I Have Seen*, vol. 81. Leiden: Brill, 2003.

Beale, G. K. *The Book of Revelation: A Commentary on the Greek Text*. The New International Greek Testament Commentary. Grand Rapids: Eerdmans, 1999.

Beale, G. K. *John's Use of the Old Testament in Revelation*. Journal for the Study of the New Testament Supplement Series, vol. 166. Sheffield: Sheffield Academic, 1998.

Beasley-Murray, G. R. *The Book of Revelation*. New Century Bible. London: Butler and Tanner, 1974.

Beckwith, Isbon T. *The Apocalypse of John: Studies in Introduction with a Critical and Exegetical Commentary*. New York: Macmillan, 1919.

Ben-Dov, Jonathan. *Head of All Years: Astronomy and Calendars at Qumran in Their Ancient Context*. Leiden: Brill, 2008.

Bernstein, Alan E. *The Formation of Hell: Death and Retribution in the Ancient and Early Christian Worlds*. Ithaca: Cornell University Press, 1993.

Berquist, Jon L. 'Critical Spatiality and the Construction of the Ancient World'. In *'Imagining' Biblical Worlds: Studies in Spatial, Social, and Historical Constructs in Honor of James W. Flanagan*. Edited by David M. Gunn and Paula M. McNutt. JSOTSup, vol. 359, 14–29. London: Sheffield Academic, 2002.

Bingham, Geoffrey C. *The Revelation of St John the Divine*. Blackwood: New Creation, 1993.

Bird, Michael F. 'Tearing the Heavens and Shaking the Heavenlies: Mark's Cosmology in its Apocalyptic Context'. In *Cosmology and New Testament Theology*. Edited by Jonathan T. Pennington and Sean M. McDonough, 45–59. London: T&T Clark, 2008.

Blenkinsopp, Joseph. *Isaiah 56–66. Anchor Bible*, vol. 19B. New Haven: Yale University Press, 1974.

Blount, Brian K. *Revelation: A Commentary*. Louisville: Westminster John Knox Press, 2009.

Boll, Franz. *Aus der Offenbarung Johannis. Hellenistische Studien zum Weltbild der Apokalypse*. Leipzig: B. G. Teubner, 1914.

Boring, M. Eugene. *Revelation. Interpretation*. Louisville: John Knox Press, 1989.

Bousset, W. *Die Offenbarung Johannes*. Göttingen: Vandenhoeck and Ruprecht, 1966.

Bowman, John Wick. *The Drama of the Book of Revelation*. Philadelphia: Westminster Press, 1955.

Box, G. H. *The Apocalypse of Abraham. Translations of Early Documents. Series I, Palestinian Jewish Texts (Pre-Rabbinic)*. London: Society for Promoting Christian Knowledge, 1918.

Brett, M. G. *Locations of God: Political Theology in the Hebrew Bible*. New York: Oxford University Press, 2019.

Brownlee, William Hugh. *Ezekiel 1–19. Word Biblical Commentary*, vol. 28. Waco: Word Books, 1986.

Bryan, David J. *Cosmos, Chaos and the Kosher Mentality*. London: Sheffield Academic Press, 1995.

Burton, Keith A. 'The Millennium: Transition to the Final Aeon'. *Andrews University Seminary Studies*, 38/2 (2000): 207–22.

Caird, G. B. *A Commentary on the Revelation of St. John the Divine*. 2nd edn. *Black's New Testament Commentaries*. London: A&C Black, 1966.

Carrington, Philip. *The Meaning of the Revelation*. London: Society for Promoting Christian Knowledge, 1931.

Carson, D. A. *The Gagging of God: Christianity Confronts Pluralism*. Leicester: Apollos, 2009.

Charles, R. H. *The Book of Enoch, or, 1 Enoch*. Oxford: Clarendon, 1912.

Charles, R. H. *A Critical and Exegetical Commentary on the Revelation of St. John*, vol. 1. *The International Critical Commentary*. Edinburgh: T&T Clark, 1920.

Charles, R. H. *A Critical and Exegetical Commentary on the Revelation of St. John*, vol. 2. *The International Critical Commentary*. Edinburgh: T&T Clark, 1920.

Charlesworth, James H., ed., *The Pseudepigrapha and Modern Research, With a Supplement*. Chico: Scholars Press, 1981.

Chatman, Seymour Benjamin. *Story and Discourse: Narrative Structure in Fiction and Film*. Ithaca: Cornell University Press, 1978.

Couprie, Dirk L. 'The Spiral Movement of the Sun on an Imaginary Cylinder According to Empedocles and Anaximander'. *Philologia Classica*, 15/1 (2020): 4–24.

Dalton, W. J. *Christ's Proclamation to the Spirits: A Study of 1 Peter 3:18-4:6*. Rome: Pontifical Biblical Institute, 1965.

Day, Peggy Lynne. *An Adversary in Heaven: Satan in the Hebrew Bible*. Harvard Semitic Monographs, vol. 43. Atlanta: Scholars Press, 1988.

DeSilva, David Arthur. *Seeing Things John's Way: The Rhetoric of the Book of Revelation*. Louisville: Westminster John Knox Press, 2009.

Dillmann, August. *Das Buch Henoch übersetzt und erklärt*. Leipzig: Vogel, 1853.

Dochhorn, Jan. "'World' (ዓለም) in the Ascension of Isaiah'. *Ephemerides theologicae Lovanienses*, 94 (2018): 241–56.

Dreyer, J. L. E. *A History of Astronomy from Thales to Kepler*. New York: Dover, 1953.

Duke, Rodney K. 'Eternal Torment or Destruction? Interpreting Final Judgment Texts'. *Evangelical Quarterly*, 88/3 (2016): 237–58.

Duvall, J. Scott. *Revelation. Teach the Text*, edited by John H. Walton and Mark L. Strauss. Grand Rapids: Baker, 2014.

Dyer, Keith. 'Beastly Hybridity: Leviathan, Behemoth, and Revelation 13'. *St Mark's Review*, 239/1 (2017): 93–104.

Dyer, Keith. 'The Four Horsemen of the Apocalypse and the Consequences of War (Revelation 6.1-11)'. In *Ecological Aspects of War: Engagements with Biblical Texts*. Edited by Anne Elvey and Deborah Guess, 132–48. London: T&T Clark, 2017.

Edwards, James R. 'The Rider on the White Horse, the Thigh Inscription, and Apollo: Revelation 19:16'. *JBL*, 137/2 (2018): 519–36.

Elar, J. J. *The Apocalypse the Antichrist and the End*. London: Burns and Oates, 1906.

Elliott, Mark Adam. *The Survivors of Israel: A Reconsideration of the Theology of Pre-Christian Judaism*. Grand Rapids: Eerdmans, 2000.

Esler, Philip Francis. *God's Court and Courtiers in the Book of the Watchers: Re-Interpreting Heaven in 1 Enoch 1–36*. Eugene: Cascade, 2017.

Evans, Craig A. *Mark 8:27-16:20. Word Biblical Commentary*, vol. 34B. Nashville: Thomas Nelson, 2001.

Evelyn-White, Hugh G. *Hesiod, the Homeric Hymns, and Homerica. The Loeb Classical Library*. London: Heinemann, 1914.

Fair, Ian A. *Conquering with Christ: A Commentary on the Book of Revelation*. Abilene: Abilene Christian University Press, 2011.

Fee, Gordon D. *Revelation: A New Commentary*. Eugene: Cascade, 2011.

Ferguson, William Scott. 'Legalized Absolutism en Route from Greece to Rome'. *The American Historical Review*, 18/1 (1912): 29–47.

Fischer, Ulrich. *Eschatologie unt Jenseitserwartung im hellenistischen Diasporajudentum*, vol. 44. *BZNW*. Berlin: de Gruyter, 1978.

Fitzmyer, Joseph A. *First Corinthians. Anchor Bible*, vol. 32. New Haven: Yale University Press, 2008.

Ford, J. Massyngberde. *Revelation*. 1st edn. *The Anchor Bible*, vol. 38. Garden City: Doubleday, 1975.

Frazer, James George. *Apollodorus, The Library*. London: Heinemann, 1921.
Friesen, Steven J. *Imperial Cults and the Apocalypse of John: Reading Revelation in the Ruins*. Oxford: Oxford University Press, 2001.
Friesen, Steven J. 'Myth and Symbolic Resistance in Revelation 13'. *JBL*, 123/2 (2004): 281–313.
Friesen, Steven J. *Twice Neokoros: Ephesus, Asia, and the Cult of the Flavian Imperial Family*. Leiden: Brill, 1993.
Gebhardt, Hermann. *The Doctrine of the Apocalypse and its Relation to the Doctrine of the Gospel and Epistles of John*. Translated by John Jefferson. *Clark's Foreign Theological Library*, vol. 58. Edinburgh: T&T Clark, 1878.
Genette, Gérard. *Narrative Discourse: An Essay in Method*. Ithaca: Cornell University Press, 1980.
Giblin, Charles Homer. 'The Millennium (Rev 20.4-6) as Heaven'. *New Testament Studies*, 45 (1999): 553–70.
Goodspeed, Edgar J. 'Some Greek Notes: IV. Enoch in 1 Peter 3:19'. *Journal of Biblical Literature*, 73/2 (1954): 91–2.
Gore-Jones, Lydia. 'Animals, Humans, Angels and God: Animal Symbolism in the Historiography of the "Animal Apocalypse" of 1 Enoch'. *Journal for the Study of the Pseudepigrapha*, 24 (2015): 268–87.
Graves, Robert. *The Greek Myths*. Middlesex: Penguin, 1955.
Greenberg, Moshe. *Ezekiel 1–20: A New Translation with Introduction and Commentary*. 1st edn. Garden City: Doubleday, 1983.
Greenwood, Kyle. *Scripture and Cosmology: Reading the Bible between the Ancient World and Modern Science*. Downers Grove: IVP Academic, 2015.
Grelot, Pierre J. 'La géographie mythique d'Hénoch et ses sources orientales'. *Revue Biblique*, 65/1 (1958): 33–69.
Grudem, W. A. *Systematic Theology: An Introduction to Biblical Doctrine*. Grand Rapids: Zondervan Academic, 2009.
Gwyther, Anthony. 'New Jerusalem Versus Babylon'. Griffith University, 1999. https://research-repository.griffith.edu.au/handle/10072/367847.
Hagner, Donald Alfred. *Matthew 1–13*. *Word Biblical Commentary*, vol. 33A. Dallas: Word Books, 1993.
Hagner, Donald Alfred. *Matthew 14–28*, vol. 33B. *Word Biblical Commentary*. Dallas: Word Books, 1995.
Hahne, Harry Alan. *The Corruption and Redemption of Creation: Nature in Romans 8.19-22 and Jewish Apocalyptic Literature*. *Library of New Testament Studies*, vol. 336. London: T&T Clark, 2006.
Hall, Robert G. 'The Ascension of Isaiah: Community Situation, Date, and Place in Early Christianity'. *Journal of Biblical Literature*, 109/2 (1990): 289–306.
Hall, Robert G. 'Living Creatures in the Midst of the Throne: Another Look at Revelation 4.6'. *New Testament Studies*, 36/4 (1990): 609–13.
Hansen, Ryan Leif. *Silence and Praise: Rhetorical Cosmology and Political Theology in the Book of Revelation*. Minneapolis: Fortress Press, 2014.
Hard, Robin. *The Routledge Handbook of Greek Mythology*. London: Routledge, 2004.
Harlow, Daniel C. *The Greek Apocalypse of Baruch (3 Baruch) in Hellenistic Judaism and Early Christianity*. *Studia in Veteris Testamenti pseudepigrapha*, vol. 12. Leiden: Brill, 1996.
Harrington, Wilfrid J. *Revelation*. *Sacra Pagina Series*, vol. 16. Collegeville: Liturgical Press, 1993.

Harrisville, R. A. 'The Concept of Newness in the New Testament'. *Journal of Biblical Literature*, 74 (1955): 69–79.
Harvey, W. J. *Character and the Novel*. Ithaca: Cornell University Press, 1965.
Heath, T. L. *Aristarchus of Samos: The Ancient Greek Copernicus*. Oxford: Clarendon Press, 1913.
Helgeland, John. 'Time and Space: Christian and Roman'. *Aufstieg und Niedergang der römischen Welt*, 23/2 (1980): 1285–1305.
Henderson, Jeffrey, ed., *Pliny: Letters and Panegyricus: With an English Translation by Betty Radice*. Loeb Classical Library. Cambridge: Harvard University Press, 1969.
Hengel, Martin. *The Zealots: Investigations into the Jewish Freedom Movement in the Period from Herod I until 70 A.D.* Translated by David Smith. Edinburgh: T&T Clark, 1989.
Henning, Meghan. 'Eternal Punishment as Paideia: The Ekphrasis of Hell in the Apocalypse of Peter and the Apocalypse of Paul'. *Biblical Research*, 58 (2014): 29–48.
Himmelfarb, Martha. *Ascent to Heaven in Jewish and Christian Apocalypses*. New York: Oxford University Press, 1993.
Hobbs, Herschel H. *The Cosmic Drama*. Waco: Word Books, 1971.
Hongisto, Leif. *Experiencing the Apocalypse at the Limits of Alterity*. Leiden: Brill, 2010.
Houtman, C. *Der Himmel im Alten Testament: Israels Weltbild und Weltanschauung*. Oudtestamentische studiën. Leiden: Brill, 1993.
Howard-Brook, Wes, and Anthony Gwyther. *Unveiling Empire: Reading Revelation Then and Now*. Maryknoll: Orbis, 1999.
Hughes, Philip Edgcumbe. *The Book of the Revelation: A Commentary*. Leicester: Inter-Varsity Press, 1990.
Isaac, E. '1 (Ethiopic Apocalypse of) Enoch'. In *The Old Testament Pseudepigrapha*. Edited by James H. Charlesworth, vol. 1. Garden City: Doubleday, 1983, 5–90.
Janko, Richard. 'Tithonus, Eos and the Cicada in the Homeric Hymn to Aphrodite and Sappho fr. 58'. In *The Winnowing Oar: New Perspectives in Homeric Studies*. Edited by Christos Tsagalis and Andreas Markantonatos, 267–96. Berlin: De Gruyter, 2017.
Jordaan, Gert J. C. 'Cosmology in the Book of Revelation/Kosmologie in die boek van Openbaring'. *In die Skriflig*, 47/2 (2013): 1–8.
Kahl, Brigitte. *Galatians Re-Imagined: Reading with the Eyes of the Vanquished*. Minneapolis: Fortress Press, 2010.
Kiddle, Martin. *The Revelation of St. John. The Moffat New Testament Commentary*. London: Hodder and Stoughton, 1940.
Kitchin, Rob, and Phil Hubbard, eds., *Key Thinkers on Space and Place*. London: Sage, 2010.
Knibb, M. A. 'The Martyrdom and Ascension of Isaiah'. In *The Old Testament Pseudepigrapha*. Edited by James H. Charlesworth, vol. 2. Garden City: Doubleday, 1985, 143–76.
Knight, Jonathan. *The Ascension of Isaiah*. Guides to Apocrypha and Pseudepigrapha. Sheffield: Sheffield Academic Press, 1995.
Knight, Jonathan. *Revelation. Readings: A New Biblical Commentary*. Sheffield: Sheffield Academic Press, 1999.
Koester, Craig R. *Revelation: A New Translation with Introduction and Commentary. The Anchor Yale Bible*, vol. 38A. New Haven: Yale University Press, 2014.
Kraybill, J. Nelson. *Apocalypse and Allegiance: Worship, Politics, and Devotion in the Book of Revelation*. Grand Rapids: Brazos Press, 2010.
Kraybill, J. Nelson. *Imperial Cult and Commerce in John's Apocalypse*. Sheffield: T&T Clark, 1996.

Kulik, Alexander. *3 Baruch: Greek-Slavonic Apocalypse of Baruch*. Berlin: Walter de Gruyter, 2010.

Kulik, Alexander. *Retroverting Slavonic Pseudepigrapha: Toward the Original of the Apocalypse of Abraham*. Atlanta: Society of Biblical Literature, 2004.

Labahn, Michael. '"Apokalyptische" Geographie: Einführende Uberiegungen zu einer Toponomie der Johannesoffenbarung'. In *Imagery in the Book of Revelation*. Edited by Michael Labahn and Outi Lehtipuu. Contributions to Biblical Exegesis and Theology, vol. 60. Leuven: Peeters, 2011.

Ladd, G. E. *A Commentary on the Revelation of John*. Grand Rapids: Eerdmans, 1972.

LaHaye, Tim. *Revelation Unveiled*. Grand Rapids: Zondervan, 1999.

Lattimore, Richmond. *The Iliad of Homer*, edited by Richard Martin. Chicago: University of Chicago Press, 2011.

Lefebvre, Henri. *La production de l'espace*. Paris: Éditions Anthropos, 1974.

Lefebvre, Henri. *The Production of Space*. Oxford: Blackwell, 1991.

Lehtipuu, Outi. *The Afterlife Imagery in Luke's Story of the Rich Man and Lazarus*. Supplements to Novum Testamentum, vol. 123. Leiden: Brill, 2007.

Liddell, Henry George, Robert Scott, Henry Stuart Jones, Roderick McKenzie and Eric Arthur Barber. *A Greek-English Lexicon*. Oxford: Clarendon Press, 1968.

Lilje, Hans. *The Last Book of the Bible*. Translated by Olive Wyon. Philadelphia: Fortress Press, 1957.

Lopez, Davina C. *Apostle to the Conquered: Reimagining Paul's Mission*. Minneapolis: Fortress Press, 2008.

MacRae, George W. 'Some Elements of Jewish Apocalyptic and Mystical Tradition: And Their Relation to Gnostic Literature'. Cambridge, MA: Andover-Harvard Theological Library, 1981.

Maier, H. O. *Picturing Paul in Empire: Imperial Image, Text and Persuasion in Colossians, Ephesians and the Pastoral Epistles*. London: Bloomsbury, 2013.

Malina, Bruce J. *On the Genre and Message of Revelation: Star Visions and Sky Journeys*. Peabody: Hendrickson, 1995.

Malina, Bruce J., and John J. Pilch. *Social-Science Commentary on the Book of Revelation*. Minneapolis: Fortress Press, 2000.

Mangina, Joseph L. *Revelation. Brazos Theological Commentary on the Bible*. Grand Rapids: Brazos Press, 2010.

Mathewson, Dave. 'A Re-Examination of the Millenium in Rev 20:1-6: Consummation and Recapitulation'. *JETS*, 44/2 (2001): 237–51.

McDonough, Sean M. 'Revelation: The Climax of Cosmology'. In *Cosmology and New Testament Theology*. Edited by Jonathan T. Pennington and Sean M. McDonough, 178–88. London: T&T Clark, 2008, 178–88.

McGiffert, Arthur Cushman. *The History of the Church, By Eusebius*. Overland Park: Digireads, 2018.

McKelvey, R. Jack. 'The Millenium and the Second Coming'. In *Studies in the Book of Revelation*. Edited by Steve Moyise. Edinburgh: T&T Clark, 2001, 85–100.

McKenzie, John L. *Second Isaiah*. Anchor Bible. Garden City: Doubleday, 1968.

Michaels, J. Ramsey. *Interpreting the Book of Revelation*. Guides to New Testament Exegesis. Grand Rapids: Baker Academic, 1998.

Milik, Józef T. *The Books of Enoch: Aramaic Fragments of Qumran Cave 4*. Oxford: Clarendon Press, 1976.

Milik, Józef T. *Dead Sea Scrolls Study: The Book of Enoch Aramaic fragments, Qumran Cave 4*: Oxford Clarendon Press, 1976.

Minear, Paul S. 'The Cosmology of the Apocalypse'. In *Current Issues in New Testament Interpretation*. Edited by William Klassen and Graydon F. Snyder. London: SCM Press, 1962, 23–37.

Minear, Paul S. *I Saw a New Earth: An Introduction to the Visions of the Apocalypse*. Washington: Corpus Books, 1968.

Moo, Jonathan. 'The Sea That Is No More: Rev 21:1 and the Function of Sea Imagery in the Apocalypse of John'. *Novum Testamentum*, 51 (2009): 148–67.

Morray-Jones, Christopher R. A. 'Paradise Revisited (2 Cor 12:1-12): The Jewish Mystical Background of Paul's Apostolate. Part 1: The Jewish Sources'. *HTR*, 86/2 (1993): 177–217.

Morray-Jones, Christopher R. A. 'The Temple Within'. In *Paradise Now: Essays of Early Jewish and Christian Mysticism*. Edited by April. D. De Conick. SBL Symposium Series 11. Leiden: Brill, 2006, 145–78.

Morris, L. *The Revelation of St. John*. Tyndale New Testament Commentaries. Grand Rapids: Eerdmans, 1987.

Mounce, Robert H. *The Book of Revelation*. The New International Commentary on the New Testament. Grand Rapids: Eerdmans, 1977.

Moyise, Steve. *The Old Testament in the Book of Revelation*. Journal for the Study of the New Testament Supplement Series, vol. 115. Sheffield: Sheffield Academic Press, 1995.

Murphy, Frederick J. *Fallen is Babylon: The Revelation to John*. Harrisburg: Trinity Press International, 1998.

Newton, Jon K. *A Pentecostal Commentary on Revelation*. Pentecostal Old Testament and New Testament Commentaries. Eugene: Wipf and Stock, 2021.

Newton, Jon K. *The Revelation Worldview: Apocalyptic Thinking in a Postmodern World*. Eugene: Wipf and Stock, 2015.

Nickelsburg, George W. E. *1 Enoch 1: A Commentary on the Book of 1 Enoch*. Hermeneia. Minneapolis: Fortress Press, 2001.

Nickelsburg, George W. E. 'Enoch, Levi, and Peter: Recipients of Revelation in Upper Galilee'. *Journal of Biblical Literature*, 100 (1981): 575–600.

Nickelsburg, George W. E. 'Revisiting the Rich and the Poor in 1 Enoch 92–105 and the Gospel According to Luke'. *Society of Biblical Literature Seminar Papers*, 134/37 (1998): 579–605

Nickelsburg, George W. E., and James C. VanderKam. *1 Enoch 2: A Commentary on the Book of 1 Enoch*. Hermeneia. Minneapolis: Fortress Press, 2012.

Nicolet, Claude. *Space, Geography, and Politics in the Early Roman Empire*. Ann Arbor: University of Michigan Press, 1991.

Norelli, Enrico. 'L' Ascension d'Esaïe est-elle vraiment un écrit unitaire?: une discussion avec Richard Bauckham'. *Annali di Storia dell'Esegesi*, 32 (2015): 11–37.

O'Hear, Natasha, and Anthony O'Hear. *Picturing the Apocalypse: The Book of Revelation in the Arts over Two Millennia*. Oxford: Oxford University Press, 2015.

Olson, Daniel C. *A New Reading of the Animal Apocalypse of 1 Enoch: All Nations Shall Be Blessed*. Studia in Veteris Testamenti Pseudepigrapha, vol. 24. Boston: Brill, 2013.

Orlov, Andrei A. *Heavenly Priesthood in the Apocalypse of Abraham*. New York: Cambridge University Press, 2013.

Osborne, Grant R. *Revelation*. Baker Exegetical Commentary on the New Testament. Grand Rapids: Baker Academic, 2002.

Papaioannou, Kim Gary. 'Places of Punishment in the Synoptic Gospels'. PhD thesis, University of Durham, Durham, 2004.

Parke, Herbert William. *A History of the Delphic Oracle*. Oxford: Basil Blackwell, 1939.

Pearson, Birger A. 'A Reminiscence of Classical Myth at 2 Peter 2:4'. *Greek, Roman, and Byzantine Studies*, 10 (1969): 71–80.
Pennington, Jonathan T., and Sean M. McDonough. *Cosmology and New Testament Theology*. Edited by Jonathan T. Pennington and Sean M. McDonough. London: T&T Clark, 2008.
Perriman, Andrew. *The Coming of the Son of Man: New Testament Eschatology for an Emerging Church*. Eugene: Wipf and Stock, 2012.
Peterson, Erik. 'Die Taufe im Acherusischen See'. *Vigiliae Christianae*, 9/1 (1955): 1–20.
Portier-Young, Anathea E. *Apocalypse Against Empire: Theologies of Resistance in Early Judaism*. Grand Rapids: Eerdmans, 2011.
Powell, Mark Allan. *What is Narrative Criticism? Guides to Biblical Scholarship*. New Testament Series. Minneapolis: Fortress Press, 1990.
Pratchett, Terry. *Strata*. Gerrard's Cross: Colin Smythe, 1981.
Rad, Gerhard von. *Genesis: A Commentary*. Rev. edn. *Old Testament Library*. London: SCM Press, 1972.
Reed, Annette Yoshiko. *Fallen Angels and the History of Judaism and Christianity: The Reception of Enochic Literature*. Cambridge: Cambridge University Press, 2005.
Reese, Ruth Anne. 'Narrative Method and the Letter of Second Peter'. In *Reading Second Peter with New Eyes: Methodological Reassessments of the Letter of Second Peter*. Edited by Robert L. Webb and Duane Frederick Watson. London: T&T Clark, 2010.
Reeve, C. D. C. *De Caelo*. Indianapolis: Hackett, 2020, 119–46.
Resseguie, James L. *Revelation Unsealed: A Narrative Critical Approach to John's Apocalypse. Biblical Interpretation*, vol. 32. Leiden: Brill, 1998.
Robbins, Vernon K. 'Rhetography: A New Way of Seeing the Familiar Text'. In *Words Well Spoken: George Kennedy's Rhetoric of the New Testament*. Edited by C. Clifton Black and Duane Frederick Watson, vol. 8. Waco: Baylor University Press, 2008, 81–106.
Robbins, Vernon K. *The Tapestry of Early Christian Discourse: Rhetoric, Society, and Ideology*. London: Routledge, 1996.
Robertson, A. T. *A Grammar of the Greek New Testament in the Light of Historical Research*. London: Hodder and Stoughton, 1919.
Roloff, Jürgen. *The Revelation of John: A Continental Commentary*. Translated by John E. Alsup. Minneapolis: Fortress Press, 1993.
Rubinkiewicz, R. 'Apocalypse of Abraham'. In *The Old Testament Pseudepigrapha*. Edited by James H. Charlesworth, vol. 1, 681–706. Garden City: Doubleday, 1983.
Russell, David M. *The New Heavens and New Earth: Hope for the Creation in Jewish Apocalyptic and the New Testament. Studies in Biblical Apocalyptic Literature*. Philadelphia: Visionary Press, 1996.
Ryan, Sean Michael. *Hearing at the Boundaries of Vision: Education Informing Cosmology in Revelation 9*. London: T&T Clark, 2012.
Schmid, Konrad. 'Himmelsgott, Weltgott und Schöpfer'. *Jahrbuch für Biblische Theologie*, 10 (2005): 111–48.
Schüssler Fiorenza, Elisabeth. *The Book of Revelation: Justice and Judgment*. 2nd edn. Minneapolis: Fortress Press, 1998.
Skinner, John. *A Critical and Exegetical Commentary on Genesis*. 2nd edn. *International Critical Commentary on the Holy Scriptures of the Old and New Testaments*. Edinburgh: T&T Clark, 1930.
Stephens, Mark B. *Annihilation or Renewal?: The Meaning and Function of New Creation in the Book of Revelation. Wissenschaftliche Untersuchungen zum Neuen Testament 2 Reihe*, vol. 307. Tübingen: Mohr Siebeck, 2011.

Struckenbruck, Loren T., and Gabriele Boccaccini, eds, *Enoch and the Synoptic Gospels: Reminiscences, Allusions, Intertextuality. Early Judaism and Its Literature*, vol. 44. Atlanta: SBL Press, 2016.
Sweet, J. P. M. *Revelation. Westminster Pelican Commentaries*. Philadelphia: Westminster Press, 1979.
Swete, Henry Barclay. *The Apocalypse of St. John*. 3rd edn. London: Macmillan, 1906.
Sylva, Dennis D. 'A Unified Field Picture of Second Peter 1.3-15: Making Rhetorical Sense Out of Individual Images'. In *Reading Second Peter with New Eyes: Methodological Reassessments of the Letter of Second Peter*. Edited by Robert L. Webb and Duane Frederick Watson. London: T&T Clark, 2010, 91–118.
Szkredka, Sławomir. 'Postmortem Punishment in the Parable of Lazarus and the Rich Man (Luke 16: 19-31): Between Coherence and Indeterminacy of Luke's Eschatology'. *Verbum Vitae*, 36 (2019): 109–32.
Talbert, Charles H. *The Apocalypse: A Reading of the Revelation of John*. Louisville: Westminster John Knox Press, 1994.
Theisohn, J. *Der auserwählte Richter: Untersuchungen z. traditionsgeschichtl. Ort d. Menschensohngestalt d. Bilderreden d. Äthiopischen Henoch*. Gottingen, Germany: Vandenhoeck und Ruprecht, 1975.
Thomas, John Christopher, and Frank D. Macchia. *Revelation. The Two Horizons New Testament Commentary*. Grand Rapids: Eerdmans, 2016.
Thompson, Leonard L. *Revelation. Abingdon New Testament Commentaries*. Nashville: Abingdon Press, 1998.
Ureña, Lourdes García. *Narrative and Drama in the Book of Revelation*. Translated by Donald Murphy. *Society for New Testament Studies Monograph Series*, vol. 175. Cambridge: Cambridge University Press, 2019.
VanderKam, James C. '1 Enoch, Enochic Motifs, and Enoch in Early Christian Literature'. In *The Jewish Apocalyptic Heritage in Early Christianity*. Edited by James C. VanderKam and William Adler. Minneapolis: Fortress Press, 1995, 33–101.
Villiers, Pieter G. R. de, ed., *Studies in 1 Enoch and the New Testament*. Stellenbosch: University of Stellenbosch Press, 1983.
Vinson, Richard B. 'The Sea of Glass, the Lake of Fire, and the Topography of Heaven in Revelation'. *Perspectives In Religious Studies*, 45/2 (2018): 127–38.
Waal, Kayle B. de. *A Socio-Rhetorical Interpretation of the Seven Trumpets of Revelation: The Apocalyptic Challenge to Earthly Empire*. Lewiston: Edwin Mellen Press, 2012.
Walcot, P. 'Greek Attitudes towards Women: The Mythological Evidence'. *Greece and Rome*, 31/1 (1984): 37–47.
Walton, John H. *Genesis 1 as Ancient Cosmology*. Winona Lake: Eisenbrauns, 2011.
Wan, Wei Hsien. *The Contest for Time and Space in the Roman Imperial Cults and 1 Peter: Reconfiguring the Universe. Library of New Testament Studies*. London: T&T Clark, 2020.
Watts, John D. W. *Isaiah 1–33. Word Biblical Commentary*, vol. 24. Nashville: Thomas Nelson, 2005.
Watts, John D. W. *Isaiah 34–66. Word Biblical Commentaries*, vol. 25. Nashville: Thomas Nelson, 2005.
Wenham, Gordon J. *Genesis 1–15. Word Biblical Commentary*, vol. 1. Waco: Word Books, 1987.
Westermann, Claus. *Genesis 1–11: A Commentary*. Translated by John J. Scullion. Minneapolis: Augsburg, 1984.

Whitaker, Robyn J. *Ekphrasis, Vision, and Persuasion in the Book of Revelation.* Wissenschaftliche Untersuchungen zum Neuen Testament. Tübingen: Mohr Siebeck, 2015.

Williamson, Peter S. *Revelation. Catholic Commentary on Sacred Scripture.* Grand Rapids: Baker Academic, 2015.

Wink, Walter. *Naming the Powers: The Language of Power in the New Testament.* Philadelphia: Fortress Press, 1984.

Wink, Walter. *Unmasking the Powers: The Invisible Forces that Determine Human Existence.* Philadelphia: Fortress Press, 1986.

Wintermute, O. S. 'Apocalypse of Zephaniah'. In *The Old Testament Pseudepigrapha.* Edited by James H. Charlesworth, vol. 1. Garden City: Doubleday, 1983, 497–506.

Witherington, Ben. *Revelation. New Cambridge Bible Commentary.* Cambridge: Cambridge University Press, 2003.

Wood, Barry. 'Imagining the Unimaginable: Narratives of the Big Bang: Time, Space, Matter, Energy'. *Journal of Big History*, 2/1 (2018): 1–13.

Woodington, J. David. 'Crafting the Eschaton: The Second Death and the Lake of Fire in Revelation'. *Journal for the Study of the New Testament*, 41 (2019): 501–18.

Wright, J. Edward. *The Early History of Heaven.* Oxford: Oxford University Press, 2000.

Wright, M. R. *Cosmology in Antiquity.* London: Routledge, 1995.

Wright, N. T. *Jesus and the Victory of God.* Minneapolis: Fortress Press, 1996.

Wright, N. T. *The New Testament and the People of God.* Minneapolis: Fortress Press, 1992.

Wright, N. T. *Revelation for Everyone.* Louisville: Westminster John Knox Press, 2011.

Yarbro Collins, Adela. *The Combat Myth in the Book of Revelation.* Missoula: Scholars Press, 1976.

Yarbro Collins, Adela. *Cosmology and Eschatology in Jewish and Christian Apocalypticism.* Supplements to the Journal for the study of Judaism. Leiden: Brill, 1996.

Yarbro Collins, Adela. 'The Political Perspective of the Revelation to John'. *Journal of Biblical Literature*, 96/2 (1977): 241–56.

Yarbro Collins, Adela. 'The Seven Heavens in Jewish and Christian Apocalypses'. In *Death, Ecstasy, and Other Worldly Journeys.* Edited by John J. Collins and Michael A. Fishbane. Albany: State University of New York Press, 1995, 57–92.

Yonge, C. D. *The Works of Philo Judaeus, the Contemporary of Josephus.* London: H. G. Bohn, 1854.

Yu Yap, Marlene. 'Three Parables of Jesus through the Shame-Honor Lens'. *Asian Journal of Pentecostal Studies*, 19/2 (2016): 207–23.

Index of Ancient Literature

HEBREW SCRIPTURES AND SEPTUAGINT

Genesis
1	44, 96
1.2	11, 41
1.6-10	148
1.11-12	51
1.14	51, 80
1.14-18	45
1.14-25	97
1.20	51, 80
1.24-25	51
3	109
4.10	134
4.10-11	76
5	43
5.24	102
7	39
7.11	11, 41, 45, 48, 148
9.4	76
21.30	89
25.8	40
37.35	38, 40
42.38	38, 40
44.29	38, 40
44.31	38
47.30	40
49.29	40

Exodus
12.22	46
12.23	92
20.4	39
24.6	76
24.10	63
29.12	76
29.16	76
26.20	76
39.3	45

Leviticus
1.5	76
1.11	76
1.15	76
3.2	76
3.8	76
3.13	76
4.7	76
4.18	76
4.25, 76	
4.30	76
4.34	76
5.9	76
7.2	76
8.15	76
8.19	76
8.24	76
9.9	76
9.12	76
9.18	76
11.9	91, 117
17.6	76
17.10-16	76
17.11	76
17.13	76

Numbers
16.30	38
16.33	45
16.38-39	45
18.17	76
21.18	89
22	107, 109

Deuteronomy
4.32	36
8.7	11, 41
12.23	76
12.27	76
13.7	36
28.49, 64	36

31.16	40	37.3	36, 60
32.8-9	13	37.18	45
33.17	36	38.10	148
		38.13	36, 60
Joshua		41.23-24	11
10.13	97		
		Psalms	
1 Samuel		17.5-6 LXX	94
2.6	38	18.4-5	94
2.8	37	24.1-2	37, 91, 117
29	107	30.4	38
		54.24 LXX	89
2 Samuel		55.16	38
19	107	66.6	91
22.8	46	70.21 LXX	94
22.43	37, 45	74.14	106
		75.3	37
1 Kings		77.49 LXX	92
2.10	40	78.23-24	49
2.6, 9	38	78.49	92
5	107	87.4-8 LXX	94
11	107	88.3-7	94
		89.26	91
2 Kings		104.2	46, 63
16.13	76	104.5	37
16.15	76	104.5-9	148
		104.9	148
1 Chronicles		104.26	93
21	107, 109	109	107
21.15	92	136.6	37, 45
		148.7	41
2 Chronicles			
29.22	76	*Proverbs*	
		1.12	38
Ezra		5.5	38
2.68	37	7.27	38
		8.27	37
Job		8.29	148
1–2	113		
1.6–2.7	55	*Isaiah*	
2	107, 109	5.14	38
2.1-5	39	6.2	69
7.9	38	11.12	36, 60
9.8	46, 63	11.15	92
17.16	38	13.4-5	88, 148
26	46	13.5	36, 46
26.7.	46	13.13	46
28.24	36	14	109

14.2	109	*Daniel*	
14.11	38	7.1–8.4	93
14.12	86	8.10	109
14.12-20	106	10.13	13
14.15	38	10.20-21	13
24.16	36, 60		
24.18	49	*Joel*	
34.4	46, 63	2.10	46
38.18	38		
40.19	45	*Amos*	
40.22	46, 63	9.2	38
42.5	37, 45, 46, 63	9.6	46
44.24	63		
45.12	63	*Nahum*	
50.2	92, 117	1.4	92, 117
51.13	63		
44.24	37, 45, 46, 63	*Habakkuk*	
45.12	46, 63	3.8	92, 117
51.13	63		
66.24	41, 128, 129	*Zechariah*	
		3	107, 109, 113
Jeremiah		3.2	113
1.9	105	4.10	70
5.22	148	12.1	46, 63
7.32-33	41		
10.9	45	*Epistle of Jeremiah*	
10.12	46, 63	54	98
15.16	105		
25.36	36	*1 Maccabees*	
51	147	7.19	89
51.15	46, 63		
		2 Maccabees	
Ezekiel		5.1-4	15
1	46		
1.4-28	69, 112, 123	*3 Maccabees*	
1.18	69	6.18	50
1.22	46, 73		
1.22-26	63, 64	*Psalms of Solomon*	
2.8–3.3	105	1.5	86
6.11	45	17.19	91
25.6	45		
31.15-17	38	APOCALYPSES, TESTAMENTS AND ORACLES	
32.21, 27	38		
37	134		
38.22	128	*1 Enoch*	
41.22	36	1–36	3, 49, 60, 84, 102, 133, 148
43.20	36		
45.19	36	2.1	3, 84
46.21-22	36	3.2-3	50

6.1-8	52, 84	18.12-15	42
8.1	107	18.12-16	84
9.1-3	133	18.13-15	50, 52, 84, 85, 87, 99
9.4	91	19.1	84
9.6	107	20.2	91
9.9-10	133	21.1-6	42, 84
10.4	107	21.1-10	54, 84, 129, 132
10.4-5	54, 56, 129, 134	21.3-6	50, 52, 84, 85, 87, 99
10.4-6	4	21.7	91
10.6	128, 129	21.7-10	4, 42, 56, 84
10.8	107	22	75
10.9-15	134	22.1-4	129
10.11-12	54	22.1-7	133
10.11-13	4, 134	22.1-14	40
10.12	56, 129	22.4	42
10.12-14	134	22.5-12	76
10.13	128	26.1–27.5	129
10.14	134	33.1	48
11.1	56	33.1-4	52, 80, 84, 99
12.4	52, 84	33.2-4	49
12.5-6	134	34.2	50
13.1	107	36.1	50
14.5	54, 55, 87, 134	36.2-3	49
14.6	134	37–71	102
14.8	102	39.1	102
14.8-18	74, 123	41.4	50
14.9-25	104	43.1	50, 102
14.10	63	43.1–44.1	87
14.14-25	71	47.1-2	76
14.15-17	74	48	135
14.17	63	48.9	135
14.22	71	51	75
15.1-7	52, 84	51.1	129
17–36	3	54.1-6	91, 129
17.2	38	54.5	107
17.7	91	54.6	107
17.8	89	54.7-9	45
17.10–21.10	125	55.4	107
18.1	50	56.8	129
18.1–36.4	36	60.11-23	50
18.4	80	60.12	50
18.10	11	63.10	129
18.10-15	132	66.1-2	56
18.10–19.1	54	67.4-13	129
18.10–19.3	129	69.2	107
18.10–22.14	129	69.21	50
18.11	42, 84	69.24	50
18.11–19.1	4, 56, 84	70	102
18.12	84	71.7	69

72–82	3, 49, 85, 152	22.1	54
72.1-3	50	23–38	37, 38, 48, 62
72.2–73.37	49	25–26	48
72.3	49	25.4	66, 74, 123
74.1-9	49	27	48, 64
75.1	50	30.4	80
75.1-6	49	38	102
75.3	80	39–73	38, 48
76.1-14	50	40.10	50
78.1–79.6	49	40.12	125
79.1–80.8	50	47	48
80.4-6	84, 87, 99	47.3	37
80.4-7	152	67	102
80.5-6	3	68.1-3	102
81.5	102	73.4	49
81.6	102		
82.1-9	152	2 Baruch	
82.4	3	10.11	50
82.19	85	11.6	42
83–90	83, 91	21.24	42
83.4	91	50.2	42
83.7	91	59.3	54, 97
83.11	36, 60		
85–90	42, 50, 84, 85, 134	3 Baruch	
88.1	83, 91	1.3-7	60, 81, 105
90.2	98	2.1	36, 48
90.20	123	2.1-7	53
90.21	91	2.2	47, 48, 50, 51, 62
90.24-26	83, 91	2.2-3	48
90.24-27	129, 134	2.2-7	4
108.3	132	2.5	47
		3.1	50, 51, 62
2 Enoch		3.1-2	48
1–22	38, 43, 48	3.1-8	4, 53
1.1–2.2	60, 81, 105	3.2	47, 48
3–6	73	3.7	48, 64
3.3–4.2	80	4.1-5	4
5.1–6.1	50	4.2	43, 47, 50, 51, 62
7.1-5	43, 54, 89	4.2-5	53
8.1–10.6	43	5	95
10.1	104	5.3	43, 53
10.2	128, 129	6–9	80
11.1-3	80	6.1	53, 104
11.3	50	6.1–8.5	49
13–16	125	6.1–9.7	4
13.1–15.4	49	8.1	104
16.1-8	49	10.1-5	4, 53, 73
18.3	43, 89	10.1-9	53, 63
18.7	43	10.5	43

10.6-9	4, 50	*Apocalypse of Moses*	
11–17	53, 87	37.3	130
11.1-2	51, 62		
11.1-6	50	*Apocalypse of Paul*	
14.1	51	22	130
16.2	102	23–29	131
		31	131, 132
4 Ezra			
2.39-45	76	*Apocalypse of Peter*	
4.35	42	14	130
4.41	42		
7	95	*Apocalypse of Zephaniah*	
7.32	40, 42	6.16-7.9	107, 109
7.36	41, 42		
7.75-101	42	*Ascension of Isaiah*	
7.95	40	1–5	56
8.23	91	1.3	43, 56, 135
		2.7-9	4
Apocalypse of Abraham		3.30-31	35
1–8	150	3.31	12
1–9	5	4.1-13	4
9–22	150	4.1-19	128
10.1–11.6	60, 81, 105	4.2	52, 151
15.1	93	4.14	43, 56, 135
15.4-5	49	4.14-18	4
15.4-7	51, 73	4.18	4, 53, 56, 135, 151
15.5	49	5.13	4
15.6-7	54	6.6-9	60, 81, 105
17–18	67, 73	6.10-14	34
17.1	104	7–9	151
17.1–18.14	112, 123	7.9	151
17.3-5	49	7.9-10	4
18.1	49	7.9-12	52
18.1-3	51, 54	7.9-17	51
18.3-6	69	7.10	4, 151
18.10	92	7.13	53
19.1-9.	48, 51	8.1	51, 52
19.3	5	8.16	52
19.4	49, 150	9.1	51, 52, 53
19.5-9	151	9.6	51, 52, 53
19.9	50, 80	9.7	53
21.1-2	49	9.9	76
21.1-5	125	9.19-26	4
21.4	60, 95	9.28	104
21.6	75	9.33-34	104
24.6	125	9.39	104
30.1	102	9.41	104
31.1-3	56	10.8	43, 56, 135
31.3	54, 93	10.24-27	50

11.35	102	*Testament of Levi*	
		2.6	50, 62
History of the Rechabites		2.7	73
4.9	91	3.1-3	56
		5.1	50, 62
Jubilees		5.7	102
2.2	91		
2.16	91	*Testament of Solomon*	
4.17-18	4	20.14-17	86
6.32-38	4		
7.34-37	4	QUMRAN	
8.19	144		
10.8	107	1QS	
10.11	107	4.13	134
11.5	107		
11.11	107	4QEn^c	
17.16	107	10.12-14	134
18.9	107		
18.12	107	EARLY CHRISTIAN LITERATURE	
19.28	107		
23.17-18	4	*Matthew*	
48.2	107	4.1-11	107
48.9	107	4.8	36, 60
48.12	107	5.22	41, 128
48.15	107	5.29	41
49.2	107	10.25	107
50.1-5	4,	10.28	41
		11.23	40
Shepherd of Hermas		12.22-32	107
1.1.3	147	13.42	128
2.1.1	147	13.50	128
		16.23	107
Sibylline Oracles		12.26	107
2.202	86	18.9	41, 128
2.334-338	130	22.10	153
2.331-338	131	23.15	41
2.337-338	131	23.33	41
3.51-62	128	24.29	86
3.82	63	25.41	4, 56, 128
5.72	86	26.26-29	155
5.208	97		
8.190	86	*Mark*	
8.233	63	1	47
8.341	86	1.10	47, 63
8.413	63	3.13-27	107
14.269	86	3.22	107
		4.22-25	155
Testament of Asher		9	41
7.2	36	9.43	41, 128, 129

9.48	128, 129	12.2-4	34, 54
13	137	12.7	107
13.25	86		
15	47	*2 Thessalonians*	
15.38	47	1.5-12	128
Luke		*1 Timothy*	
2.14	158	1.20	107
4.5	36, 60		
8.21	41	*Hebrews*	
8.31	4, 11, 91	1.12	63
10.12	128		
10.15	40	*James*	
10.18	86, 107	3.6	41
11.18	107		
11.14-23	107	*1 Peter*	
12.5	41	2.5	149
13.16	107		
16.23	40	*2 Peter*	
17.29-30	128	2.4	42, 89
19.38-40	158	2.6	128
22.14-20	155		
24.30-35	155	*Jude*	
		9	107, 113
Acts		13	50, 86
2.2	65	14	34, 52, 84, 87, 99
2.27	40		
2.31	40	*Revelation*	
15.20	76	1	67, 118
15.29	76	1–3	13
20.7	155	1.1-3	26
		1.3	12, 155
Romans		1.4	12, 34, 60, 127
8	138	1.4–20.10	88, 117, 122, 125, 141–2
10.6-7	40		
10.7	94	1.5-7	34
		1.6	139, 149, 155
1 Corinthians		1.7	70, 108
5.5	107	1.9	59, 155
8.1-13	154	1.9-16	105
10.14-21	154	1.9-20	65, 81, 84, 85, 105
10.16-17	155	1.9–22.5	26
11.20-34	155	1.10	60, 65, 155
15.35-41	51, 55	1.11	26, 60, 105
15.53	76	1.12	26, 60, 74
		1.14	70, 82
2 Corinthians		1.18	75, 95, 108
5.1-4	76	1.18–3.22	60, 81
12.1-7	35	1.19	105

Index of Ancient Literature

1.20	81, 85	5.8-10	72, 96
2.1–3.22	105	5.8-14	155
2.2	34	5.9	114
2.2-3	155	5.10	139, 149, 155
2.4-5	155	5.11	64, 65, 72, 96, 123
2.6	34	5.11-12	71, 90, 96
2.9-10	107, 114	5.11-13	72
2.13	107, 114	5.13	10, 65, 73, 90, 96, 120, 127, 138
2.14	150, 154		
2.14-15	34	6.1	64, 65, 96
2.18	70, 82	6.1-8	96
2.19	155	6.2	76, 108
2.20	150, 154	6.3	64, 65, 96
2.20-24	34	6.5	64, 65, 96, 108
3.4	76	6.6	64
3.9	107, 114	6.7	64, 65, 96
3.10	155	6.8	95, 108
3.12	8, 149	6.9	75, 76, 114, 150
3.18	70, 76	6.9-11	67, 81
4–5	118	6.12	64, 82
4–6	83	6.12-14	80, 82
4.1	22, 61, 64, 103, 108	6.12-17	82, 83, 119, 137
4.1-2	34, 62	6.13	8, 64, 86, 87, 112, 120
4.2	29, 67, 74, 83, 96, 105, 108, 118, 119, 127, 136	6.14	62, 63, 96, 119
		6.14-16	64
4.2-3	122, 124	6.16	127
4.2-11	67, 81	7–8	83
4.2–9.21	64, 96, 102	7.1	60, 64, 83, 98, 148
4.3	72, 123	7.1-3	87, 92, 148
4.4	76	7.2	64, 80, 112, 127
4.5	73, 127	7.9	83, 98, 108, 127
4.6	63, 72, 73, 123, 126	7.9–8.5	67, 81
4.8	72	7.11	98, 127
4.9	127	7.13	104
4.9-10	71	7.13-14	68
4.10	71, 127	7.15	71, 127, 149, 150
4.11	139–40	7.16	80
5.1	70, 127	7.17	70
5.1-14	67, 81	8.2	83, 98
5.2-3	138	8.3	98, 104, 150
5.3	96	8.3-4	155
5.5	108	8.3-5	71
5.6	70, 74, 82, 85, 98	8.5	150
5.6-10	34	8.7-12	88, 117
5.6-14	79, 96–7, 99, 154	8.7–9.19	109
5.6–6.8	73	8.8	87
5.7	104, 127	8.8-9	147
5.8	69	8.10	86, 87, 112

8.12	8	12	13, 15, 74, 75, 82, 97,
8.13	96, 97, 98, 112, 127		101, 105, 106, 108,
8.16	10		109, 115
9	22, 93		
9.1	8, 10, 64, 83, 87, 88,	12.1	74, 102
	108, 112, 120	12.1-3	110
		12.1-4	151
9.1-2	94, 121	12.1-6	34, 106, 109, 110,
9.1-11	59, 79, 83, 87–93,		111, 113
	98, 121	12.1-9	15, 108, 114
9.11	92	12.1-13	34
9.12	108	12.1-18	59
9.13	64, 65, 73, 150	12.3	74, 108
9.13-15	92	12.3-4	124
9.13-19	30, 88, 147, 148	12.3-9	150
9.14	148	12.4	8, 87, 98, 108, 109,
9.14-16	87		110, 112, 120,
9.20	88, 150		148, 151
9.21	155	12.5	110
10	103, 105	12.6	102, 103, 110, 122
10–14	118	12.7	8, 93, 124
10.1	29, 65, 83, 102,	12.7-9	106, 109, 111,
	103, 105, 112, 118,		113, 151
	121, 127	12.7-12	15
10.1-7	105, 120	12.9	111, 113
10.1-11	105	12.10	26, 65, 105
10.1–11.13	105	12.10-12	106, 107, 108, 111,
10.1–15.1	65		112, 113
10.4	65, 104, 105	12.11	114
10.5	98	12.12	61, 120
10.6	73, 120, 139	12.13-14	103, 110
10.8	65, 98, 105	12.13-17	34, 106, 150
10.9	103, 105	12.13-18	106
10.10	104	12.14	110, 122
10.11	105	12.17	114, 150
11.1	105, 150	12.18	98
11.1-2	149	12.18–13.1	148
11.1-3	105	13	13, 34, 87, 93
11.1–15.1	105	13.1	11, 73, 74, 93, 148
11.4	105	13.1-8	147, 148
11.4-6	87	13.3	148
11.7	11, 93, 121, 148	13.4	151
11.9	26	13.7	93
11.11	98	13.10	155
11.12	26, 65, 105	13.12	139
11.14	108	13.13	120
11.16	26	14 126–8	
11.16-18	65, 105	14.1	108
11.18	60	14.1-5	16
11.19	26, 67, 71, 81, 150	14.2	65

14.3	127	17.12	85
14.6	10, 97, 98	17.16	136
14.6-10	112, 127	18–19	127
14.7	73, 117, 120, 139	18.1	103, 112, 118, 120, 121, 127
14.8	136		
14.8-11	136	18.1-8	127, 128
14.9-11	93, 128, 135	18.1–19.3	136
14.10	126	18.2	61
14.12	155	18.2-24	148
14.12-13	155	18.3	136
14.13	65	18.4	65, 118, 136
14.14	74, 108	18.9	26, 136
14.15	71, 150	18.9-19	136
14.17	71, 150	18.11-19	148, 154
14.17-19	112	18.13	85
14.18	150	18.17	148
15	118	19.1	118
15.2	29, 63, 73, 83, 93, 98, 105, 118, 129	19.1-3	128
		19.3	127
15.2-4	155	19.4	69
15.2-8	67, 81	19.4-5	118
15.5	150	19.6	118
15.5-8	71, 104	19.9	155
15.5–16.1	71	19.10	149, 155
15.5–16.21	73	19.11	74, 108
15.8	71, 150	19.11-16	67, 128
16.1	64, 71, 150	19.12	70, 82
16.2	93	19.16	34
16.2-9	88, 117	19.17	10, 97, 98, 112
16.4-6	87	19.19	93
16.7	64, 150	19.19-20	93
16.10	93	19.20	135
16.10-11	88	19.20-21	136
16.12	88	19.21	126
16.12-16	147, 148	20.1	87, 88, 103, 112, 118, 121, 127
16.13	93		
16.14	88, 93	20.1-3	87, 89, 94, 121, 151
16.15	108, 155		
16.17	150	20.1-15	59, 122, 136
17	13, 85	20.2-3	113
17–19	118, 127	20.4	118
17.1	104	20.5	139
17.1-3	112, 127	20.6	155
17.1-5	136	20.7	121
17.3	29, 67, 118, 126, 143, 147	20.8	93
		20.9-10	136
17.3-18	93, 148	20.10	93, 126, 135
17.3–20.10	65	20.11	118, 120, 127, 138, 141, 142
17.8	60		

20.11-15	117, 119–21, 138, 140–2	*Didache* 14.1	155
20.11–22.5	138, 141		
20.12	120, 127	*Gospel of Thomas*	
20.13	76, 95, 120	11.1	52
20.14	121, 135	111.1	63
20.14-15	131		
20.15	124	GRAECO-ROMAN LITERATURE	
21	123		
21–22	123	*Homeric Hymn to Apollo*	
21.1	8, 11, 73, 120, 121, 122, 137–42	316–321	133
21.1-4	65, 93	*Homeric Hymn to Aphrodite*	
21.1-5	140	218–238	133
21.1–22.5	64, 117, 121, 132, 140, 141	Apollodorus	
21.2	103, 118, 121, 122, 141	*Library* 1.1.2.	39
21.3	65, 108, 122	1.1.4	133
21.3-8	122	1.2.1	133
21.4	70, 76, 139	1.3.5	133
21.5	108, 127, 137, 139, 140	1.6.1-3	55
		1.9.2	39
21.5-8	132		
21.8	124, 126, 131, 132, 150	Aristotle *De Caelo*	
21.9–22.5	28, 59	278b10-20	7, 155
21.10	29, 67, 103, 112, 118, 121, 122, 127, 147	278b10–279a	132
		278b12-15	80
21.11	117	292a15-b19	52, 84, 99
21.18	155	294b13-21	37
21.22	65, 122	294a28-34	37
21.27	124		
22.1-2	65	Dionysius of Halicarnassus	
22.1-5	122	*Roman Antiquities*	
22.4	124	1.3.3.	145
22.7	108, 155		
22.8-9	149, 155	Hesiod	
22.12	108	*Theogony*	
22.15	132, 150, 155	160–181	133
22.18	12	492–506	133
22.20	139	519–521	47
		617–720	39
1 Clement		720	39
20.5	91	721–725	55
28.3	91	820–868	39
59.3	91		
		Works and Days	
		609	97

Index of Ancient Literature

Homer		2.13.11	47
Iliad		2.14.3	47
1.590-594	55, 133		
5.504	46, 47	Pliny the Younger	
8.13-16	39	*Epistle to Trajan*	
17.425	46, 47	10.96.7	155
18.395-405	133		
18.607	47	Ptolemy	
23.51	39	*Tetrabiblos*	
		1.10	37
Odyssey			
1.52-54	47	Quintilian	
10.513	130	*Institutio Oratoria*	
10.560	39	8.3.67-9	127
11	39		
11.582-600	39	Strabo	
15.329.	46	*Geographica*	
24.204	39	1.3.11	97
		2.5.1	97
Plato		5.4.5	89
Gorgias		14.1.11	89
523b	39		
		Valerius Flaccus	
Laws		*Argonautica*	
898d–899b	55, 84, 99	2.82-97	133
Timaeus		Virgil	
39e–40b	51, 55, 84, 99	*Aeneid*	
		1.236-237	10, 11
Phaedo		6.274	89
107d-e	40	6.548	131
108e-109a	36, 37		
109b 9–10		EARLY JEWISH AND CHRISTIAN	
109b–111c	52	AUTHORS	
110d	78		
112e	10	Hippolytus of Rome	
113b 130–1		*Refutation of All Heresies*	
113d	40	1.5	6, 36, 37
114a	131	1.6	37
Phaedrus		Josephus	
247b-c	53	*Against Apion*	
		2.240	39
Republic			
614–621	53	*Antiquities of the Jews*	
		18.14	40
Pseudo-Plutarch			
Placita Philosophorum		*Jewish War*	
2.11.2	47, 64	5.212-214	47

Justin Martyr
Dialogue with Trypho
61 91
129 91

Philo of Alexandria
De gigantibus
6–8 9, 97, 98

Theophilus of Antioch
To Autolycus
1.4 91
1.7 91

Index of Modern Authors

Adams, Edward 137
Aune, David E. 10, 11, 23, 61, 79, 109, 119, 128, 129

Bal, Mieke 25, 26, 28, 29, 60
Barker, Margaret 106
Barnett, Paul 76
Barr, David L. 22, 28, 60, 92, 102, 103, 132, 155
Bauckham, Richard 56
Beale, G. K. 10, 39, 71, 73, 86, 87, 92, 93, 101, 125, 135, 139
Beckwith, Isbon T. 103, 120, 126
Berquist, Jon L. 144
Bingham, Geoffrey C. 124
Bird, Michael F. 47
Boll, Franz 7, 36, 95, 98, 110
Boring, M. Eugene. 111, 114, 132
Bousset, W. 11, 93
Bowman, John Wick 67, 68, 72, 92
Box, G. H. 75
Brett, M. G. 54
Brownlee, William 46
Bryan, David J. 5, 96

Caird, G. B. 8, 63, 73, 114, 136
Carrington, Philip. 69, 82
Charles, R. H. 11, 61, 69, 71, 76, 79, 86, 87, 88, 92, 93, 96, 102, 108, 110, 120, 127, 132
Chatman, Seymour 25, 28, 29, 30, 31
Couprie, Dirk L. 47

Day, Peggy Lynne 55, 109, 114
DeSilva, David Arthur 10, 16, 88, 97, 108
Dillmann, August 84
Dochhorn, Jan 56
Duke, Rodney K. 135
Dyer, Keith 89, 149

Edwards, James R. 34
Elar, J. J. 126, 130

Elliott, Mark Adam 134
Esler, Philip Francis 51, 74, 104
Evans, Craig 41

Fair, Ian 86
Ferguson, William Scott 146
Ford, J. Massyngberde 64, 69
Friesen, Steven J. 1, 6, 10, 11, 17, 27, 30, 31, 34, 117, 131, 143–7, 153, 154

Gebhardt, Hermann 8, 15, 101, 126
Genette, Gérard 26, 68
Gore-Jones, Lydia 85
Greenwood, Kyle 37, 45, 63
Grudem, W. A. 126
Gwyther, Anthony 14, 15, 19, 74, 101, 145, 152, 154, 158

Hagner, Donald Alfred 154
Hall, Robert G. 69, 75
Hansen, Ryan Leif 10, 18, 24, 30, 98, 138, 141
Harrington, Wilfrid J. 114
Harrisville, R. A. 139
Helgeland, John 146
Henning, Meghan 31
Himmelfarb, Martha 55
Hongisto, Leif 25
Houtman, C. 45

Janko, Richard 133
Jordaan, Gert 8, 9, 15, 74, 114, 157

Kiddle, Martin 76
Knibb, M. A. 43, 56
Knight, Jonathan 56, 63, 75
Koester, Craig R. 23, 33, 34, 61, 86, 89, 92, 99, 101, 103, 108, 137, 149, 154, 155
Kraybill, J. Nelson 146, 154
Kulik, Alexander 48, 54

Labahn, Michael 25, 31, 60, 108
Lefebvre, Henri 30, 143
Lehtipuu, Outi 41
Lilje, Hans 88

MacRae, George W. 49
Malina, Bruce J., 2, 11, 12, 62, 64, 68, 69, 82, 90, 97, 105, 110, 118, 119, 130
McDonough, Sean M. 2, 7, 9, 15, 30, 114, 125, 131
Michaels, J. Ramsey 26-7
Milik, Józef T. 125, 143
Minear, Paul S. 15, 101, 102, 152
Moo, Jonathan 45, 63, 73
Morray-Jones, C. R. A. 74, 104
Mounce, Robert H. 69
Murphy, Frederick J. 71, 124

Newton, Jon 19
Nickelsburg, G. W. E. 48, 50, 98, 134, 87, 102, 123, 152

Olson, Daniel C. 85
Orlov, Andrei A. 49, 54

Papaioannou, Kim Gary 40
Perriman, Andrew 41
Peterson, Erik 131
Pilch, John J. 2, 11, 12, 62, 64, 68, 69, 82, 90, 97, 105, 110, 118, 119, 130
Powell, Mark Allan 22, 29

Rad, Gerhard von 45
Reed, Annette Yoshiko 85
Reese, Ruth Anne 24
Resseguie, J. L. 22, 101
Robbins, Vernon K. 18, 21, 25

Rubinkiewicz, R. 54
Russel, David 4
Ryan, Sean Michael 6, 9, 10, 11, 13, 19, 22, 42, 69, 83

Schüssler Fiorenza, E. 16
Schmid, Konrad 54
Skinner, John 45
Stephens, Mark B. 138
Sweet, J. P. M. 14, 33, 67, 76, 127
Swete, Henry Barclay 71, 103, 135, 136, 141
Sylva, Dennis D. 21
Szkredka, Sławomir 40

Ureña, Lourdes García 12, 23, 25, 26, 27, 29, 61, 62, 65, 67, 68, 74, 76, 82, 123

VanderKam, James C. 50, 87, 102, 123, 152
Vinson, Richard B. 63, 71, 125, 126

Walcot, P. 144
Walton, John H. 45
Wan, Wei Hsien 5, 17, 30, 88, 143-7, 149, 151, 153, 154
Watts, John D. W. 86
Wenham, Gordon J. 44
Whitaker, Robyn 25, 68, 70
Wink, Walter 13, 14, 19, 74, 151
Witherington, Ben 101, 125
Wood, Barry 140
Woodington, J. David. 129, 130, 135
Wright, J. Edward 42, 61
Wright, M. R. 46, 55, 66, 80, 146
Wright, N. T. 137, 140-1

Yarbro Collins, Adela 7, 34, 44-5, 106, 107
Yu Yap, Marlene 40-1

www.ingramcontent.com/pod-product-compliance
Lightning Source LLC
Chambersburg PA
CBHW051524230426
43668CB00012B/1734